The
Tabernacle
of
Moses

The Tabernacle of Moses

Kevin J. Conner

Published by City Christian Publishing
9200 NE Fremont
Portland, Oregon 97220

Printed in U.S.A.

City Christian Publishing is a ministry of City Bible Church, and is dedicated to serving the local church and its leaders through the production and distribution of quality materials.

It is our prayer that these materials, proven in the context of the local church, will equip leaders in exalting the Lord and extending His kingdom.

For a free catalog of additional resources from
City Christian Publishing please call 1-800-777-6057
or visit www.CityChristianPublishing.com

The Tabernacle of Moses
© Copyright 1976 by Kevin J. Conner
All Rights Reserved

ISBN 0-914936-93-X

THE TABERNACLE IN THE WILDERNESS

Chart from LECTURES ON THE TABERNACLE by Samuel Ridout

Published by LOIZEAUX BROTHERS. New York

INDEX
TABERNACLE OF MOSES

TABERNACLE OF MOSES
FOREWORD

"Of making many books there is no end" (Ecclesiastes 12:12). So said the wise King Solomon. As long as God continues to unfold and open His Book, the Holy Bible, so long will other books continue to be written.

In approaching this study of the Tabernacle of Moses, it is well to remember the words of the following proverb: "It is the glory of God to conceal a thing: but the honor of kings is to search out a matter" (Proverbs 25:2). With respect to the Tabernacle of Moses as revealed by God to Israel it is no different. In the very structure, furniture, and material of this Tabernacle it has pleased God in His glory to conceal and veil eternal truths. It then becomes the honor of believers, who are Kings and Priests unto God and His Christ (Revelation 1:6; 5:9-10 and I Peter 2:5,9), to search out these glorious truths.

It is very important that we know what God has hidden for us in the Tabernacle of Moses. Much of the Word of God as we find it in the Old and New Testaments becomes meaningless to us without a general knowledge, understanding and interpretation of that which pertains to the Tabernacle of Moses. The whole Bible is built on the service, ordinances and ceremonies connected with this structure, yet for many of God's people, this is one of the most neglected areas of study.

There is no need for ignorance concerning the spiritual realities hidden in the external form. For God's Word is its own commentary and interpreter. In this study we will attempt to simply allow God's Word to have free course, so that we will interpret as God's Word interprets and not go beyond.

Under the Mosaic Covenant God revealed truth to His people, the Children of Israel in five chief areas. They are (1) the **Law,** moral, civil and ceremonial; (2) the **Priesthood,** both the Aaronic and Levitical; (3) the **Five Offerings** or sacrificial ceremonials; (4) the **Three Chief Feasts**—Passover, Pentecost and Tabernacles and (5) the **Tabernacle of the Lord** with its particular service. Each of these are vast subjects in themselves. The subsequent *Outline Studies* have to do basically with the fifth one—the Tabernacle of Moses (N. B. In the Scripture this is referred to as the Tabernacle of the Lord. We will in this study be referring to it as the Tabernacle of Moses to distinguish it from other Tabernacles in Scripture, and because the actual pattern was given to Moses on the mount.).

For nearly 400 years the entire nation of Israel functioned around this structure. Why was it so important? How could gold, silver, brass, wood and skins play such an important role in the life of a people? Because it was here that God had chosen to dwell, and in it He had demonstrated in picture form all revelation and knowledge of Himself. The Tabernacle was virtually God's 'visual aid' for instructing the nation of Israel.

In this volume we have endeavoured to set forth *Outline Studies* which would be valuable to both the teacher and to the individual student. For the teacher these notes are laid out in a manner which gives flexibility and ample room to develop the 'seed-thoughts' expressed. For the student these notes have been prepared in as general an outline as possible, giving the basic points in a reasonably concise manner. For everyone it is important that all the Scripture references be read. Unless we see the truth from the Word of God itself our time spent is meaningless.

In this approach we have sought to refrain from too much detail, unnecessary comment, fanciful and questionable interpretations, seeking to let clear Scriptures speak for themselves to confirm the truths typified in the most prominent points. These notes are simply *"handfuls of purpose"* (Ruth 2:16) for the gleaner in God's wonderful Word.

In these Studies will be found **"Seed to the sower, and Bread to the eater"**. (Isaiah 55:10).

The Tabernacle of Moses and its furnishings will be viewed in the following manner:

1. TYPICALLY of the Lord Jesus Christ

The first and primary interpretation and application of all that pertains to the Tabernacle of Moses is found in the person of the Lord Jesus Christ, the Son of God. The **Word** made flesh which "dwelt (lit. tabernacled) among us" (John 1:14). Jesus Himself declares, "In the volume of the book it is written of Me" (Hebrews 10:7). Jesus also bore witness that "He (Moses) wrote of Me" (John 5:46). The **Law**, the **Psalms**, and the **Prophets** all foretold of the Lord Jesus Christ in His redemptive ministry (Luke 24:44). (Ezekiel 11:16; Isaiah 8:14) **"I will be to them a Little Sanctuary".**

2. PROPHETICALLY of the Church, local and universal

The second application is that which finds fulfillment in the Church, which is the Body of Christ. That which is fulfilled in the Head of the Church must now find its fulness in His Body, which is the fulness or completeness of Him which filleth all in all (Ephesians 1:22-23). The New Testament Church. Local and Universal, is now God's dwelling place—His Habitation. Thus, the Tabernacle and its furnishings are a shadow of that which finds fulfillment in the Church Hebrews 8:5 . "That Christ might **Dwell** (Grk. Tabernacle) in your hearts". (Ephesians 3:16,17; Colossians 1:19; 2:9; 1:27).

3. DISPENSATIONALLY of the ages of time

There is further application in the measurements found in the structure of the Tabernacle and in the Outer Court. These, as will be seen, become typical and prophetical of the Dispensations of the Law Covenant and the New Covenant times, consummating in the eternal ages to come.

4. HEAVENLY, of the True & Heavenly Sanctuary

It must be remembered that the Tabernacle of Moses was simply the shadowy outline and silhouette on earth of the **true** and **Heavenly Sanctuary.** There is a Sanctuary in Heaven. There is a True and Real and Spiritual Tabernacle. The Scriptures are expressively clear as to this truth. (Hebrews 9:21-24, Revelation 15:5; Jeremiah 17:12; Hebrews 8:1-4). All the ministrations of Aaron in the Holy Places of the Earthly Sanctuary were but the shadow of the reality of the ministrations of Christ, our Great High Priest, in the Heavenly Sanctuary. It is this aspect which is the predominant theme in the Book of Hebrews. Christ ministering in the Heavenly Sanctuary, the Heavenly Tabernacle and Temple. The three Places in the temporal Tabernacle point to the three Heavens in the eternal Tabernacle.

5. PRACTICALLY and EXPERIENTIALLY

The whole purpose in the declaration and interpretation of spiritual truth, as in Tabernacle types, is the application of it to the heart and life of the believer, both individually and collectively. Truth must become practical and experiential, or else it remains but the Letter of the law. *Theory* without *life* is preaching doctrine without experience and ministers death to the hearer. It is the Spirit which gives life.

A final word of exhortation—

The importance of reading and studying the Scripture passages that are referred to in this study relative to the thoughts laid down cannot be overemphasized for the serious student of the Word of God. It is not just our comments on the Word, But **the Word** itself is the "Sword of the Spirit" and that which brings about the renewal of the believer's life. Therefore, read and meditate upon the Scriptures as you follow the study.

ACKNOWLEDGMENT

It would be impossible to acknowledge the various teachers, preachers and ministers in the Body of Christ, plus the writers of notes and authors of books from which we have drawn over the years concerning this wonderful subject. In the words of the Apostle Paul, anyone who takes the responsibility of writing must say, "Came the Word of God **out from** you, or came it **unto** you only?" (I Corinthians 14:36). One can only give full glory to the Lord Jesus Christ, who brings understanding, revelation and illumination to the Church by the ministry of the Holy Spirit, whose ministry it is to take the things of the Lord and make them real to our hearts and lives.

These studies have been given in Australia and New Zealand, and they have been used as a general text book in Portland Bible College, Portland, Oregon.

Kevin J. Conner

MT. SINAI

HEB 12:18-29

OLD TESTAMENT
BOOK OF EXODUS

NEW TESTAMENT
BOOK OF HEBREWS

MOSAIC COVENANT

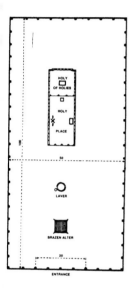

1. THE TABERNACLE
   Outer Court
   Holy Place
   Most Holy Place

2. THE FEASTS
   Passover
   Pentecost
   Tabernacles

3. THE FIVE OFFERINGS
   Burnt Offering
   Meal Offering
   Peace Offering
   Sin Offering
   Trespass Offering

4. THE LAW
   Moral Law
   Ceremonial Law
   Civil Law

5. THE PRIESTHOOD
   High Priesthood
   Aaronic Priesthood
   Levitical Priesthood

TABERNACLE OF MOSES
INTRODUCTION

Many Christians immediately ask, **"Why study the Tabernacle of Moses?"** or "Why use the Old Testament?" When the New Testament writers wrote their books they continually appealed to the **Law**, the **Prophets** and the **Psalms** to interpret what God was doing in their time. We have good New Testament evidence for using the Old Testament. The following are 17 New Testament reasons giving us good Scriptural ground for using and studying that which pertains to the Tabernacle of Moses as we find it in the Old Testament.

We study the Tabernacle of Moses—

1. **Because** the revelation of the Tabernacle of Moses is part of the **"All Scripture** given by inspiration of God, and is profitable for **doctrine,** for reproof, for correction, for instruction in righteousness" (II Timothy 3:16).

2. **Because** "whatsoever things were written aforetime were written for our **learning,** that we through patience and comfort of the scriptures might have hope" (Romans 15:4).

3. **Because** "all these things happened unto them for ensamples, (Grk. Types) and they are written for our **admonition,** upon whom the ends of the world are come" (I Corinthians 10:6,11).

4. **Because** when Christ gave the disciples His own three-fold division of the Scripture and said that "all things must be fulfilled concerning me," He included the **Law of Moses, the Psalms,** and **the Prophets.** The revelation of the Tabernacle is part of the Law of Moses and, hence, contains prophecy concerning Christ, (Luke 24:26, 27, 44-46). Moses wrote of Me, (John 5:45,46; Acts 3:22,23), Prophetically and Typically.

5. **Because** Jesus said, "In the volume of the Book it is **written of Me"** (Hebrews 10:7 and Psalms 40:6-8). Therefore the Tabernacle, being part of the Book, is also prophetic of Christ and the Church.

6. **Because** "the law was our **Schoolmaster** to bring us to Christ" (Galatians 3:24). The law containing the Tabernacle acts as a guardian with the purpose of leading us to Christ or revealing Christ to us.

7. **Because** Jesus said, "Think not that I am come to destroy the Law, or the Prophets: I am not come to destroy, but to **fulfill.** For verily I say unto you, Till heaven and earth pass, one jot or one tittle shall in no wise pass from the Law, till all be fulfilled" (Matthew 5:17-18).

8. **Because** "the Prophets and the Law prophesied" Matthew 11:13. All speak of His glory (Psalms 29:9). All were prophetical of "the sufferings of Christ and the glory that should follow" (I Peter 1:11).

9. **Because** the Law was "a shadow (Grk. Outline) of good things to come." It is the purpose of the shadow to bring us to the substance. Just as it is the purpose of prophecy is to bring us to fulfillment. It is the purpose of the type to bring us to the antitype. The law was the age of the 'shadow' to point us to the real. The shadow of a thing has no reality in and of itself. It can only point to that which casts the shadow.

One has to trace the shadow with light before you arrive at the substance. If one turns his back on the light, then one gets lost in the shadow, getting further away from the realities.

The only purpose in looking at the "Shadow of the Law" is to follow the shadow through until we come to **Him** whose shadow it was.

The Tabernacle could be likened to a silhouette, an outline of things to come.

Check the following Scriptures in this regard: (Hebrews 8:5; 9:9,23-24; 10:1; I Corinthians 10:11 and Colossians 2:17).

10. **Because** the Tabernacle was a *pattern* (Grk. Type) of heavenly realities—the Heavenly Tabernacle (Hebrews 8:5; 9:23).

11. **Because** in the Law was the *external form* of knowledge and truth (Romans 2:20, Amp. N.T.).

12. **Because** the Tabernacle, its measurements, its furnishings and its curtains were all "separate revelations—each of which set forth **a portion of Truth**" (Hebrews 1:1-2, Amp. N.T.)

13. **Because** the Tabernacle was **a Figure** of the True Tabernacle. "Christ is not entered into the Holy Places made with hands, which are **Figures** (Grk. Antitypes) of the True," (Hebrews 9:24).

14. **Because** "The Priests serve unto the **Example** (Grk. Copy) and Shadow of Heavenly things." (Hebrews 8:5).
    "It was therefore necessary that the **Patterns** (Grk. Copies) of things in the Heavens should be purified with these, but the Heavenly things themselves with better sacrifices than these." (Hebrews 9:23).
    The Earthly Sanctuary was simply a Copy of the Heavenly Sanctuary.

15. **Because** the Tabernacle was also *a Parable*. "The First Tabernacle standing was a Figure (Grk. Parable) for the Time then present." (Hebrews 9:9).
    A Parable is an extended simile or story in historical form for the purpose of comparison or illustration.

16. **Because** all things in the Tabernacle were *Types* of that which was to come, even Christ Himself.
    "Make it according to the **Fashion** (Grk. Type)", God said to Moses. (Acts 7:44).

17. **Because** a principle of God is "First the **Natural, afterwards that which is Spiritual**". (I Corinthians 15:46,47).
    We look at the Natural, the Material, which is the Temporal, the things seen; in order to discover, by the Spirit, the Truth, which is Spiritual, and the Eternal; things not seen by the natural mind of man. (II Corinthians 4:18).

In the Old Testament God gave Israel, His children, the letters of His alphabet. In the New Testament, the Church can put these letters together, and they all spell **"Christ Himself"**, which ever way they may be arranged.

In order to exemplify what we mean, let us look at a few quick examples of how God in His wisdom used natural things of the Old Testament to reveal Christ and the Church.

1. The *Smitten Rock* from which the Children of Israel drank pointed to Christ (I Corinthians 10:1-4).

2. The *Manna* which came from heaven pointed to Christ (John 6:45-67).

3. The Sacrificial *Passover Lamb* typified **The Lamb** of God that took away the sin of the world (John 1:29).

4. The High Priestly ministry of *Aaron* demonstrated Christ's Priestly ministrations (Hebrews 4:14; 5:1-5; 6:19-20).

5. The Tabernacle and all its furnishings, metals, curtains, coverings and operations typified the Lord Jesus Christ in His ministry in the Church.

Though the Tabernacle and its furnishings have perished and have ceased to exist, the spiritual truths and eternal realities shadowed forth in this Habitation of God still remain; for **Truth is Eternal!**

It is for these reasons that we study *the revelation of God in the Tabernacle of Moses.*

All of these things are applicable to any areas that are studied in using the Old Testament.

In (Romans 1:20) Paul declares, "For the **invisible things** of Him from the creation of the world are clearly seen, being understood **by the things that are made,** even His eternal power and Godhead." God wants to make it clear that He has given us the visible things of creation to help us understand spiritual things (invisible). The things that are seen are temporal, while the things that they point to are eternal (II Corinthians 4:18). The Tabernacle of Moses was composed of many different elements of creation—gold, silver, brass, wood and precious stones. It had coverings and curtains. It had array of furniture from the Ark of the Covenant to the Brazen Altar. All of these things from creation now become symbols, hiding or revealing truth and different facets of revelation concerning Christ and His Church.

Jesus often taught deep spiritual truths by means of parables. It was one way that finite man could comprehend some of the things of God, an infinite being. In all the parables that Jesus spoke there was veiled truth which the Spirit is still unfolding to us. Even as Jesus spoke in parables in His earthly ministry, so God speaks to us in the parable of the Tabernacle of Moses, taking the natural elements of creation and transforming them into a symbolic language to depict eternal truths. The Tabernacle becomes God's secret code for revealing truth to the sincere and yielding seeker after God. In fact, the whole of the Mosaic system becomes God's 'flannelgraph' to teach Divine Truth to the people of God.

The New Testament gives the doctrinal exposition of the Types. Abstract statements of truth are much easier to lay hold upon if some visible representation, as in the Tabernacle, is used. Thus the Tabernacle is full of illustrative types. Types, as already noted, are shadows, and shadows involve substance. All these things were object lessons, material symbols setting forth spiritual truths. The Lord Jesus Christ is the key to understanding "The Gospel according to Moses".

PRELIMINARY AND GENERAL OBSERVATIONS

(1) Israel, the Church in the wilderness (Acts 7:38)

The Nation of Israel is spoken of in the New Testament as being the "Church in the wilderness." Thus, Natural or National Israel is set forth as a type and shadow of the New Testament Church, which is the Spiritual Israel of God (Romans 9:6-8). The principle of interpretation is set forth by Paul in (I Corinthians 15:46-47)where he indicates that the *natural* preceeds or points to the *spiritual*, (i.e. First the natural, then the spiritual). The "Israel of God" (Galatians 6:16) is now the Church which is the New Creature in Christ Jesus (Galatians 3:16, 28-29).

God's Israel is pictured in the Bible as an olive tree into which all believers in Christ are grafted. This grafting in comes about by faith in Christ Jesus (See especially Romans 11:1-12 and 9:1-10). However, just as in Christ all believers are grafted into the olive tree (the Israel of God,) even so after the Cross all of the unbelieving Jews are cast off from the tree. Belief in the Christ, the Son of the Living God becomes the only criterion for membership in this planting into the tree of God.

For these reasons Paul is able to tell us that everything that happened to Natural Israel happened unto them for types and ensamples and were written for our admonition (I Corinthians 10:11). Therefore we are justified in looking at the truth in the Tabernacle as a type and shadow of the good things to come in the New Testament or New Covenant Church.

(2) The Mosaic Covenant and the Mosaic Economy

When we look at the Book of Exodus we see that the book is basically divided into two sections. In chapter 1-19 the material is *Historical* in nature. This section deals primarily with the bondage and deliverance of the nation under God by the hand of Moses and Aaron who brought them through to Mt. Sinai in the wilderness. The second section covers chapters 20-40. This section is mainly *Legislative*. That is, it deals primarily with the laws which were to govern the life of the nation. These laws included the Moral Law, the Civil Law and the Ceremonial Law. The Moral Law basically involved the Ten Commandments. The Civil Law included the Book of the Law or the Book of the Covenant. And the Ceremonial Law ordered the religious life of the nation manifest in the giving of the Tabernacle, the Priesthood and Offerings. (See section on Contents of the Ark for further material).

The "Church in the wilderness" was built upon a five-fold foundation laid down in the Mosaic Covenant or Economy of God, which finds its fulfillment first in Christ and then in the Church. This five-fold foundation is as follows:

1. The *Tabernacle* of Moses — Exodus 25-40
2. The *Law Covenant* (also called Old and Mosaic) — Exodus 20
3. The *Priesthood*, both Aaronic and Levitical — Exodus 28,29,39
4. The *Five Offerings* and sundry Sacrifices — Leviticus 1-7
5. The *Three Feasts* of the Lord,—Passover, Pentecost and Tabernacles — Leviticus 23

Upon these five things the whole epistle of Hebrews dwells, interpreting all in relation to the ministry of Christ Jesus. Each of these are vast studies in themselves. We will be dealing with the first one, the *Tabernacle of Moses*. (See Diagram)

(3) General description of the Tabernacle

The Tabernacle of Moses was simply a portable tent with various curtains and coverings over a wooden structure. It had three apartments or places to it. The Scripture refers to each of these as (1) the Holiest of All or Most Holy Place, (2) the Holy Place and (3) the Outer Court. In each of these apartments there were particular pieces of furniture, as follows:

    1. The Holiest of All contained:

        The Ark of the Covenant

8

2. The Holy Place contained:

    a. The Golden Altar of Incense
    b. The Table of Shewbread
    c. The Golden Candlestick

3. The Outer Court contained:

    a. The Brazen Altar
    b. The Brazen Laver

It was in the Holiest of All that God's very Presence and Shekinah Glory dwelt. It was here that God communicated with man, dwelling in the midst of His people Israel, Just as even now the presence of Christ dwells in the midst of His people, the Church. "Where two or three are gathered together in MY NAME, there I AM in the midst of them" (Matthew 18:20).

(4) The Divine Purpose of the Tabernacle

The Divine purpose in the building of the Tabernacle is summed up in the key verse found in Exodus 25:8 and 29:46-47. "Let them make me a Sanctuary that I may dwell among them." This verse is the key thought of all that pertains to the Tabernacle. God's desire is to dwell in the midst of His redeemed people on His own terms and His own grounds. God follows the pronouncement of His purpose by giving a pattern that is to be followed in the construction of His dwelling place.

God made a dwelling place for man when He created the earth. The details of this creation are contained in two consecutive chapters in Genesis 1 and 2. Mankind marvels at the vastness of this material product of the creation of man's dwelling. Scientists spend lifetimes studying and exploring the mysteries and wonders of this created dwelling. Yet infinitely greater is the mystery and wonder of God's dwelling place, the Tabernacle. The Bible affords about 43 consecutive chapters, Exodus 25-40 and Leviticus 1-27 plus many other portions of Scripture (See Numbers, Hebrews and Revelation) to the subject of God's dwelling. If the two chapters concerning man's dwelling place afford such a rich field of study and exploration, then the habitation of the Eternal God certainly must provide an abundance of food for the hungry student. A wealth of knowledge, truth and spiritual riches are hidden in this revelation. Externally we may see nothing but a bit of wood and skins, but as the Scripture clearly sets forth, "It is the glory of God to conceal a thing: but it is the honor of Kings to search out a matter" (Proverbs 25:2). The believer needs to place value and emphasis where God does, and this is that which concerns **His dwelling place.**

God has ever desired to dwell with and among His people. This is revealed in the typical dwelling places in the Old Testament and consummated in the New Testament where the Word was made flesh to "dwell" among us. As we look at this particular area we see a progressive revelation in the "Dwelling places" of God. We begin in the Book of Beginnings with the Garden of Eden and end in the Book of Ultimates with the City of God. Let us briefly follow this progressive thought throughout the Bible.

1. God dwelt with man before the entrance of sin in Eden's dwelling or tabernacle. God walked and talked with Adam in this Garden (Genesis 3:8,24).

2. God walked and talked with Noah and the Patriarchs in their times Genesis 6:9. God appeared to Abraham, Isaac and Jacob (Genesis 17:1; 26:24 and 35:1ff).

3. God dwelt with man in the *Tabernacle of Moses* (Exodus 25:8,22). He dwelt with redeemed Israel.

4. God gave further revelation and truth in His dwelling under King David in the *Tabernacle of David* (I Chronicles 17:1-6 and Acts 15:15-18).

5. God gave still further revelation in the *Temple of Solomon* (II Chronicles 5).

6. God's fullest and most perfect revelation was in the person of the Lord Jesus Christ. He is the "fullness of the Godhead Bodily" (Colossians 1:19 and 2:9). He is God in human form. He is **The** Tabernacle and **The** Temple (John 2:19-21). He was that Word made flesh who "**dwelt** (lit. tabernacled) among us, and we beheld His Glory" (John 1:14-18). God was in Christ (II Corinthians 5:18-19).

7. God now dwells in the tabernacle or dwelling place of the *Church.* He dwells individually in each

believers heart (II Corinthians 5:1; Ephesians 3: 17 and II Peter 1 :13-14). He also dwells corporately or collectively in the Church as a body (I Timothy 3:15; John 14:23; I Peter 2:5; II Corinthians 6:15-18; I Corinthians 3:16-17 and Ephesians 2:20-24).

We have seen that God has dwelt *with* men, *amongst* men and, finally, *in* men. Fellowship between God and man is necessary to fulfill God's purpose and plan in redemption. [In the beginning (Genesis) we see God coming down to earth to dwell and fellowship with Man eternally.] God desires to fellowship with man, and yet God can only dwell with man on His own grounds and His own terms. That is, Divine holiness having dealt with man's sinfulness, "Be ye holy, for I am holy" (Leviticus 11:44 and I Peter 1:15-16).

8. The ultimate revelation of the dwelling of God is seen in the revelation of the *Foursquare City of God*. This is the New Jerusalem. "The Tabernacle of God is with men, and He will dwell with them, and they shall be His people, and God Himself shall be with them, and be their God" (Revelation 21:3. See also: Hebrews 8:2, 5; 9:11, 24; Revelation 11:19; 21:1-3).

In all this we see the Scripture fulfilled, "But have gone from **tent** to **tent,** and from one **tabernacle** to **another"** (I Chronicles 17:5).

(5) Names and Titles given to the Tabernacle

In the Old Testament we see that there were many different names by which the Tabernacle of Moses was called. Each of these names brings out its own particular aspect of the truth, even as the various names for the New Testament Church speak of different aspects of the Church. This Tabernacle was called:

1. *The Tabernacle* (Exodus 25:9) — The word 'tabernacle' simply means "tent" or "dwelling place". This Tabernacle was to be the dwelling place of the Most High.

2. *The Sanctuary* (Exodus 25:8) – The word 'sanctuary' means "a holy place" or "place set apart". This Tabernacle was to be a place set apart for the habitation of a holy God.

3. *The Tent of Testimony or Witness* (Numbers 9:15; 17:7; 18:2); See also: (Exodus 25:22 and 26:33-34)— The Tabernacle received this title because it contained the Ark of the Covenant which contained the Tables of the Law. The Tables of the Law were called 'the testimony' of a holy God. They were His moral standard for redeemed Israel.

4. *The House of God* (Exodus 34:26, Deuteronomy 23:18; Joshua 9:23; Judges 18:31) — This was God's house in which He was to be Lord.

5. *The Tent of the Congregation* (Exodus 40:34-35)— This was to be the place where the congregation gathered together at the door for festival days and worship. Even as they gathered unto the door of the Tabernacle, so also we gather to **the Door,** the Lord Jesus Christ who declared, "I am the door."

We might also note that in two of these titles the word 'tent' occurs. Those that dwell in tents are called pilgrims. Tents are not permanent homes. All this is significant of the pilgrimage life in the Wilderness. The Church is also made up of strangers and pilgrims in this world. They stand with Abraham in the company of those who have no continuing city but look "for a city which hath foundations, whose builder and maker is God" (Hebrews 11:10).

All these aspects of truth found in the various names of the Tabernacle find their spiritual fulfillment in the New Testament Church, local and universal. The Church is God's dwelling place. It is a peculiar people set apart unto God, for He dwells in the praises of His people. The Church is the House of God made up of living stones. The Church is the place of the New Testament gathering.

(6) The sevenfold requirements for building the Sanctuary

There were seven particular requirements necessary for the building of the Sanctuary of the Lord in the Old Testament. The dwelling place of God was to be built:

1. *By Freewill Offerings* — "Speak unto the children of Israel, that they bring me an offering: of every man that giveth it willingly with his heart ye shall take my offering" (Exodus 25:2).

The Spirit of giving came upon the Israelites in thankfulness to the Lord who had delivered them out of the House of Bondage in Egypt through the blood of the Passover Lamb. This is the kind of offering in which God is interested.

It is interesting to notice where the Children of Israel got all of this material to build the sanctuary. They got it from the Egyptians themselves. This was a direct fulfillment of the prophecy given to Abraham years before that Israel should come out with great substance (Genesis 15:12-16), See also: (Exodus 3:21-22 and 12:33-36).These blessings that the people receive from the hands of the Egyptians were not received to make the people rich, but they were given to them to be given back to the Lord. There came a time to give, and the people responded.

2. *By a people stirred up* — "And they came, every one whose heart stirred him up" (Exodus 35:21,26 and 36:2).
   The people were stirred up about the building of the Lord's Sanctuary. Likewise should every Christian be stirred up about the building of God's House today (Isaiah 64:7 and II Timothy 1:6).

3. *By a people made willing* — "Every one whom his spirit made willing" (Exodus 35:5,21-22,29; 25:1-2).
   God's people are to be a people willing to do His will (Psalms 51:10-17 and Psalms 110:3).

4. *By a free-hearted people* — A study of Exodus 35 and 36 reveals that the word "heart" or "hearted" is used at least 12 times. The people gave these offerings freely as a heart response to the goodness of the Lord (Exodus 36:3).It is the condition of the heart which counts before the Lord (Psalms 51:10,12, 17 and Mark 7:6).

5. *By the wisdom of God* — "And every wise hearted man, in whom the Lord put wisdom and understanding to know how to work all manner of work for the service of the sanctuary" (Exodus 36:1-8 and 35:10,25).
   The Tabernacle was built by the wisdom of God through Moses. The Temple was later built by the wisdom of God through Solomon (I Kings 3:12-13).And likewise the New Testament Church will only be built by the wisdom of God   (Proverbs 1:1-6; 9:1; I Corinthians 3:9-11 and Ephesians 1:14-18).   It is important to know that although Moses was learned in all the wisdom of the Egypt-world, he depended upon the wisdom of God alone for the building of God's Sanctuary (Acts 7:22)! The wisdom of this world is foolishness to God (I Corinthians 1:18-25).

6. **By the Spirit of God** — "He hath filled him with the Spirit of God, in wisdom, in understanding, and in knowledge, and in all manner of workmanship" (Exodus 35:30-35 and 36:1-3).

   The Tabernacle was built by the enabling and equipping of the Holy Spirit upon men. The New Testament Church can only be built accordingly. We are now living in the Dispensation or Age of the Spirit. More than ever before it is necessary for God's people to be totally available to and dependent upon the ministrations of the Holy Spirit of God   (I Corinthians 12:1-13 and Galatians 5:16-26). This is the way in which God accomplishes His works among men. "Not by might, nor by power, but by **my spirit**"(Zechariah 4:6).

7. **According to the Divine Pattern.** "See, saith He, that thou make all things according to the **pattern** shewed to thee in the mount" (Hebrews 8:5; Exodus 25:40; 26:30; 27:8; Numbers 8:4 and Acts 7:44).

   A study of Exodus 39-40 reveals that seventeen times we are told that Moses built the Tabernacle "as the Lord commanded Moses." In addition, at least seven times in other places he is told to make all things according to God's pattern. Nothing was left to the mind or imagination of man. Everything was to be made according to God's pattern. God can only bless and seal with glory that which is done according to the standard of His Word. The New Testament Church will also have to measure up to the pattern of God.

   Moses is a beautiful example of a man sold out to the will and Word of God. Moses gave complete and full obedience to the instructions and revelation of the Sanctuary. He fulfilled God's Word to him to the letter. As a result we have the following progression in Moses experience:

   a. Moses did "as the Lord commanded".

   b. "Moses finished the work" (Exodus 39:32,42,43; 40:33).

c. "The Cloud of Glory filled the Tabernacle" (Exodus 40:34-38).

God can only fully bless and place His Shekinah Glory upon that which is according to His Word and Divine Pattern. (Colossians 4:17; Zechariah 4:9; John 17:1-6 and 19:30). The Church will in the same way measure up to the Divine standard. And as a result it will be finished work!

If all of these qualities were so necessary then in the building of a temporary dwelling of God, how much more are they requirements in the building of the New Testament Sanctuary of the New Testament Church which is in the eternal purpose of God.

(7) The Builders of the Tabernacle

There were primarily two individuals involved in the construction of the Tabernacle. The first man was Bezaleel (Exodus 31:1-5 and 35:30-35). He was a man filled with wisdom, understanding and knowledge. He was a skilled workman. He was a man filled with the Spirit of God with a vision of God's plan in his heart (Exodus 35:34).In his very name we see that the hand of God was upon this man's life. Whenever God calls a person by name it is always significant of a spiritual truth. Divinely given names are significant of the nature of the individual. This principle is set forth in (Hebrews 7:2). By interpreting the name we interpret the nature and the message behind the name.

God says of Bezaleel, "See, I have called by name Bezaleel the son of Uri, the son of Hur, of the tribe of Judah" (Exodus 31:2). Bezaleel means "in the shadow of God" or "God is my protection." (Compare Isaiah 49:1-2). The name 'Uri' means "light" or "splendor" and calls to mind that Jesus was to be the Brightness of the Father's glory and the express image of His person (Hebrews 1:3). The name 'Hur' means "noble, whiteness or free". We remember that Jesus was anointed to set people free (Luke 4:18). He was the **Truth,** and knowing the truth is able to set men free (John 8:32,36).Bezaleel was of the tribe of Judah which means "praise". Jesus was the Lion of the tribe of Judah (Revelation 5:5). He alone is worthy to receive praise.

The other man involved in the building of the Tabernacle was Aholiab (Exodus 31:6 and 35:34-35). He was also a skilled man who was filled with wisdom. Aholiab was "the son of Ahisamach, of the tribe of Dan." Aholiab means "tabernacle or tent of my father". Jesus was that Tabernacle or Temple of His Father (John 1:14 and 2:19-21).Jesus is the one who builds the Tabernacle which is the Church for His Father. The Church becomes a habitation of God by the Spirit of God (Ephesians 2:20-22). The name Ahisamach means "brother of support" pointing to the ministry of the Holy Spirit who is called to be our support or helper (John 14:26 and 15:26). Aholiab was of the tribe of Dan which means "judge". This also speaks of one aspect of the Spirit's ministry. He is to reprove the world of sin, righteousness and judgment (See also I Corinthians 2:15).

God Himself was the Divine Architect. Moses, Bezaleel and Aholiab built to the Divine Pattern.

(8) The Revelation of the "Cross" in the Arrangement:
of the Camp (Numbers 1-4)

Natural Israel is often referred to as the 'Camp'. This is a military term and speaks to us of the truth that Israel was to be the "Armies of the Lord". Israel was under the leadership of the Lord, and as long as they obeyed the Word of the Lord there would be victory in the camp. The Church or Spiritual Israel is the present day Camp of the Lord. It is "the Camp of the Saints" (Revelation 20:9) under the leadership of the captain, Jesus Christ (Hebrews 2:10; II Corinthians 10:3-4 and Joshua 5:14). The believers are soldiers in the Army of the Lord (II Timothy 2:3-4 and Ephesians 6:12).

God is a God of order, and if He is going to have an army, the Camp is going to have to be in order. God never does things promiscuously or haphazardly. Israel was a large Camp and God set forth a prescribed order for the camp. The first thing that we notice about the order is that the Tabernacle was "in the midst" of the Camp (Numbers 2:17 and 3:5-10).With respect to the New Testament Camp, this speaks to us of the centrality of Christ in the camp of the saints. The Lord Jesus Christ is "in the midst" of His people (Matthew 18:20).Everyone is to be camped in relation to the Son of God.

In Israel there were Twelve Tribes. These Twelve Tribes were divided into four groups in regard to their positioning around the Tabernacle. Each group of three Tribes had their own particular standard under which they encamped. The four groupings were as follows:

1. On the **East** side under the standard of the **Lion** were positioned the Tribes of Judah, Issachar and Zebulon (Numbers 2:3-9). These armies totaled 186,000 individuals and comprised the largest of the groups.

2. On the **West** side of the Tabernacle under the standard of the **Ox** were the three Tribes of Ephraim, Mannasseh and Benjamin (Numbers 2:18-24). This was the smallest group of tribes involving 108,100 people.

3. On the **North** side the Tribes of Dan, Asher and Naphtali camped under the standard of the **Eagle** (Numbers 2:25-31). This camp was comprised of 157,000 individuals.

4. Opposite to the above camp we find the Tribes of Rueben, Simeon and Gad on the **South** side of the Tabernacle under the standard of the **Man** (Numbers 2:10-16). We notice that the individuals in this camp have a similar total to that of the camp on the North. This total is 151,450.

(**Note:** It is important to add here that in a Hebrew Encyclopedia it is pointed out that the four faces in Ezekiel's vision were the four standards under which the nation of Israel encamped. The four faces were those of a Lion, an Ox, an Eagle and a Man — See Ezekiel 1 and Revelation 4-5.)

Therefore, with all the Tribes in their place we have a very interesting picture, not in man's view, but in God's. For with all the Tribes so arranged on the North, South, East and West with the Tabernacle in the midst from a heavenly view we would see the camp of Israel arranged in the shape of **the Cross!** (See Diagram)

The New Testament fulfillment is that God's camp of His Saints around the world are seen in relation to each other and in relation to Jesus Christ in **the Cross.** This is Divine Order! Just as God had order then, He has order in His New Testament Church. The "Cross Principle" must be maintained for full blessing to life (Matthew 16:16-25; I Corinthians 2:1-2; I Corinthians 14:40 and Colossians 2:5).   No wonder Paul said, "God forbid that I should **Glory, save in the Cross** or our Lord Jesus Christ" (Galatians 6:14).

Of the Furniture

Further confirmation of "The Cross" principle is that seen in the placing and Divine positioning of the Furniture in the Tabernacle itself. God gave express instructions as to the position of the Furniture. Divine arrangement is seen throughout the whole of the structure and enclosure.

The **Ark** of the Covenant was positioned at the *"Head* in the Most Holy Place, or the Holiest of All.
The Staves were on the sides. Exodus 25:13
The Cherubims were on the ends. Exodus 25:18
The Mercy Seat faced the East. Leviticus 16:14
The Staves were left in the rings. Hence the Ark was placed with the Staves running North and South.

The **Golden Altar** of Incense was placed in the following position:
It was before the Veil. Exodus 30:6
It was also before the Ark. Exodus 40:5
It is spoken of as being before the Mercy Seat. Exodus 30:6. This would place the Incense Altar in line with the Ark of the Covenant, or at the *"Heart"* of the Tabernacle, in the Holy Place.

The **Shewbread Table** was placed on the North side of the Tabernacle. Exodus 40:22

The **Golden Candlestick** was placed on the South side of the Tabernacle. Exodus 40:24. It is specifically placed opposite the Table. Both were in the Holy Place. Thus Table and Candlestick were opposite each other. Exodus 26:35.

Coming out to the Outer Court we find that the **Brazen Altar** was placed before the Door. Exodus 40:6,29. That is, at the *"Foot"*, the beginning of man's approach to God. Then the **Brazen Laver** was placed in the Outer Court "between" the tent of the Tabernacle and the Brazen Altar. Exodus 40:7. Thus in line with the Brazen Altar.

Though the Scripture does not expressly state all in their position, yet it can be seen that if a straight line is drawn from the Ark of the Covenant, passing through the Incense Altar, and through the Brazen Laver to the Brazen Altar, and then another straight line is drawn from the Golden Candlestick across to the

THE CROSS IN THE TABERNACLE FURNITURE

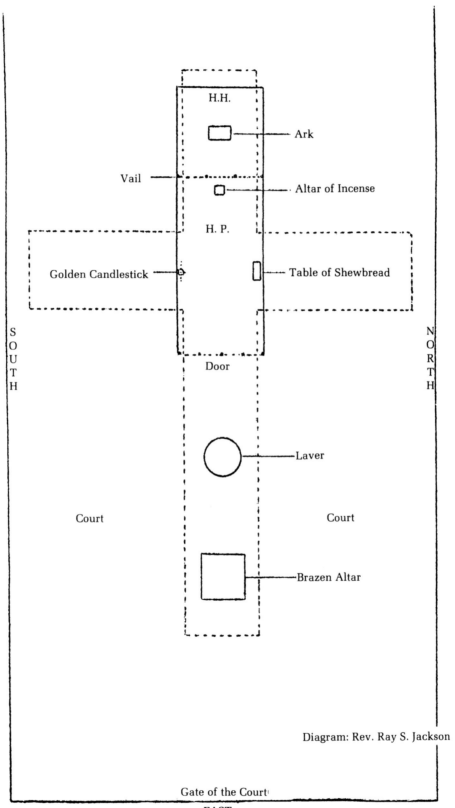

Diagram: Rev. Ray S. Jackson

Scale: 1 cu:3mm

A VIEW FROM THE MOUNT OF THE CAMP OF ISRAEL
IN THE WILDERNESS

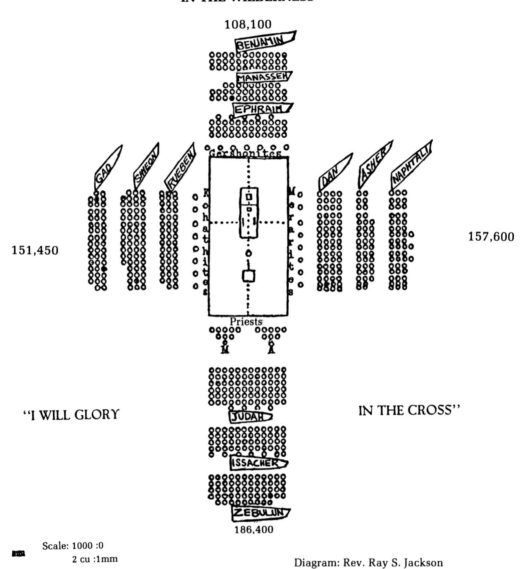

108,100

151,450

157,600

"I WILL GLORY

IN THE CROSS"

186,400

Scale: 1000 :0
2 cu :1mm

Diagram: Rev. Ray S. Jackson

THE CROSS IN THE ARRANGEMENT OF THE CAMP

Table of Shewbread, the revelation of the Cross is beheld in the positioning of the furnishings. Evidence thus shows the furniture in the form of *the Cross.*

Refer to the following Diagram for the illustration of the Camp in the form of the Cross, and the Tabernacle furniture in the form of the Cross.

The Divine Message is evident! All of God's dwelling with His people is upon the basis of the work of **the Cross** which is in Christ Jesus. Note these Scriptures on 'The Cross' — I Corinthians 1:17-18. Galatians 5:11. Colossians 2:14.

Ephesians 2:6 "And that he might reconcile both unto God in one body by **the Cross**, having slain the enmity thereby."

Colossians 1:20 "And having made peace through the blood of **his Cross**, by him to reconcile all things unto himself; . . . ."

Hebrews 12:2 ". . . . who for the joy that was set before him endured **the Cross**, by him to reconcile all things unto himself; . . . ."

Hebrews 12:2; ". . . .who for the joy that was set before him endured **the Cross** despising the shame, and is set down at the right hand of the Throne of God."

Philippians 2:8 "And being found in fashion as a man he humbled himself, and became obedient unto death, even the death of **the Cross**."

See also: I Corinthians 1:17-18; Galatians 5:11 and Colossians 2:14.

(9) The Order of the Revelation and Construction of the Tabernacle

The chapters in the Book of Exodus dealing with the complete revelation and construction of the Tabernacle are as follows:

1. Exodus 25-31 — In this section we have the actual revelation of the Tabernacle to Moses in the Mount closing with the giving of the Ten Commandments on the Two Tables of Stone.

2. Exodus 32-34 — Here we find the Golden Calf erected and the idolatry of Israel followed by the judgment of God. This closes with the intercession of Moses and the second giving of the Ten Commandments on the second Tables of Stone.

3. Exodus 35-40 — The final section includes the actual construction of the Tabernacle and closes with the placement of the Ten Commandments in the Ark of God. When all is done after the pattern the Glory of God fills the Sanctuary.

We offer the following chart to summarize the accounts of the revelation and the construction of the Tabernacle pieces:

	Revelation	Construction
1. Offerings and material commanded to be brought	Ex. 25:1-9	35:4-29
2. The Ark and the Mercyseat	Ex. 25:10-23	37:1-9
3. The Table of Shewbread	Ex. 25:23-30	37:10-16
4. The Golden Candlestick	Ex. 25:31-40	37:17-24
5. The Curtains and Coverings	Ex. 26:1-14	36:8-19
6. The Boards, Bars and Sockets	Ex. 26:15-30	36:20-34
7. The Veil	Ex. 26:31-35	36:35-36
8. The Tabernacle Door	Ex. 26:36-37	36:37-38
9. The Brazen Altar	Ex. 27:1-9	38:1-7
10. The Court, Pillars, Sockets, Pins and Cords	Ex. 27:9-19	38:9-20
11. The Oil for the Candlestick	Ex. 27:20-21	39:27
12. The Priests' Garments	Ex. 28	39:1-32
13. The Consecration of the Priests	Ex. 29	Lev. 8:1-36
14. The Golden Altar of Incense	Ex. 30:1-10	37:25-28
15. The Soul-Atonement Money	Ex. 30:11-16	38:21-31
16. The Brazen Laver	Ex. 30:17-21	38:8
17. The Holy Anointing Oil	Ex. 30:22-23	37:29
18. The Incense	Ex. 30:34-38	37:39

(10) The Time in Building

Our God is the sovereign ruler of the universe, and when He tells us that "**all these things happened unto them for ensamples**", He means **All** things. God is a God of detail. Every detail in the Tabernacle speaks some truth to this end of the age. And so we find that even in the time that it took to construct the Tabernacle there is important revelation. The time factor itself is prophetic of what was to take place 1500 years later in the incarnation of the Lord Jesus Christ.

When we correspond Exodus 19:1 and Numbers 9:1 with tradition in Jewish history, we find that the Tabernacle took approximately *nine months* to complete. After nine months it became the habitation of God.

In the Lord Jesus Christ, the **Word** made flesh we see that He was in preparation for nine months in the Virgin Mary (Matthew 1:21-23 and Colossians 1:19). In this we see the truth of Hebrews 10:5-8, "**A Body hast Thou prepared Me.**" Jesus Christ is the fulness of the Godhead Bodily. In Him dwells or tabernacles the fulness of the Divine nature, giving complete expression of God in flesh.

As the Tabernacle took nine months to complete and was built by the **Word** and by the **Spirit of God,** so did the incarnation. Mary was overshadowed by the *Spirit* and The *Word* was made flesh. Jesus is that perfect and suitable habitation for God the Father to dwell, Luke 1:30-38. Colossians 1:19. 2:9.

OUR STUDY APPROACH

There are basically two ways in which a study of the Tabernacle of Moses may be approached.

The first approach is to begin with the Gate of the Outer Court, proceeding through, from the Brazen Altar unto the Ark of the Covenant, in the Holiest of All.

This would be to approach the truth from **Man unto God,** that is, the walk of **Faith.**

As man comes to God, he must begin at the Gate, accept the Blood sacrifice of Jesus Christ. From there on he progresses step by step, line upon line, until he comes to the ultimate, the full Glory of God as seen in the Most Holy Place.

The second approach would be to follow the general order of revelation, and to begin where God began, that is, with the Ark of the Covenant, and then proceed on out to the Brazen Altar and Court Gate.

This would be approaching the truth from **God unto Man,** that is, the path of **Grace.**

Unless God first comes in Grace to man, man will in no wise be able to stand in the Presence of a Holy God.

In this present study we will be following the second approach. We begin where God began. This is the order of Sovereign Grace. God coming out from His Throne in Heaven to earth to meet the sinner in redeeming love.

From the Brass Altar to the Ark of the Covenant — Man's Approach, Faith.
From the Ark of the Covenant to the Brass Altar — God's Approach, Grace.

(Note — The Teacher may take either of these approaches, as the notes are designed to be suitable for both ways.)

Materials Used in Construction

Preliminary to any study of the Tabernacle of Moses must be a consideration of the actual materials that God set forth to be used in the structure of the Tabernacle itself, for in the very materials of the structure God was revealing eternal Truth. God uses the elements of *Creation* to set forth a portion of *Redemption* truth (Romans 1:20). We must never forget that there is eternal significance in every word that proceeds out of the mouth of God. Whether or not we fully understand the significance of each word in no way changes this fact. *God's Word is Truth.*

And so, as we look at the materials of the Tabernacle we see that God used another avenue to express His Truth. God is always progressive in His revelation to man. He always moves from the lower to the higher level. God moves from the ritual to the reality, from the shadow to the substance, from the type to the antitype, from the prophecy to the fulfillment, from the symbol to its spiritual truth, from the natural to the spiritual, from the first to the second and from the earthly to the heavenly.

The actual materials of the Tabernacle of Moses are given for us in two places — Exodus 25:1-7 and Exodus 35:4-9, "Speak unto the children of Israel, that they bring me **an offering:** of every man that giveth it willingly with his heart ye shall take my offering. And this is the offering which ye shall take of them; **gold, and silver, and brass, and blue, and purple, and scarlet, and fine linen, and goats' hair, and rams' skins dyed red, and badgers' skins, and shittim wood.** Oil for the light, **spices** for anointing oil, and for **sweet incense, onyx stones,** and **stones** to be set in the ephod, and in the breastplate." (Note: These materials were to be free-will offerings from the people. God is not interested in lip-service, but He wants a response from the heart.)

The materials listed by God divide into three natural categories or Kingdoms, and we will deal with them in this order—the Mineral Kingdom, the Plant Kingdom and the Animal Kingdom.

The materials of the Tabernacle relating to the *Mineral Kingdom* are the following:

1. **Gold** — In the Old as well as the New Testament, we find that gold speaks to us in Deity, Divine nature, the Kingly nature, the Glory of God and God the Father. (Check the following Scriptures: Job 23:10; I Peter 1:7; II Peter 1:4 and Revelation 21:21-22).

2. **Silver** — This precious metal speaks to us of Redemption, the atonement, ransom money and God the Son. This is best seen in the price paid for the betrayal of Christ who was our ransom (See also: Exodus 30:11-16; Zechariah 11:12-13 and I Peter 1:18-20).

3. **Brass** — This metal symbolizes strength, judgment against sin, and God the Holy Spirit. God tells us that if we do not listen to His voice that the heavens will be as brass (Deuteronomy 28:13-23) which is the judgment of God on man. If we will not listen to His voice, He will not listen to our voice (Additional Scriptures include: Numbers 21:5-9; Job 40:18; Isaiah 4:4 and Revelation 1:12-15).

4. **Precious stones** — These precious stones which were mainly to be used in connection with the priestly garments speak of the various gifts of the Holy Spirit, the glories of the saints, the preciousness of God's own people and the righteous acts of the children of God. They are witness to both the Word and the Spirit (I John 5:6-11),for additional reference see: Proverbs 17:8; I Corinthians 3:9-17 and Revelation 21:18-20.

The materials of the Tabernacle relating to the *Plant Kingdom* are the following:

1. **Fine Linen** — Revelation 19:7-8 clearly tells us that the fine linen is the righteousness of the saints. The saints, however, only experience this righteousness as they put on Christ. So this symbol first speaks of the righteousness of Christ (See also: Revelation 15:5-6).

2. **Shittim Wood** — This was a very durable wood used in connection with the Tabernacle. The Septuagint translates this as "incorruptible" or "non-decaying" wood. Wood being a product of the earth would then speak to us of the human nature of Christ. Shittim wood or incorruptible wood would speak to us of the incorruptible, sinless humanity of the Lord Jesus Christ, who is the righteous

Branch. As in Christ, it also speaks of the redeemed humanity of His Body, the Church (See: Isaiah 11:1-3 and Jeremiah 25:5-6).

3. **Oil for Light** — Oil is always symbolic of the Holy Spirit. Here it is used in connection with light, suggesting to us the ministry of illumination that the Holy Spirit renders. It is the ministry of the Holy Spirit to enlighten our eyes to the Word of God (I John 2:20,27; John 1:41).

4. **Spices for the Anointing Oil** — The anointing oil itself speaks to us of the ministry of the Holy Spirit who anoints us to minister. The spices, therefore, would speak of the graces, character, fruit and different operations of the Holy Spirit (I John 2:20,27; Galatians 5:22-23 and Song of Solomon 4:16).

5. **Spices for Sweet Incense** — The incense itself speaks to us of prayer which ascends unto the Lord as incense (Psalms 141:2). The spices for this sweet incense would include the various aspects or types of prayer. This would also include intercession, praise and worship unto God. Incense always moves from man to God (Luke 1:10; Romans 8:26-27 and Revelation 5:8).

The materials of the Tabernacle relating to the *Animal Kingdom* are the following:

1. **Blue** (shellfish) — One only has to look up on a clear day to see that naturally speaking blue is the color of the heavens. In the Word of God the same is true. Blue is the heavenly color. If a color would be assigned to each of the Gospels, blue would be descriptive of the Gospel of John which portrays Christ as the Lord from heaven. Exodus 24:10; Ezekiel 1:26 and I Corinthians 15:47-49.

2. **Purple** (shellfish) — This was the most precious of the colors in ancient times and speaks to us of royalty and kingship. Purple would be descriptive of the Gospel of Matthew which deals with the King and His Kingdom Judges 8:26; Luke 16:19 and John 19:1-3.

3. **Scarlet** (worm or insect) — Scarlet is the color of Blood which speaks to us of sacrifice. It speaks of the Redemptive work of Christ in the Atonement when He became the sacrifice and shed His own Blood for the sins of many (Leviticus 17:11 and Isaiah 1:18). Scarlet speaks to us of the Gospel of Mark which portrays the suffering Servanthood of Christ.

4. **Goats' hair** — Goats were used primarily in the sin offering of the Old Testament. Thus, the goat's hair covering speaks to us of sin (Leviticus 4:22-29 and 16:15-16).

5. **Rams' skin dyed red** — The ram like the lamb was a sacrificial animal. Abraham offered a ram in the stead of his son Isaac. The rams' skins speak to us of consecration, dedication and substitution (Genesis 22:13-14; Exodus 29).

6. **Badgers' skins** — Badger skins are not considered to be a precious fur. They were used on the outside of the Tabernacle to protect it. They were what the outside observer would see if he were to look upon the Tabernacle. If we apply this to Christ we see that the Badger skins speak to us of the humanity of Christ. They point to His earthly body which had no form or comeliness or beauty the we should desire Him. His beauty was behind the external (Isaiah 52:14 and 53:1-3).

It would be well for the reader to refer back to this section frequently, for these symbolic truths will be maintained in all of the teaching that follows.

THE ARK OF THE COVENANT

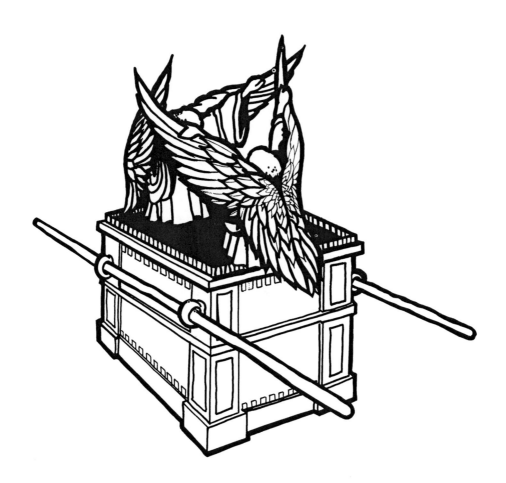

Read the following: Exodus 25:10-22; 37:1-9; 40:20-21 and Leviticus 16:13-15.

The Ark of the Covenant

(1) The Ark in General

In the Old Testament God has set forth revelation of Divine truth in three distinct Arks. Each of these Arks carries with it the thought of *preservation*. The first Ark mentioned in the Scriptures is the *Ark of Noah* (Genesis 6:13 - 9:18) This Ark was made of gopher wood, pitched within and without. It speaks most emphatically to us of preservation; for in it the animals and eight souls were preserved from the water of judgment and death (I Peter 3:20).

The second Ark mentioned in the Old Testament is the Ark prepared for the baby Moses, which we will call the *Ark of Moses* (Exodus 2:3-6). This Ark was made of reeds and pitched within and without just as Noah's Ark. Here, too, we see that the Ark was a means of preservation for the baby Moses from the waters of death. It is interesting to note that the Hebrew word 'tebah' is used in reference to both the Ark of Noah and the Ark of Moses. The literal meaning of this word is 'Box, chest, vessel or ark.'

The third Ark referred to in the Bible is the *Ark of the covenant*. An altogether different Hebrew word is used when this Ark is referred to. The word used in reference to the Ark of the covenant is 'arown'. This word means 'chest or ark', but it also carries with it a couple of other connotations. In Genesis 50:26, this same word is used in regard to the coffin (mummy-case) of Joseph. In another reference in II Kings 12:10-11 we find this word used in reference to a money chest. However, this word is used most often in regard to the Ark of the covenant. This Ark is referred to by many different titles or names in the Old Testament. It was called:

1. The Ark of the Testimony, Exodus 25:22
2. The Ark of the Covenant of the Lord, Numbers 10:33
3. The Ark of the Lord God, I Kings 2:26
4. The Ark of the Lord, the Lord of All the Earth, Joshua 3:13
5. The Ark of God, I Samuel 3:3
6. The Holy Ark, II Chronicles 35:3
7. The Ark of Thy Strength, Psalms 132:8
8. The Ark of the Covenant of God, Judges 20:27
9. The Ark of the Covenant, Joshua 3:6
10. The Ark of the Lord, Joshua 4:11
11. The Ark of God the God of Israel, I Samuel 5:7
12. The Ark of Shittim Wood, Exodus 25:10

This Ark of the Covenant was made of shittim wood, overlaid with gold within and without. This Ark also carries with it the thought of preservation. We see this particularly when the children of Israel were crossing the Jordan (Joshua 3-4). As the Ark led the way, the children of Israel were preserved from the waters of the Jordan (death). In addition to this, the thought of preservation is seen in regard to the Tables of the Law, the Golden Pot of Manna and Aaron's Rod that budded which were preserved in the Ark of the covenant.

(2) And they shall make an ark . . . Exodus 25:10

In Exodus 25:8 God expresses His desire to live among His called or chosen people, He instructs Moses to build Him a Sanctuary that He might dwell among them. He instructs Moses to follow the pattern that He reveals to him to the letter. Why? Because in it all, in the very order, materials, dimensions and colors God has hidden Divine and eternal truth. So in verse 10 God begins with the Ark of shittim wood. This Ark is to prove to be the most important piece of furniture in all of the Old Testament. The fact is that it is the only piece of furniture to inhabit three different Tabernacles or Sanctuaries (I Chronicles 16:1 and I Kings 8:9).There are about 185 references to this article in the Old Testament, all of which show the emphasis that God placed upon it. The reference here in Exodus is the first mention of the Ark. The last mention of it in the Old Testament is found in Jeremiah 3:14-16, and the final mention of the Ark in the Bible is in Revelation 11:19 where the true Ark of His Testament is seen in heaven.

But why would God begin here with this Ark or chest of wood overlaid with gold? Why would God specify this piece of His sanctuary to be made first? In order to understand this more fully we must see what this Ark represents. The Ark of the covenant of the Lord represents the following:

1. The Ark represents the *Throne of God* in the earth.
2. The Ark represents the *Presence of God* in Christ, by the Spirit in the midst of His redeemed people.
3. The Ark represents the *Glory of God* revealed in Divine order and worship.
4. The Ark represents the *Fullness of the Godhead Bodily* revealed in the Lord Jesus Christ (Colossians 1:19 and 2:9). All that the Ark was to Israel in the Old Testament, Jesus Christ is to His Church, Spiritual Israel, in the New Testament).

God begins the revelation of His Sanctuary with Himself, "in the beginning God" (Genesis 1:1). God begins in the Holiest of all or the Most Holy Place, in His own Throne Room, with the Ark of the Covenant. It was upon this piece of furniture that the High Priest sprinkled the Blood of atonement once a year (Leviticus 16 and Hebrews 9:7). It was from this piece of furniture that God's audible voice was heard speaking to Moses the Lawgiver and Aaron the High Priest (Leviticus 1:1). Every other article took a place of subordination in relation to the Ark of the Lord. If the Ark of God's Presence were to be removed from this Tabernacle (as it was when the Tabernacle of David was established), all that would remain would be empty form. For without the Presence of the Lord, as upon that Ark and Mercy Seat, all our ritual is meaningless and powerless. All of Israel's worship was directed to **Jehovah** who dwelt upon that Blood-stained Mercy Seat (Psalms 80:1).

God begins with Himself, where He must begin. For He alone is God, who is from everlasting to everlasting. This is a picture of the grace of God. God dwelling in eternity becomes flesh and Tabernacled among us (John 1:14). God begins first with His Throne, the Ark of the Covenant, and proceeds in grace to man and the place of sacrifice — the Brazen Altar. This is the opposite of man's approach to God. Man must begin at the Brazen Altar and experience the Cross and the Blood before he can approach the Ark of His Glory. This indeed, is a true picture of the grace of God. For unless God first comes out to man, man has no access whatsoever to God. Any man that tried to come straight into the presence of God without approaching the prescribed way through the Blood was slain. Violation of God's order means death. The Ark and all it contains are representative of the holiness of God. The Brazen Altar is necessary because of man's sinfulness. But because of the provision of God in the Brazen Altar, there is a Day when the High Priest can enter beyond the veil to the very Throne of God (Hebrews 9).

(3) of shittim wood . . . Exodus 25:10

Shittim wood most likely comes from the Acacia trees which are still common in the Sinai desert region. The Acacia tree grows in the desert in arid conditions, and a medicinal gum comes from it. It is a hard, orange-brown wood that is extremely durable. In fact, the Septuagint version of the Old Testament translates the word as "incorruptible" or "non-decaying" wood.

This wood, then, becomes a fitting type or symbol of the sinless, incorruptible humanity of the Lord Jesus Christ. He was "a root out of dry ground" and "hath no comeliness . . . no beauty that we should desire Him" (Isaiah 53:2). In the midst of desert conditions of evil and corruption, **He** remained uncorrupted, incorruptible and unstained in His nature and character (Psalms 16:10; Luke 1:35; I Peter 1:23 and I John 3:5).

This wood also speaks to us of Christ as **"the branch"** revealed throughout the Old Testament. God continually promised to raise up a righteous **"branch"** to rule over His people (Isaiah 4:2; 11:1; Jeremiah 23:5; Zechariah 3:8 and 6:12).

(4) Two cubits and a half shall be the length thereof, and a cubit and a half the height thereof. Exodus 25:10

The measurements of the Ark of the Covenant suggest spiritual significance in the numbers.

The Ark-chest measured 2½ cubits in length, by 1½ cubits width, by 1½ cubits height, or 2½ cubits x 1½ cubits x 1½ cubits.

The Mercy Seat fitted as a perfect lid on the top of the box-like Ark.

Thus 2 x 1½ = 3, the Number of the Godhead.

2 x 2½ = 5, the Number of the Atonement, the Grace of God.

The Circumference of the end, 1½ + 1½ + 1½ + 1½ = 6, the Number of Man.
The Circumference of the top, 2½ + 1½ + 2½ + 1½ = 8, the Number of Ressurection.

The top and bottom of Ark, 4 x 2½ = 10, the Number of Law, Order, Judgment.
The two ends together, 8 x 1½ = 12, the Number of Perfect Government, Order of Israel.

The Height of the Ark was 1½ cubits; the same height as the Table of Shewbread, and the Grate of the Brazen Altar in the Outer Court.

Thus three articles, one in the Outer Court, the Holy Place, and the Holiest of All are connected in the same height; the same truth.

It is only as we come to the Blood sacrifice (Brazen Altar grate, 1½ cubits), that we may come to the Mercy Seat (Ark of Covenant, 1½ cubits) and then may have the Communion as in the Shewbread (Table, 1½ cubits).

In the numbers 3, 5, 6, 8, 10, and 12 we understand the combined significance of truth as fulfilled in the Lord Jesus.

Jesus Christ is God (No. 3), and the Grace of God personified (No. 5). He became Man, the Union in One Person, the God-Man (No. 6).

He alone perfectly kept and fulfilled the Law, God's Order and was judged for our sin, in our breaking of the Law (No. 10).

In Him God's perfect and eternal Order of Israel, perfect Government, will be manifested. He chose 12 Apostles. (No. 12).

(Refer to Significance of Numbers — Appendix)

(5) and thou shalt overlay it with pure gold . . .Exodus 25:11

In addition to the shittim wood, the Ark of the Covenant was composed of pure gold. As we have seen (Introduction/3) gold is always symbolic of Deity or the Divine nature. Wood, on the other hand, speaks to us of Humanity or Human nature coming from natural growth in the earth. Hence, we have a blending of the two materials in the Ark. We have **two** materials in **one** ark. The gold is always gold, and the wood is always wood. This is significant of the **two** natures in **one** person as seen in the person of the Lord Jesus Christ—"God manifest in the flesh"(I Timothy 3:15-16). The gold symbolized His Divine nature(Hebrews 1), and the wood symbolizes His Human nature Hebrews 2. These two natures remain separate though brought together in one Person. God and Man are united in one Person, the **new** creature, the Firstborn of every **new** creation, Immanuel (God with us), The **Word** made flesh, the God-Man, the Lord Jesus Christ (Matthew 1:21-23; Isaiah 7:14; 9:6 and John 1:14).

(6) within and without shalt thou overlay it . . . Exodus 25:11

A second picture that we see here is that of the Fulness of the Godhead Bodily(Colossians 1:19; 2:9).When the wood was overlaid with gold within and without it produced a three layered Ark—**gold, wood** (central), **gold.** this is symbolic of the Three Persons of the Godhead—The Father, the Son, and the Holy Spirit. The gold without it typical of the Father-God who created all the universe. The gold within is typical of the Holy Spirit who dwells within. And the central material or the wood represents the central figure of the Godhead who was crucified on a Cross of wood "in the midst" (John 19:18) the Son. All of these together united in one Ark speak of the "Fulness of the Godhead bodily—the Lord Jesus Christ." Peter proclaimed the marvelous truth on the great day of Pentecost that God had made this "same Jesus . . . both Lord and Christ"(Acts 2:36)— See also: John 14:7-10, 18 and John 3:33-34.

Thus:—

Gold without —	Type of the Father God	)	The **Lord**	(**Fulness of**
Wood central —	Type of the Son (The Cross)	)	**Jesus**	(**the Godhead**
Gold within —	Type of the Holy Spirit	)	**Christ**	(**bodily**

(7) and shalt make upon it a crown of gold round about. Exodus 25:11

Three pieces of furniture in the Tabernacle receive Crowns—the Golden Altar of Incense, the Table of Shewbread and the Ark of the Lord. The Crown of gold tells us what the Father thinks of His Son. When the Son of God became flesh man Crowned Him with thorns(Mark 15:17),but God Crowned Him with glory and honour (Hebrews 2:9).

A Crown always speaks of Kingship. It is only natural then that we should see a Crown in connection with God's Throne Room in the earth relative to Israel.

The Holiest of All was the Throne Room for the King of Kings and the Lord of Lords.

The Crown signifies the Kingship of the Lord Jesus Christ.

He was born King of the Jews. (Matthew 2:2).

He was revealed as King in the Gospel of Matthew, the Gospel of the Kingdom.

He was crucified as King. (John 19:14).

He is the King-Priest forever sitting at the right hand of God (Psalms 110:1).

He is King in Zion,(Psalms 2:6),the Church (Hebrews 12:22-23).

We notice that it is the Lord Jesus Christ in His ministry as the King-Priest after the Order of Melchisedek who positions the mercy of God, even as the Crown of gold positioned the Mercy Seat on the Ark of God.

Ultimately, when Jesus comes again, He will be Crowned with many Crowns (Revelation 19:11-21),and we will lay our Crowns at His feet in worship (Proverbs 4:9; Isaiah 28:5-6; I Peter 5:4; Revelation 3:11 and 5:5-10).

Jesus is the King of Kings and Lord of Lords. May His Kingdom endure forever! Hallelujah!

(8) and thou shalt cast four rings of gold for it, and put them in the four corners thereof: and two rings shall be in the one side of it, and two rings in the other side of it. Exodus 25:12

These four rings were built for the staves which we will look at next. There were a total of **four** rings. The number four is usually symbolic of the creation or the world. It speaks to us of the four corners of the earth, with a world-wide or a universal appeal.

We give several illustrations of the number four suitable to the **four rings of gold,** in the Ark, to keep a balanced Ark.

1. *The Gospel to the 4 Corners of the earth.* (Acts 1:6).
   1. Jerusalem,   )
   2. Judea,   )
   3. Samaria,   )   The Power of the Gospel is universal.
   4. Uttermost part of the earth)

—Jerusalem, Judea, Samaria, and the uttermost part of the earth—four. It speaks to us of the fact that Christ has all power in all the earth.

The four rings were absolutely necessary for keeping the Ark evenly balanced. This speaks to us of the importance of a balanced presentation of our Lord Jesus Christ.

2. *The 4 Gospels in the New Testament.*
   1. Gospel of Matthew   —   Christ as The King   —   Son of David.
   2. Gospel of Mark   —   Christ as The Servant   —   Son of Man.
   3. Gospel of Luke   —   Christ as The Perfect Man —   Son of Adam.
   4. Gospel of John   —   Christ as God the Son   —   Son of God.

Such balance is seen in the **four** Gospels of the New Testament. In Matthew's Gospel we see Jesus as the King or Anointed One(Matthew 1:6; 4:17).In Mark's Gospel we see Jesus pictured as the *Servant* of many. Just in the fact that Mark records no geneology which in those days was so important shows this emphasis. In Luke's Gospel Jesus is seen as the *Son of Man,* while in John Jesus is portrayed as the *Son of God,* the Eternal Once.

3. *The 4 descriptions of God in the Bible.*

Balance is also seen in connection with the number four in regard to the description of God in the Bible.

In John 4:24 we are told that "God is a **Spirit**: and they that worship Him must worship Him in spirit and in truth." In another place, I John 1:5, we are told "That God is **light**, and in Him is no darkness at all." Again in I John 4:16 we see a third description of God, "God is **love**; and he that dwelleth in love dwelleth in God, and God in Him." Finally, there is a fourth description of God found in Hebrews 12:29. Here we see that "our God is a **consuming fire.**" When all these descriptions of God are seen, we have a balance in the presentation of God. To stress one above the other is to distort the very nature of God.

1. God is Light   I John 1:5
2. God is Spirit   John 4:24
3. God is Love   I John 4:16
4. God is a Consuming Fire   Hebrews 12:29

4. *The 4 Moral Attributes of God relative to His Creatures.*

This is also true of the four moral attributes of God in dealing with His creatures. There must be a balanced presentation of the nature and being and attributes of God.

1. Perfect Holiness
2. Perfect Righteousness
3. Perfect Love
4. Perfect Faithfulness

First, God dwells in perfect *holiness*. God is sinless perfection in the strictest sense. He has an absolute hatred for sin. Second, God manifests perfect *righteousness* or justice. Righteousness is holiness in action. It is holiness dealing with sin. Third, God is seen as having perfect *love*. The goodness, mercy, grace and kindness of God to His creatures is related to His love for them. Finally, God manifests perfect *faithfulness*. God is absolutely trustworthy. He always keeps His Word.

There are many such pictures of four qualities of God coming together in His dealings with man. One of the most graphic examples is that found in Psalms 85:10 where **"mercy and truth are met together; righteousness and peace have kissed each other."** All of these concepts must be maintained if we are to keep a balanced picture of the Lord Jesus Christ. Most heresy is not only the result of false teaching, but it is the result of an over-emphasis of one truth over and above the body of truth. As the Gospel message goes forth it must be a *balanced* message.

Thus **four rings of gold** — Balanced Truth relative to the things of **God.**

(9) And thou shalt make staves of shittim wood, and overlay them with gold. And thou shalt put the staves into the rings by the sides of the Ark, that the Ark may be borne with them. The staves shall be in the rings of the Ark: they shall not be taken from it. Exodus 25:13-15.

God instructs Moses to makes staves of shittim wood, overlaid with gold. Here, again, we have the blending of the two natures, the Divine and the Human or earthly (See section #5). The staves were to be put through the rings so that the Ark could be carried upon the shoulders of the Priest without actually touching the Ark itself (I Chronicles 15:15). The staves were to remain in the rings of the Ark significant of an earthly pilgrimage or an unsettled Ark. The staves remain in the Ark until we come to Solomon's Temple where the Ark was finally set (I Kings 8:8). This was significant for Israel that the wilderness wanderings and their journey was over. It speaks to us of the fact that we are but strangers and pilgrims in a foreign land (Matthew 8:20; John 15:19; I Peter 2:11 and I John 3:1), and with Abraham we are looking "for a city which hath foundations, whose builder and maker is God" (Hebrews 11:10). This world is not our eternal home; we are just passing through.

(10) And thou shalt make a mercy seat of pure gold: two cubits and a half shall be the length thereof, and a cubit and a half the breadth thereof. And thou shalt put the mercy seat above upon the Ark: and in the Ark thou shalt put the testimony that I shall give thee. And there I will meet with thee, and I will commune with thee from above the mercy seat, from between the two cherubim which are upon the Ark of the *testimony, of all things which I will give thee in commandment unto the children of Israel.* Exodus 25:17, 21-22.

Realizing that the New Testament writers are the infallible interpreters of the Old Testament, we see in Romans 3:25 exactly *who* this mercy seat is, "(Christ Jesus) whom God hath set forth to be a **propitiation through faith in His Blood.**" The Greek word used here for 'propitiation' is the same Greek word that is used in Hebrews 9:5 which is translated "Mercy-Seat". So we see that Jesus was set forth by God to be our Mercy-Seat. When we see what was involved in this Mercy Seat, it can only make this conclusion more apparent.

It was here, from above the Mercy Seat that God spoke to Aaron (Exodus 25:22; Numbers 7:89). This is where the Blood of the slain bullock was sprinkled as atonement for the sin of the nation (Leviticus 16). The Priest could never enter the Most Holy Place without the Blood. And so we see that the voice of God from off the Mercy Seat was only heard through Blood atonement. God has nothing to say to man apart from Jesus Christ and His redeeming Blood.

It was the **Blood** that changed the Throne of Judgment into a Throne of Grace (Hebrews 4:14-16). It is through faith in the **Blood** that Jesus becomes our propitiation—Mercy Seat (Romans 3:25). The word 'propitiation' means "to appease, placate or to make satisfaction." God is a holy God, full of righteousness and judgment. This is the picture of God that we see in the **Law**. When Israel broke the Law, they stirred up the wrath of God. Divine wrath is the holiness of God in action again sin. Sin must be judged; the demands of a holy God must be appeased. God's holiness and righteousness must be vindicated. The wages of sin is death! The Blood which was sprinkled on the Mercy Seat testified that a death had taken place. The judgment of God had been executed. Hence God's wrath was appeased. His righteousness was vindicated and now, God's mercy can flow.

Under the Old Covenant (Mosaic Covenant) God accepted the Blood of a sinless animal as atonement for sin, **but** this was only a shadow of the sinless Blood of Christ which would be for us a propitiation. As we stand sprinkled in the Blood of Christ God can be merciful, just and the justifier of all who believe or have faith in the Blood (I John 2:2,4:10 and Romans 3:20-27). Now we can stand with the publican who prayed in the temple, "God be **merciful** to me a sinner" (Luke 18:9-14), or as the literal suggests, "God be **'mercy-seated"** to me a sinner." The Blood shed at the Brazen Altar (which is seen as a type of the Cross) is brought to the Ark and Mercy Seat (the Throne of God), and God is propitiated.

In the Tabernacle we see a blending of judgment and mercy. Mercy and truth, righteousness and peace have been reconciled here (Psalms 101:1; 85:10; 86:5,13,15 and James 2:13). The grate on the Brazen Altar of sacrifice which was one and one half cubits high was the *Judgment Seat*. Here the sin of the whole nation was judged in that substitutionary death. Yet we see the Ark of the Covenant which was also one and one half cubits high as the *Seat of Mercy*. Here the whole nation of Israel was reconciled.

To remove the Blood-stained Mercy Seat, as did curious Israelites (I Samuel 6:19-20), is to expose and to bring into operation the ministration of death as seen in the 10 Commandments. In order to look upon the Tables of Stone, which had no life in them, one had to remove or put aside the Blood. If we reject the Blood, (the Law of the Spirit of Life,(Romans 8:2), we fall to the level of the Law (the Law of sin and death, Romans 8:2) which can only bring death to fallen man (II Corinthians 3). The Law could only thunder, demand command and condemn. It was God's perfect standard of righteousness, but it was powerless to give life or grace. In Christ alone can life be found, "*for Christ is the end of the law for righteousness to every one that believeth*"(Romans 10:4).Therefore since Christ has died to vindicate the righteous claims of a holy God and to satisfy divine justice (His Blood being the evidence that sin has been judged), we can once again be restored to a position of fellowship with God (Revelation 5:8-10).

It is important to notice also that this structure is called a Mercy **Seat**. This is the one and only seat in the whole of the Tabernacle. It was called a seat, and yet no man ever sat upon this seat. Paul, or the writer to the Hebrews, clearly identifies the truth set forth here, "And every priest **standeth** daily ministering and offering . . . but this man, after he had offered one sacrifice for sins forever, **sat down** on the right hand of God,"(Hebrews 10:11-12),See also: Psalms 110:1; Mark 16:19; Hebrews 8:1-3 and 12:1-2. The fact that Jesus sat down is significant of His **finished work** (Isaiah 16:5 and John 19:30). Christ presented His own Blood at the Throne of God, and having done so, He sat down. He is now seated as our Heavenly High

Priest after the order of Melchizedek. He is now seated on a Throne of pure gold, a seat for Deity, even the **Eternal Son of God.**

To sum up, we have seen that the Mercy Seat involved the following:

1. A place of holiness, justice and righeousness
2. A place of atonement and propitiation
3. A place of mercy and reconcilation
4. A place of communion of God with redeemed man
5. A place of the Glory of God
6. A place where God recorded His Name (II Samuel 6:1-2).

(11) And thou shalt make two cherubims of gold, of beaten work shalt thou make them, in the two ends of the mercy seat. And make one cherub on the one end, and the other cherub on the other and even of the mercy seat shall ye make the cherubims on the two ends thereof. And the cherubims shall stretch forth their wings on high, covering the Mercy Seat with their wings and their faces shall look one to another: toward the Mercy Seat shall the faces of the cherubim be. Exodus 25:18-20.

In the Cherubim and the Mercy Seat which were but one piece of gold, we have the most magnificent representation of the Godhead in all of the typical triangles in Scripture! Having identified who the Mercy Seat is, we identify the Two Cherubim at each end of the Mercy Seat. Nowhere does the Bible ever speak of these as angels. Angels have no part in the Mercy Seat because they are not one with Jesus. Hence, we cannot identify them as angels desiring to look into the mystery of our salvation(I Peter 1:12). The Cherubim are referred to as ''Cherubim of Glory'' (Hebrews 9:5).

The lid of the Ark of the Covenant was made of **one** piece of gold fashioned into **three** figures. We have Two Cherubs and a Blood-stained Mercy Seat. This is significant of the fulness of the Godhead, that is, the Father, the Son and the Holy Spirit (Tri-Unity). Just as there is one piece of gold, there is only one God. Just as there are three representations, there are Three Persons in the Godhead (See diagram below).

Thus: **One Cherub — Mercy Seat — One Cherub**
    The Father   The Son   The Holy Spirit

One Piece of God — Typical of One God.
Fashioned in a Tri — Typical of the Eternal Godhead,
    (angle)   the Eternal *Tri*, even the Father, **(three)** the Son, and the Holy Spirit.

The **Tri**-angle well illustrates the truth.

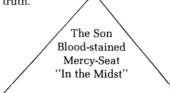

    One Cherub   One Cherub
    The Father   The Son   The Holy Spirit
                        Blood-stained
                        Mercy-Seat
                        "In the Midst"

Only the Father, the Son and the Holy Spirit are *one* in the plan of Redemption (I John 5:5-8). Thus, the Father and the Holy Spirit gaze with satisfaction upon the Blood-stained Mercy Seat and the finished work of Redemption. God said to Moses, ''When I see the Blood, I will pass over you''(Exodus 12:13). As God sees the Blood-sprinkled Mercy Seat, He is appeased and He withholds the judgment of death.

All throughout the Old Testament the Cherubim are seen in relation to judgment on sin. They are the guardians of the holiness of God, as well as that which pertains to the work of Redemption. The following are some examples:

1. Genesis 3:21-24 — The Cherubim guard the *tree of life* with the flaming sword at the Gate of Eden.
2. Exodus 26:31-33 — The Cherubim are inwrought within the veil(Hebrews 10:20),and are seen guarding any presumptuous intrusion, without Blood in to the Holiest of all, God's Throne Room.
3. Psalms 80:1 — The Shepherd of Israel dwells between the Cherubim.
4. Psalms 99:1 — The Lord reigns and *sits* between the Cherubim.

The only conclusion that we can come to is that the Cherubim are significant of the Father and the Holy Spirit, while the Mercy Seat, the Shepherd-King is none other than the Blessed Son of God, the Redeemer.

This is not a new concept, but others searching in the **Word** have come to similar conclusions. One such example is extremely interesting. In a book of doctrine published in 1804 by a man named Jones there is a section on the "Names and Titles of Christ" from which we glean the following excerpts:

"The Ark of the Covenant, the first object to be constructed, preached the Covenant of grace entered into between the Divine Persons, or Elohim in Jehovah, whose sensible representations, respecting their gracious offices, the Cherubim were. The **Father** and the **Spirit** were thus described, looking upon and shadowing with wings, the **Mercy Seat**, the propitiation, the Mediator, the place of their feet, all synonymous terms, expressing the **Human Nature** assumed by the **Divine** in the person of **Jesus Christ**, who was crowned, who crowned, who was connected with, and who covered the Ark or **Church** beneath Him, and with whom all the Church were thus to be represented as **One**, even as Christ and God are one, and as partakers in Him of the divine nature and glory. (John 17)

To be a true believer was to have a place by faith in God's Ark, to be covered with Christ, the Mercy-Seat, and to be under the wings or protection of the Elohim, or **three persons in the Covenant.** Thus it is said of Ruth that she came to trust in or under the wings of Jehovah, the Elohim of Israel His people.

Thus to seek the faces of Jehovah was to appear before the Ark where only was the **Shekinah**, the Divine manifestation under the Law. This was the Psalmist's sense of the shadow of the wings of God (God's wings), which he frequently mentions as his own trust and joy, and which he earnestly exalts before others.

And our Lord Himself, carrying the same idea of affection of a bird, laments over the Jews, as persons who refused to be gathered under His protection, though He had borne with them, and borne their fathers on Eagles' wings (i.e. the power of the Spirit) and brought them unto Himself. (Exodus 19:4; 25:20).

In short, the fabric of this Ark gave birth to many spiritual ideas for the use of the Ancient Church(Acts 7:38) which caused them to prize it above all the sacred economy.

The Ark of the Covenant (or, as it is otherwise called), the Ark of Elohim Jehovah, or of the Covenanters in Jehovah, was the standing symbol or testimony on the Ancient Church of this fundamental truth (of the Godhead Three in One) and so God was represented to us, inhabiting the very Cherubim (for thus it should have been translated) and who is to be called on there. (Deuteronomy 6:4; I Chronicles 13:6; Leviticus 16:2; Numbers 7:89; Exodus 25:22)" (End of Quotes).

(12) The Shekinah

Between this **Tri-une** piece of gold, there was the very Presence and Glory-Brightness of God in visible manifestation upon the Blood-stained Mercy Seat. As we have said, it was here that God spoke in an audible voice (Exodus 29:42; 30:6, 36 and Numbers 7:89).The Hebrews called this manifestation of the visible Glory or Brightness of God "the Shekinah". Although this word never occurs in the Bible, it does occur in extra-Biblical Hebrew writings. In Shabbath 22b we are told that the burning lamps outside the veil were a witness "that the Shekinah abides in the midst of Israel." Apart from this, however, the Old Testament is saturated with the thought of the visible presence and brightness of God. The word 'Shekinah' means "the one who dwells". It refers to God's dwelling visibly among His people.

The record of this visible manifestation coming down to the Ark is found in Exodus 40:33-38 where "the Glory of the Lord filled the Tabernacle." Prior to this Moses journeyed into the Presence of the Lord, and he was visibly changed by the experience (Exodus 34:29-35).The Presence was so manifest on the Ark that when the Ark set forth or when it rested Moses addressed it as **"Lord"** (Numbers 10:35-36). All through the wanderings and conquest this thought is maintained. When the Ark is lost in I Samuel 4, the children of Israel realize full well that they had lost much more than a material Ark, but they knew that the "Glory" had departed with it (I Samuel 4:21-22).

Asaph refers most assuredly to this manifestation as he begins Psalm 80 with the words, "Give ear, O Shepherd of Israel . . . thou that dwellest between the Cherubims, shine forth" (See also, Isaiah 37:16)

The Ark of the Covenant is the only piece of furniture upon which God dwelt in Brightness. All the other pieces of furniture were but powerless forms if "The Presence" in the Ark was not there. So everything in the Church becomes empty form and meaningless ceremony if "The Presence" is not there(Matthew 18:20). So what is "The Presence" in the Church?

In the New Testament the Shekinah speaks to us of the Glory of God in the face of Jesus Christ (II Corinthians 4:6). Jesus was the "Brightness of His Glory, and the express image of His Person" Hebrews 1:3. He was the Word made flesh who "dwelt" among us, and "we beheld His Glory, the Glory as of the only Begotten of the Father, full of grace and truth" (John 1:14). He was the "Lord of Glory" (I Corinthians 2:8). In fact, His Glory will one day light the earth (Revelation 18:1).

The Most Holy Place in the Tabernacle was the most unique section of the Tabernacle. The Outer Court experienced the natural light of day. The Holy Place was lighted by the seven lamps. But the Most Holy Place had no artificial or no natural light, and yet it was the brightest section of the Tabernacle. It was lighted by the light of I Timothy 6:15-16, "the light which no man can approach unto; whom no man hath seen, nor can see." It was lighted by the very *Glory* of God.

(13) The Place of the Ark

The Ark of the Covenant was placed in the Holiest of all or the Most Holy Place. This area measured 10X10X10 or 1000 cubical content. It was *foursquare,* as was the Brazen Altar, the Golden Altar and the Breastplate of Judgment on the Priest. The Shekinah Glory of God filled that four squareness and covered the *earth floor* within the veil. All of which is significant of the whole earth being "filled with the knowledge of the glory of the Lord, as the waters cover the sea" (Habakkuk 2:14). The 1000 cubits point to the full glory of the Kingdom as set forth in the 1000 years spoken of in Revelation 20:1-6. The ultimate fulfillment and revelation is the **Glory of God** in the **New** and **Heavenly** Jerusalem, which is the *foursquare* and **Eternal City of God** and the **Redeemed** (Revelation 21-22).

(14) And the Ark of the Covenant overlaid round about with gold, wherein was the golden pot that had manna, and Aaron's rod that budded, and the Tables of the Covenant.
Hebrews 9:4

The Ark of the Covenant was a place of preservation for the Tables of the Law (Exodus 25:21; Deuteronomy 10:5 and Exodus 40:20), the Golden Pot of Manna (Exodus 16:33-34) and Aaron's Rod that Budded (Numbers 17:10). Not only does the Ark itself represent the Lord Jesus Christ as the Fulness of the Godhead bodily, but the contents of the Ark also give us further revelation. The contents of the Ark reveal two distinct pictures. That is, they are typical of the Godhead, and they are typical of the Fulness of the Godhead bodily, the Lord Jesus Christ.

First of all, we see the contents of the Ark as typical of the Godhead. The contents of the Ark included **three** articles in **one** Ark. Each of these three articles can be seen as a revelation of a different Person of the Godhead. Each declare the characteristics and symbolism of a distinct member of the Godhead, as follows:

1. *The Tables of the Law* — Here we see a type of the Father-God, the Lawgiver. It was by His voice that the Law was first given. The Law is symbolic of all authority and power which is in the hands of the Father.

2. *The Golden Pot of Manna* — In the Manna we are directed to God the Son who is the Bread of life and the Bread of heaven which came down from above (John 6:48-45).

3. *Aaron's Rod that Budded* — Aaron's Rod is a type of God the Holy Spirit, for in Aaron's Rod we see the principle of fruitfulness and life (Galatians 5:22-23).

Second, the contents of the Ark speak to us of the "Fulness of the Godhead bodily." Everything in the Old Testament finds fulfillment in the Lord Jesus Christ, for "in Him dwelleth all the fulness of the Godhead bodily" (Colossians 2:9). We should also be aware that which is fulfilled in Christ, the Head is also to come to fulfillment in His Body, the Church. Each of these articles in the Ark tell us something of the nature of Christ and His ministry to and through His Body.

1. *The Tables of the Law* — In Israel there were three aspects of the Law:

    a. *Moral Law* — This was the Ten Commandments which were written on Tables of Stone. This Law was given to Israel three times. It was given orally to the nation of Israel as they gathered at Sinai (Exodus 19-20; Deuteronomy 4-5 and Hebrews 12:18-20). Later it was written by the finger of God on two Tables of Stone (Exodus 31:18 and Exodus 32:16). These Tables of the Law were broken by Moses symbolizing to the people of Israel how they had already broken those commandments in their sinful idolatry in making the golden calf (Exodus 32:19). Finally, these commandments were written a second time on Stone(Exodus 34:1-4) and placed in the Ark by Moses (Deuteronomy 10:1-5).They were placed beneath the Blood-stained Mercy Seat.

b. *Civil Law* — This is commonly referred to as the Book of the Law. These laws were an amplification of the Moral Law. It proceeded from the basis of the Moral Law and applied it to specific situations. These laws were written in a Book and placed in the side of the Ark (Deuteronomy 31:24-26).

c. *Ceremonial Law* — This law was the manifestation of the grace of God. It had to do with all the regulations in regard to sacrifical blood, the Priesthood, the Sanctuary service, the Feasts of the Lord and the Sabbaths.(Exodus 25-40)and the Book of Leviticus cover these ceremonials.

In these three aspects of the law, we are able to see shadowed forth the truth of John 1:17, "For the law was given by Moses, but **grace and truth** came by Jesus Christ." Just as in the grace of God the Law (the ministration of death) was covered by a Blood-stained Mercy Seat, even so Christ, **the** Blood-stained Mercy Seat became a curse to remove for us the curse of the Law (Galatians 3:13).

All the Law was perfectly kept and fulfilled in Jesus Christ. He is the one and only person who has ever kept the Law, for it was in His heart Psalms 40:7-8. He was a just God and a Saviour, (Isaiah 45:21).

In the Sermon on the Mount (Matthew 5-7) Jesus assumes His role as Law-giver. He is the one who magnifies the law and makes it honorable (Isaiah 42:21).He fulfills the Moral, Civil and Ceremonial Law, and at the Cross He abolishes the Ceremonial Law (for He is the ultimate expression of the grace of God) when His Body was broken and His Blood was shed. He now calls us to a higher Law. This is not a Law written on two Tables of Stone, but it is written by the finger of God (the Holy Spirit) upon the fleshly Tables of the Heart (Jeremiah 31:31-34; II Corinthians 3 and Hebrews 8). This is the law of the New Covenant. It is a much higher law—the *Law of Love.*

Thus, the two Tables of the Law point to the One who only perfectly kept the Father's law, i.e., the Father's will (John 5:30; 6:38 and 8:29).Because of this, all judgment formerly in the Law is given over to Christ (John 5:22).

2. *The Golden Pot of Manna* (Exodus 16:11-31)— Naturally speaking, the manna was the Bread from heaven upon which Israel fed for forty years in the wilderness. It is named after the first impression the people had when they saw it on the ground. The name 'Manna' means "What is it?" The characteristics of it were as the taste of oil, coming in the stillness of the night and coming up with the dew. It was white, round and sweet as honey to the taste (Numbers 11:7-9).All of the people were responsible to gather it early in the morning for themselves. No one could eat for another.

Spiritually speaking, this symbolized the nature, character and sustaining power of the Lord Jesus as the Bread of life. Jesus is that Bread from heaven who was anointed with the oil of gladness. Jesus is sweet as honey and as fresh as the dew to the partaker (believer). Jesus is the True Mannna John 6. All must eat of Him or die. No one can eat for another. He is the source of life eternal. He sustains His people in the wildneress journey.

There are three additional observations in regard to the Manna that should be noted:

a. There was no Manna once Israel entered Canaan land (Joshua 5:11-12).

b. There was no Manna on the seventh day of the week, but there was twice as much on the sixth day(Exodus 16:25-26).In spite of what Moses declared, some thought that there would be Manna on the seventh day (Exodus 16:27).

c. There was no Manna in the Ark of the Covenant when it was taken to Solomon's Temple, the permanent resting place of the Ark (I Kings 8:9).

All of this tells us that **now** is the accepted time, **now** is the day of salvation. There will be no Gospel preaching in the Age or Ages to come.

The Lord Jesus Christ is the Golden (Divine) Pot of Manna. He is the Bread of eternal life. If any eat of Him they shall never die. Those that overcome will be once again given of the "Hidden Manna" that was preserved in the Ark (Revelation 2:17).

3. *Aaron's Rod that Budded* (Numbers 17:1-10) — In the rebellion of Korah against Aaron, God commanded Moses to take twelve rods for the twelve tribes and to write their tribal names thereon (Aaron having his own personal name therein) and lay them up in the presence of the Lord before the Ark. In the morning Aaron's rod was manifested in life having the bud, the flower and the almond fruit. There was **one** rod and yet a **three**fold manifestation of fruitfulness, again typical of the fulness of the Godhead bodily.

	(1. The Bud	— The Father, Source, Beginning.
One Rod — One God	(2. The Flower	— The Son, fragrant, crushed.
	(3. The Fruit	— The Holy Spirit, fruitfulness.

As the fruitfulness of Aaron's rod attested that he was the God-chosen, God-anointed and God-appointed High Priest in Israel, even so does the resurrection of Jesus Christ from the dead attest to His eternal Priesthood, after the Order of Melchizedek (Hebrews 7:24-25; 5:1-14; John 11:25; 14:1, 6) and (Romans 1:1-4).In Aaron's rod life came forth out of death. In the resurrection of Jesus, our Great High Priest, the only Mediator between God and man (I Timothy 2:5-6) rises out of death. In Christ is manifest all life, beauty and fruitfulness. He is the only way of approach for man unto God. (Note: Christianity is the only religion founded on a resurrected man.)

Thus, as all the contents of the Ark testify and witness to the fact of the Godhead; all witness to the fact that in Christ dwells all the fullness of the Godhead bodily(John 1:32-33; 3:34; 14:1, 6-11; 12:48-50 and Colossians 1:19).

All of this fulness is to be likewise manifested in the Church, which is the Body of Christ. The Church is "His Body, the fulness of Him that filleth all in all" (Ephesians 1:22-23, See also 3:17-21).

The Law = The Way	
The Manna = The Truth	**The Lord Jesus Christ** John 14:6
The Rod = The Life	

(15) The Ark in Transit Numbers 4:4-6

In transit the Ark had the following coverings upon it.
1. The Covering Veil — symbolic of the Veil of Christ's flesh (Hebrews 10:20).
2. The Covering of Badger's Skins — symbolic of no natural beauty (Isaiah 52:14).
3. The Cloth of Blue — symbolic of the Lord from heaven (I Corinthians 15:47).

(16) The History of the Ark seen Symbolically

The Ark of the Covenant is the most important piece of furniture in the Old Testament. God places such a great importance on it that there are more references to the Ark than to any other piece of furniture. For this reason a closer study of the history of the Ark is warranted. In fact, it will be seen that the history of the Ark is prophetic of the history of the New Testament Ark, the Lord Jesus Christ. As the Ark was first and foremost in Israel's history, so Jesus Christ is first and preeminent in all things before the Father and in the Church (Colossians 1:17-19).

The journeyings of the Ark speak of the Lord Jesus Christ in His birth, anointing, life, ministry, death, resurrection, glorification and second coming. It is in fact **His-Story.**

This is a vast subject in itself and would take a great deal of space to handle adequately. But for the student who is eager to search out the precious nuggets in God's Word, we offer the following 'seed thoughts' in chart form:

The History of the Ark of the Covenant

1. The Ark was made according to the pattern by the enablement of the Spirit of God in wisdom (Exodus 35:31 — 36:3).

2. There were three coverings for the Ark in transit.

3. The Ark was never exposed to the peoples eyes in its wilderness walk (Numbers 4:44-45).

4. The Ark of the Testimony was anointed (Exodus 30:26).

5. The voice of God spoke from off the Ark (Exodus 25:22 and Numbers 7:89).

6. The Israelites found the Ark of Strength (Psalms 132:6-8).

7. The Philistines wanted to know what they should do *to* the Ark (I Samuel 6:2).

8. The Cloud overshadowed the Ark in the Tabernacle (Exodus 40:34-38).

9. In connection with the Ark was a visible manifestation of the Glory of God (Exodus 40:33-38).

10. There was rejoicing and shouting before the Ark as it entered the city (II Samuel 6:12-18).

11. Those who despised the coming of the Ark were smitten with physical barrenness (II Samuel 6:20-23 and I Chronicles 15:29).

12. The Ark of God was carried out of Jerusalem and across the Brook Kidron with the rejected King David (II Samuel 15:23-24).

13. When the Ark was taken, Israel fled (I Samuel 4:10).

14. The Philistines wanted to know what they should do *with* the Ark (I Samuel 5:8).

15. The Ark was placed on a new cart (I Samuel 6:7-13).

16. The Ark experienced a journey of three days and three nights (Numbers 10:33-36). In this time the tabernacle was taken down and the glory departed as they went to find rest. But the glory returned when it was once again set up.

17. The Ark led the way into the Jordan, the river of judgment, 2000 cubits ahead of the others, and then held the waters back for the others to get across (Joshua 3:3-15).

18. The Ark was sprinkled in connection with atonement (Leviticus 16:14).

19. The Ark was positioned "in the midst" of the camp as they marched and at rest (Numbers 2:17 and 10:14-28).

20. Presuming to fight without the Ark meant sure defeat (Numbers 14:44-45).

21. When the Ark was lost there was no victory or Glory (I Samuel 4:3-22).

22. Israel shouted when the Ark came into the Camp (I Samuel 4:5-6), but it caused a trembling in the Camp of the enemy (vs. 8-9).

23. The Ark meant judgment in the Camp of the enemy (I Samuel 5), and yet it was a great blessing to the people of God (II Samuel 6:11).

24. The Ark was the place for enquiring after the Lord concerning His will (Joshua 20:18-28).

25. There was to be a continual ministry before the Ark with musical instruments (I Chronicles 16:4, 37, 42).

26. No god can stand before the Ark of the Living God (I Samuel 5:1-4).

27. Seven priests and seven trumpets preceeded the Ark when Jericho collapsed. At the seventh time, on the seventh day, at the sound of the seventh trumpet there was a shout and all things collapsed. The Kingdom was possessed. (Joshua 6 and Hebrews 11:30).

28. The Ark is placed "in the midst" of two companies, one on Mt. Ebal and the other on Mt. Gerizim. One company receives blessing, and the other receives cursing (Joshua 8:30-35 and Deuteronomy 37:28).

(For a detailed listing of the history of the Ark see: Soltau, *The Holy Vessels and Furniture of the Tabernacle*, pp. 40-42).

The Life Story of the Lord Jesus Christ (His-Story)

1. Christ Jesus was made (Galatians 4:4) by the wisdom and the Spirit of God (Luke 1:35).

2. Jesus was the Fulness of the Godhead Bodily (Colossians 2:9).

3. Jesus as the Son of God was hidden from view in His earthly body, the veil.

4. Jesus was anointed to be a Testimony (Luke 4:18 and Acts 10:38).

5. The voice of God confirmed the Sonship of Jesus (Mark 9:7 and Matthew 3:17).

6. Philip declared that "we have found Him" (John 1:45).

7. The scribes and Pharisees communed one with another what they might do to Jesus (Luke 6:11).

8. Jesus was overshadowed by the Cloud on the Mount of Transfiguration (Mark 9:2-8).

9. The visible manifestation of the Glory of God shown through the veil of Christ's flesh (Matthew 17:1-2 and Revelation 1:16).

10. Jesus was heralded by rejoicing and shouting as He entered the city (Matthew 21:8-9).

11. Those who despised and rejected Christ were left in spiritual barrenness (Luke 19:41-44).

12. Jesus fulfills this remarkably when He crosses the Kidron with His disciples in rejection's darkest hour. (John 18:1).

13. When Christ was taken the disciple fled (Matthew 26:31,56).

14. Pilate wanted to know what he should do with Jesus (Matthew 27:22).

15. Jesus was nailed to a cross (Matthew 7:32).

16. Jesus experienced a journey of three days and three nights. His body (the tabernacle) was taken down and the Glory departed as He died to give us rest. In the resurrection the Glory returns and He is set up at the right hand of God.

17. Jesus entered into and conquered the waters of death 2000 years before the experience of the Church at this end of the age, and he restrained its power until our crossing (Hebrews 12:1-2; Romans 6:3-4; Colossians 3:1-4).

18. By Jesus Christ we have now received the atonement (Romans 5:11).

19. Christ is also positioned "in the midst" of His Church (Matthew 18:20; John 19:18 and Revelation 1:13).

20. Attempting to stand against Satan without Christ means sure defeat.

21. When Christ is outside the Camp there is no Glory or victory.

22. When Christ comes to His Church there is great joy and rejoicing, but to the world outside it causes fear and trembling.

23. Christ and the things of God have a two-fold effect (II Corinthians 2:15-16).

24. Christ, our Ark, is the only Mediator (I Timothy 2:5 and High Priest Hebrews 7:26-27).

25. We are to minister before the Lord in like manner (Colossians 3:16 and Ephesians 5:19).

26. Every knee must bow to the Lordship of Christ (Philippians 2:1-10; John 18:6).

27. At the end of the Book we see seven angels with seven trumpets (Revelation 8:2) before the Ark (Revelation 11:18-19). There is a great shout that ushers in the end of the age and possession of the Kingdom (Revelation 11:15 and I Thessalonians 4:16).

28. A day is coming when Christ will be "in the midst" of two companies, those on the right or the sheep and those on the left or the goats. One group receives blessing, and the other receives cursing (Matthew 25:32-46).

Table of Shewbread

Read the following: Exodus 25:23-30, 37:10-16, 40:22-23 and Leviticus 24:5-9.

The Table of Shewbread

(1) The Table in General

The second article of furniture to be made in the Tabernacle was the Table of Shewbread. This table was made of shittim wood, overlaid with gold. It was placed in the Sanctuary directly opposite the Golden Candlestick in the Holy Place. Upon this Table were placed twelve loaves of bread which were for the priests of the Tribe of Levi to partake. We will see that this piece of furniture points to the Lord Jesus Christ in His ministrations in the Church.

(2) Thou shalt also make a table . . .Exodus 25:23

This is the first use of the word 'Table' in the Bible. The first use of a word is always significant, and here we see the same is true. In the Book of Genesis we find the account of man's ruin by sin. When man falls communion with God is broken. Here in Exodus we are given a picture of fallen man redeemed by the grace of God. We see God's grace coming to fallen man to re-establish the severed lines of communion. God provides the Table for His Priests in His Sanctuary. All of this tells forth the truth that God has prepared a Table in Christ for His redeemed people, the priests of the eternal Sanctuary.

In the construction of this Table in the Old Testament we find that it was given completely by revelation. Nothing was left to the mind or imagination of the builders. It was constructed according to the Divine pattern. After its construction it was set on the North side of the Holy Place, opposite the Golden Candlestick. It would take the light of the Golden Candlestick to reveal and illumine the Bread and the Table.

The Table is given several names throughout Scripture. It was called:

1. The Table of Shewbread (Exodus 25:30),
2. The Table of Shittim Wood (Exodus 25:33; 37:10).
3. The Pure Table (Leviticus 24:6) — we must be clean to partake.
4. The Table (Exodus 39:36; 40:4, 22),
5. The Table of Gold (I Kings 7:48) — in Solomon's Temple.

The Table of Shewbread is typical and significant of the Lord Jesus Christ Himself as the Bread of Life to His people (John 6:25-63), and it points to the Table of the Lord or The Communion of the New Testament Church, the Body of Christ (I Corinthians 10:15-21; 11:23-34) and (Matthew 26:26-28). This Table is what David had in mind when he declared, "Thou **preparest a Table** before me" (Psalms 23:5) — Compare Matthew 26:17-20.

(3) of Shittim Wood . . .Exodus 25:23

Once again, as seen in the Ark of the Covenant, shittim wood speaks of the sinless, incorruptible and perfect humanity of Christ. As already noted, the shittim or acacia wood is translated as "incorruptible wood" in the Septuagint version. Christ Jesus is the **root** out of dry ground, the Man whose name is **the branch** (Zechariah 6:12-13 and Isaiah 11:1-4). Christ's incorruptible character and nature is seen in the desert of this world and is portrayed for us in the four Gospels.

(4) Two cubits shall be the length thereof, and a cubit the breadth thereof, and a cubit and a half the height thereof . . .Exodus 25:23

God has Divinely established measurements for everything. All things must measure up to this standard. It is to be noted that the Table, the Brazen Altar Grate and the Ark of the Covenant are all partakers of the 1 ½ cubits in height. Thus the Brazen Altar Grate in the Outer Court, the Table of Shewbread in the Holy Place and the Ark of the Covenant and its Blood-stained Mercy seat in the Holiest of All are brought together in this similar measurement.

This same height signifies the same standard or the same level set forth before God. It speaks of the truth that we begin at the 'Judgment Seat' (1 ½ cubits of Brazen Altar,) that we may come to the

Shewbread Table and have fellowship with God and His Priests (1 ½ cubits of Table) on the basis of the Blood on the 'Mercy Seat' (1 ½ cubits of the Ark lid.)

(5) And thou shalt overlay it with pure gold . . .Exodus 25:24

The Hebrew word for 'gold' comes from an unused root word meaning "shimmer" or "from its shining." Gold therefore is typical of Deity or the Divine nature of Jesus Christ. In the Table we have two components. We have gold and wood. Two components and yet only one Table. This speaks to us of the union of the two natures in the Lord Jesus Christ. Deity and Humanity in their fulness are seen typically in the wood and gold. The Lord Jesus Christ is the God-Man. He is the **Word** (Gold) made **Flesh** (Wood) who dwelt among us (John 1:1-3, 14-18; I Timothy 3:16 and 2:5-6).

Jesus is the True Mediator between God and man. In order to meditate two parties He must of necessity partake of both. He must be Divine to represent God to man. Yet, He must be human to represent man before the throne of God. The gold and the wood come together in the Lord Jesus Christ.

(6) And make thereto a crown round about. And thou shalt make unto it a border of an hand breadth round about, and thou shalt make a golden crown to the border thereof round about. Exodus 25:24-25

By corresponding Exodus 25:24-25 with Exodus 37:11-12, we see that the Table had a double crown around the border with a handbreadth between these crowns. The *hand*-breadth was as a border between the crowns for the various vessels. It also acted as a guard to protect anything from falling off the Table. We notice that it is the *hand* of Christ that is able to keep us from falling. The hands of Jesus are nail-pierced hands (Zechariah 13:6; John 10:28 and Jude 24).

Crowns in the Old Testament speak to us of principally of two offices. First of all, we notice that the mitre on the *High Priest* was called "The Holy Crown" (Exodus 29:6). It is also spoken of as "the Crown of the Anointing" (Leviticus 21:12). The second office in the Old Testament that was crowned was the office of the *King*. The Kings were crowned after they had been anointed to their office.

The *double crown* on the Table points to the fact in Christ Jesus our Table of Shewbread the two offices of King and Priest are united. He is crowned **King-Priest** after the Order of Melchizedek. Jesus is **the branch** (Zechariah 6:1, 12-13; 3:5) who is sitting as King-Priest exercising the ministry of Mediator between God and man. Man crowned Him with thorns (the product of sin and the curse,) but God crowned Him with glory and honor (the seal of a finished work) (Hebrews 2:6-8; I Peter 5:4 and Hebrews 7:1-2).

There were three pieces of furniture that were crowned in the Tabernacle.

1. The Ark of the Covenant
2. The Table of Shewbread
3. The Golden Altar of Incense

The thought of the crown ends up in the Book of Revelation where we see the 24 elders (2x12 = 24) who cast their crowns before the Lamb. Christ comes the second time crowned with many crowns. At His first coming He came as the Man of Sorrows. At His second coming He is revealed as King of Kings and Lord of Lords (Revelation 19:11-16).

(7) And thou shalt make for it four rings of gold, and put the rings in the four corners that are on the four feet thereof. Over against the border shall the rings be for places of the staves to bear the table Exodus 25:26-27.

There were *four* rings of gold in the *four* corners of the Table on the *four* feet thereof. The number *four* is impressed here upon the Table of Shewbread (See Significance of Numbers.) Four is the number of earth including the thoughts of being worldwide or universal in influence. There are four seasons, four quarters of the moon and four corners of the earth.

The Table had —

1. *Four Corners* — This is significant of the fact that Christ is the Table of Shewbread to all the four corners of the earth. It is His worldwide ministry to feed His people as the Bread of Life. It points to

the commission of our Lord to "Go ye into all the world and preach the Gospel to every creature" (Matthew 28:18-20; Mark 16:15-20 and Acts 1:8). See also Revelation 5:9-10.

2. *Four Feet* — Feet are always significant of an *earth-walk*. The *four* feet here point to the *four* Gospels which set forth Christ in His earth-walk. They reveal Him as the true Bread of Life who established the Table of the Lord before His ascension into heaven. Just as the four legs of the Table upheld the Bread on the Table, even so Matthew, Mark, Luke and John uphold the true Bread, the Lord Jesus Christ.

3. *Four gold Rings* — In these rings we see three particular symbols. They are the following:

   a. **Gold** — This speaks of the Deity or Divine nature of the Lord Jesus Christ.
   b. **Rings** — A ring is a circle that has no beginning or end. It is a common symbol to represent eternity of being. The Lord Jesus is from everlasting to everlasting.
   c. **Four** — As we have already noted there are four descriptions of God in the Bible (1) God is Light-(I John 1:5), (2) God is *Love* (I John 4:16), (3) God is *Spirit* (John 4:24)and (4) God is a *Consuming Fire* (Hebrews 12:29). These are the eternal attributes of God and the Son of God. (See Ark, Section 8).

(8) And thou shalt make the staves of shittim wood, and overlay them with gold, that the table may be borne with them. Exodus 25:28

Again we have the thought of incorruptible wood (humanity) overlaid with pure gold (deity.) The purpose of the Staves was to carry the Table in the wilderness wanderings. The Staves also helped to keep and present a balanced Table. There must be a balanced presentation of the Gospel of Jesus as the Bread of Eternal Life. Jesus Christ Himself was a "pilgrim and a stranger" here in His earth walk. This points to the pilgrimage of the Church. We have no continuing city, but we are seeking one to come. At the present time Christ is wandering in the Wilderness of this present age with His Church (Hebrews 11:9-13; 13:14) and (I Peter 2:11).

(9) The table in transit Numbers 4:7-8.

In transit the Table was covered with the following cloths:

1. The Table was covered with a cloth of **blue.** The blue cloth is seen as a type of the Holy Spirit who was upon the true Bread (Luke 4:18). The color of blue is also seen as the color of heaven which speaks of Christ as the Lord from Heaven (I Corinthians 15:47).

2. The dishes, spoons and bowls were next and had a covering of **scarlet** upon them. Scarlet is typical of Blood Sacrifice and speaks to us of the central person of the Godhead. Jesus was the Sacrificial One.

3. The final covering was **badgers' skins.** These are typical of God who is over all. It also speaks of a third aspect of Christ. For in Christ there is no natural beauty to the unregenerate man (Isaiah 52:14-15; 53:1-3).

After the Table was properly covered, the Staves were placed in the rings for the journey. To the natural man, there is no beauty to be seen in the Wilderness walk. The only thing showing was the Badgers' skins. To the spiritual man, however, the eye of faith sees Christ who is the Bread of Life. He is seen travelling with His Church as their very life-sustaining Bread.

(10) And thou shalt make the dishes thereof, and spoons thereof, and covers thereof, and bowls thereof, to cover withal: of pure gold shalt thou make them. Exodus 25:28

There were several vessels used in connection with this Table. These are the vessels that the prophet Isaiah referred to when he said, "be ye clean, that bear the vessels of the Lord" (Isaiah 52:11). There were basically three types of vessels:

1. *Dishes* — The Dishes or Chargers were used for holding the Food-Bread (Numbers 7:13, 18-19, 25, etc.)

2. *Spoons* — The Spoons were hollow vessels of gold with incense in them. While the Priests ate at the Table of Shewbread, in the light of the Golden Candlestick, they burnt incense unto the Lord at the

Golden Altar. Thus, the three articles were connected signifying to us that as we eat at His Table in the light of His Presence we send up incense of prayer, worship and adoration to the Lord Jesus. (See: Numbers 7:14, 20, 26, etc.)

3. *Bowls and Covers* — In the Septuagint version these articles are spoken of as "flagons and chalices." In fact the very Hebrew word implies the thought of "cups." These Bowls and Covers contained strong *wine* which was poured out in connection with this Table as a libation before the Lord (Numbers 28:7). This was the *Drink Offering* of outpoured wine. It was used solely in connection with the Table of Shewbread, not with any other articles in the Holy Place (Exodus 30:9). The symbolism here is obvious. In the Table of Shewbread, **bread** and **wine** are brought together pointing to the New Testament Table instituted by our Lord Jesus Christ. Jesus referred to the Bread, "This is **My Body.**" Jesus took the cup and said, "This is **My Blood** of the New Testament" (Matthew 26:26-28; I Corinthians 10:15-21 and 11:23-34).

(11) And thou shalt set upon the table shewbread before me alway. Exodus 25:30

Throughout the Bible various names are given to this Shewbread. It was called:

1. *The Shewbread* — 'To shew' means to "tell forth" or "declare." It speaks to us of the New Testament Bread of Life who *shewed* Himself to His disciples (Matthew 16:21; John 21:2 and Acts 1:3). It also speaks of the ministry of the Church to *shew forth* His life, death, resurrection and coming again in the Table of the Lord (I Corinthians 11:26).

2. *The Bread of God* (Leviticus 21:21). — This Bread is on His Table and through it He offers fellowship to His Priests.

3. *The Continual Bread* (Numbers 4:7; II Chronicles 2:4 and Leviticus 24:8) — This Bread was to be before the Lord continually. Believers find in Christ the continual and *daily* Bread (Matthew 6:11).

The actual Hebrew word for 'Shewbread' also suggests other titles in relation to it. They include:

1. *The Bread of the Presence* or *Presence Bread* — The presence of the Lord is with us in the Table of the Lord (Matthew 18:20).

2. *The Bread of Face(s)* — In the Bread we see the truth of one God (face) and yet three persons (faces,) the tri-unity. In the New Testament we see the Glory of God in the *face* of Jesus Christ II Corinthians 4:6. As believers in the Lord we all await His coming when we shall see His *face* (Revelation 22:4).

3. *The Bread of Order* or *Arrangement* — Just as there was order at the Table in the Old Testament (II Chronicles 13:11), there is to be order concerning the New Testament Table of the Lord (I Corinthians 11:34).

All of these various aspects of truth seen in these titles are symbolic of Communion. The Lord communed with His Priests through the Bread. They were partakers of Him. What we eat becomes a part of our being. Believers in Christ are partakers of the Divine nature when they partake of His Body. (See: John 6:48-56 and II Peter 1:4).

(12) And thou shalt take fine flour . . . Leviticus 24:5

We see that there was even a Divine recipe for the loaves of Bread. First they were to take fine flour. Fine flour begins as whole kernel of wheat. In order to make this wheat useable in bread and other cooking the wheat must be crushed to powder. Thus, fine flour speaks to us of the trials, testings, temptations and sufferings of the Lord Jesus Christ as the Corn of Wheat, bruised and broken to become Bread to us(John 12:24). Just as in fine flour, there was nothing rough or uncouth in His sinless and perfect humanity. It also applies to all who are 'in Christ.' Refer to the following: Psalms 147:14; Isaiah 28:28; 52:14; 53 and Genesis 3:15.

The following quotation taken from *The Christ of God* by Robert Clark concerning the perfect humanity of Christ best sets forth the thought in the fine flour of the God-Man, the Lord Jesus Christ:

"Christ made no mistakes, committed no sins, and therefore He is unlike any other man who has ever lived. In our Lord there was:

meekness without weakness;
tenderness without feebleness;

firmness without coarseness;
love without sentimentality;
holiness without sanctimoniousness;
lowliness without lowness;
truth without error;
enthusiasm without fanaticism;
passion without prejudice;
heavenly-mindedness without forgetfulness;
care-freeness without carelessness;
service without servility;
self-exaltation without egoism;
judgment without harshness;
seriousness without sombreness;
mercy without softness."

(13) And bake . . . Leviticus 24:5

In order to make bread palatable it must be baked. The *fire* of Calvary here speaks of the intense sufferings of the Son of God. On the Cross He suffered the fire to become the Bread for us (See: Matthew 3:11; Luke 3:16; Hebrews 12:29 and 9:14).

(14) Twelve cakes thereof . . . Leviticus 24:5

There were twelve loaves of Bread on the Table before the Lord, one loaf for each Tribe in the camp of Israel. All the Tribes were represented before the Lord. In Spiritual Israel *all* are represented before the Lord as members of His Body. Every member of the Body of Christ participates in that one Bread of I Corinthians 10:17, "**We being many are One Bread** and One Body: for we are all partakers of that **One Bread**." The *unity* of the Body of Christ is set forth in the *One Bread*.

There is also significance in the number twelve used here. The number twelve is always symbolic of Apostolic Fulness and Government. This truth is particularly brought out in the selection of twelve apostles by the Lamb (Revelation 21:14 and Ephesians 2:20). It was through these twelve apostles that Jesus gave the miracle supply of Bread to the multitudes (John 6; Matthew 14:15-21; 15:32-39). The Church of today is still feeding on the revelation (the bread) of the apostles of the early Church government. The fulness of the Word of Christ (the Bread) is dispensed from the Head through to the twelve apostles and finally, to the priestly Body (Revelation 12:1).

These twelve loaves were ringshaped and perforated. The Hebrew implies the thought that they were "pierced cakes." All of this is typical of the Lord Jesus Christ who was the pierced Bread of Life (Zechariah 12:10 and John 19:34-37).

(15) Two-tenths deal shall be in one cake. Leviticus 25:5

Each of the twelve loaves had 2/10ths deal of fine flour in them. The significance of this may be discovered in the following:

1. The Manna that was to be gathered on the sixth day of the week was 2/10ths deal (Exodus 16:22, 36). In other words, it speaks of the *double portion*.

2. The Meal Offering in the Feast Day of the Sheaf of Firstfruits was to be made of 2/10ths deal of fine flour (Leviticus 23:13).

3. The Two Wave Loaves in the Feast of Pentecost were also to be made of 2/10ths deal of fine flour (Leviticus 23:17).

4. Here, in the twelve loaves of the Shewbread, we have 2/10ths deal per cake. In this we see a *double portion* of Life and Health in the Bread for the Lord's People.

5. We also see the thought of 2/10ths in the two Tables of Stone on which the Ten Commandments were written by the finger of God (Exodus 20:31:18).The Ten Commandments find their fulfillment in the Two Commandments given by Jesus in the New Testament (Matthew 22:34-40).

Additional significance can be seen in the equation given to us in this verse. We have 12 x 2/10 = 24/120. 24 and 120 are both numbers that have particular significance and fulfillment in the Last Days and unto the coming of the Lord Jesus Christ.

(16) And thou shalt set them in two rows, six on a row upon the pure table before the Lord.
Leviticus 24:6

Various diagrams show how the Bread was placed on the Table. Some set forth the Bread as being placed in two rows on the Table, while others show the Bread in two piles of six loaves. The size of the cakes themselves would seem to forbid the idea of having them in rows. Strong's Concordance states that the more correct wording of this passage would be "six loaves **on** a row, or a pile of loaves" (#4635. Refer to diagram).

(17) And thou shalt put pure frankincense upon each row . . . Leviticus 24:7.

Pure Frankincense speaks of Christ's perfect life of prayer and intercession. The fragrance of His life was pleasing in the nostrils of the Father. The Gospels reveal the Divine frankincense in His life. They reveal His life of prayer (Refer to: Song of Solomon 4:6, 12-16 and Matthew 2:11.)

(18) That it may be on the bread for a memorial . . . Leviticus 24:7

This Bread was the Bread of **Memorial.** This calls to mind what Jesus says in regard to His Table in the New Covenant. Jesus said that we were to do it in *remembrance* of Him (Luke 22:19-20).

(19) Even an offering made by fire unto the Lord . . . Leviticus 24:7

This corresponds to the thought of the Bread being baked. Jesus Christ went through the baking process at Calvary in order to become the Bread of Life for us. It is God that puts His people through the fires that they may come forth as pure gold. "Our God is a consuming fire" (Hebrews 12:29).

(20) Every sabbath He shall set it in order before the Lord continually . . . Leviticus 24:8

The Bread was to be set in order every *seventh* day. The Lord Jesus Christ is the divinely complete Bread of Life. He is all in all. In Him is the true Sabbath-rest, for He is the giver or Baptizer with the Holy Spirit. Rest is found only in His finished work (John 19:30 and Matthew 11:28-30).

The Disciples met together and broke Bread once a week on the first day of the week (Acts 20:7 and 2:41-47). See also II Chronicles 2:4.

(21) Being taken from the children of Israel by an everlasting covenant . . . Leviticus 24:8

Here we see that the *Everlasting Covenant* is involved. The Bread was to be an Everlasting Covenant. This foreshadowed the **New** Covenant in the Body and Blood of Jesus Christ (Matthew 26:26-28 and Hebrews 13:20).

(22) And it shall be Aaron's and his sons . . . Leviticus 24:9

The Bread was to be eaten by the Priests only (I Samuel 21:1-6 and Matthew 12:4). In the New Covenant in Christ all believers are called to a Spiritual Priesthood (I Peter 2:9; Revelation 1:6; 55:9-10). Only those that belong to this Spiritual House are entitled to partake of the Table.

The Table was 'Most Holy,' just as the Body of Jesus Christ is the 'Most Holy Thing' upon which to feed (Luke 1:35). Those that partake of this Table must be holy also. After the believers have experienced the Brazen Altar they are able to approach the Table worthily (I Corinthians 11:23-34).

(23) And they shall eat it in the Holy Place . . . Leviticus 24:9

The Bread was to be eaten in the Holy Place. It was never eaten in the Outer Court. The Holy Place measured 10 x 10 x 20 cubits. When this is multiplied we find the cubical content of 2000. This is prophetic of the 2000 years of the Age or Dispensation of the Holy Spirit. From Christ's first coming to His second coming is included here and commonly referred to as the Church Age.

Christ came the first time as the Corn of Wheat, to be broken for us, to endure the fire of Calvary and to be raised from the dead as the perfect and complete Bread of Life for this Dispensation. Now we may partake of the fulness of what He became for us by His death and His resurrection. In the Bread we have *Life, Healing, Divine Health, Spiritual Nourishment, Fellowship* and *Communion.* Just as Israel found all these benefits in the Manna for 40 years in the Wilderness (Exodus 16), when sickness was taken away from their midst, even so the Church of this Age is to experience that same Bread in the Lord Jesus Christ. Just as God gave Himself to them in the Bread they ate (Psalms 78:19), even so does Christ give Himself to all who will eat and receive of Him (Mark 7:27).This is the 'Children's Bread' (Matthew 4:3-4; 15:26-27 and Job 23:12).

(24) For it is most Holy unto Him of the offerings of the Lord made by fire by a perpetual statute . . . Leviticus 24:9

Again we have the thought of holiness. Jesus Christ is "that Holy Thing" (Luke 1:35 and Mark 1:24). The Believer Priest is to feed upon Him who is "Most Holy" unto God, even the Lord Jesus Christ, in all His perfections, graces, virtues and character until He becomes our very life and nature.

(25) The Tables in Solomon's Temple (See: I Kings 7:48; I Chronicles 28:16; and II Chronicles 4:8, 19

In the Temple of Solomon there were ten Tables of Shewbread. This means that there were 120 loaves of Bread in all. This number speaks to us of the *fulness* of the Bread of Life in the Church, which is now the temple of the living God by the Holy Spirit (I Corinthians 3:16; 6:19; Ephesians 2:20-22). In the end of this age (the 120th Jubilee,) we will see the fulness of the Bread of Heaven in the Church.

(26) The Singers at the table in Solomon's Temple. I Chronicles 9:27, 32-33

The Singers in the Temple of Solomon had the joy of preparing the Table of Shewbread. Song and singing was always connected with the Table of the Lord. This is also to be true in the New Testament (Matthew 26:26 and Mark 14:26).

(27) The Importance of Bread in Natural Israel.

Bread was the staff of Life in the Old Testament to the people of God. All throughout the history of the nation we are given many prophetic pictures of the significance of the Life in this Bread. The following are some examples of this importance of Bread in Natural Israel which foreshadows Christ as the Bread and Staff of Life in the Church which is Spiritual Israel:

1. Unleavened **Bread** was used in the Feast of Passover (Exodus 12:14-20, 34).
2. Manna was Israel's **Bread** for 40 years in the Wilderness (Exodus 16).
3. There were twelve loaves of **Bread** for the Priests of the Table of Shewbread (Leviticus 24:5-9 and Exodus 25:23-30).
4. The Meal Offering of fine flour was a type of **Bread** (Leviticus 2).
5. There was **Bread** in connection with the Feast of Pentecost in the two Wave Loaves (Leviticus 23:15-17).
6. The Ark of the Covenant contained **Bread** in the Golden Pot of Manna (Hebrews 9:4 and Revelation 2:17).
7. Abraham gave **Bread** (three measures of meal) to the Lord (Genesis 18:1-6 and Luke 11:5).
8. Abraham received **Bread** and wine from Melchizedek, King-Priest of the Most High God (Genesis 14:18).
9. Elijah went to the strength of the **Bread** (cake) and water that the angel ministered to him forty days' journey (I Kings 19:8).
10. David received strength from the Shew**bread** (I Samuel 21:6 and Matthew 12:1-4).
11. Mephibosheth is made to sit at the King's Table **(Bread)** as one of the King's sons (II Samuel 9:1, 7-13).
12. Hezekiah restores the Order of the Table under his reformation (II Chronicles 29:18).
13. The Shew**bread** is again restored after the Babylonian Captivity under Nehemiah (Nehemiah 10:33).
14. Jesus fed the 5000 people with the five **loaves** and two fish (Miracle **Bread,** (Matthew 14:15-21).
15. The 4000 people were fed with Miracle **Bread** and fish also (Matthew 15:32-38).

All these are evident shadowings of the True Communion. They all point to the Table of the Lord and the saints feeding upon Him who is the Bread of Eternal Life. He is the **True** Manna.

The Table of Shewbread finds fulfillment in Christ and His Church, personally and collectively. In Him is our Spiritual Meat and Spiritual Drink (I Corinthians 10:1-4, 15-21) which is the full and satisfying portion, communion and fellowship, healing and health.

"And they continued steadfastly in the Apostles' doctrine . . . and in **Breaking of Bread . . .**"

The Golden Candlestick

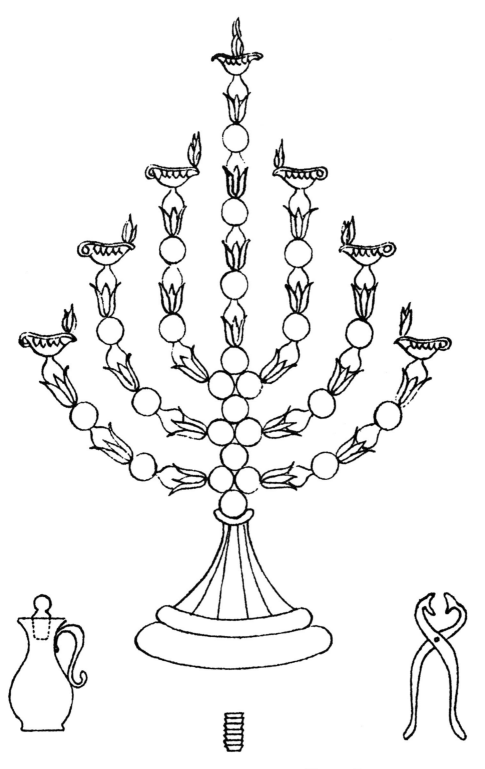

Diagram: Rev. Ray S. Jackson

Read the following: Exodus 25:31-40; 27:20-21; 30:7-8; 37:17-24; Numbers 8:1-4

The Golden Candlestick

(1) The Candlestick in General

The Golden Candlestick was the next article to be made after the Table of Shewbread. It was positioned immediately opposite the Golden Table on the South side of the Holy Place in the Sanctuary (Exodus 26:35 and 40:4, 24).When we think of a Candlestick we usually think of burning candles. This is not the case here. The Golden Candlestick was more particularly a Lampstand upon which were seven lighted lamps. This was a Candlestick having oil lamps not candles. Candles burn by self-consumption, while lamps burn by the continual supply of oil being poured into them.

The Church is not merely to be a 'candle' or to give 'candlelight,' but it is to be a Lampstand, shedding forth Divine light by the continual supply of the Oil of the Holy Spirit.

The chief purpose of the Lampstand was to give light and to illumine all that was in the Sanctuary.

(2) And thou shalt make a Candlestick of pure gold . . . Exodus 25:31

The Candlestick was called several names:

1. The Candlestick (Exodus 35:14; 40:4, 24)
2. The Candlestick of Gold (Exodus 25:31),
3. The Pure Candlestick (Exodus 31:8; 39:37; Leviticus 24:4).

We notice here that no measurements were given for the Candlestick. Later we will see that the Brazen Laver corresponds to this same thought. Both of these articles are described without reference to their measurements or size. The thought here is that we cannot measure the *light* of God which is to be revealed in the Church for time and eternity, nor can we measure the power of the *cleansing* of the Water of the Word (See Laver).

Another connection we see in these two pieces of furniture is in the fact that both the Candlestick and the Laver were constructed wholly of metal. The Candlestick was made wholly of gold, while the Laver was composed of solid brass. There was no wood used in these structures at all. The gold of the Candlestick speaks to us of deity and Divine nature as seen first in Christ (**The** Light of the world) and second in the Church(Matthew 5:14). Gold is found in the Church because the Church is the product of God, and it is in the Church that the Divine nature will be revealed, for the Church is wholly of God (Matthew 16:16-18; Colossians 1:27 and II Peter 1:4).

In connection with the Candlestick as a whole, the Lord Jesus has given an unmistakable interpretation of the symbolic significance. In Hebrews 9 we notice that the Candlestick was the first object mentioned by Paul who associated it with the Sanctuary. This 'Mystery' was revealed to John in the Book of Revelation (chapter 1). The Candlestick is typical and prophetic of:

1. The Lord Jesus Christ as the Light of the world (John 8:12; 9:5, and
2. The New Testament Church both local and universal (Matthew 5:14-16 and Revelation 1:12-20).

(3) of beaten work shall the Candlestick be made . . . Exodus 25:31 and the tongs thereof, and the snuffdishes thereof, shall be of pure gold. Of a talent of pure gold shall he make it, with all these vessels. Exodus 25:38-39.

When gold is taken out of the earth, it is fit for practically nothing. In order to make it useable it must pass through the purifying fires. It is at this point that the impurities are removed, for it is in the fires where that which is pure gold is manifest. After the gold is brought to this point it can be fashioned in the hands of the goldsmith. This process is also painful, for the gold must submit to the hammers and beating work of the smith. In this process the gold has to go through a lot, but when the work is done, it is a thing of rare beauty.

This process is typical of that which God works in His Church. God, by His Spirit, is purifying and sanctifying His Church by means of fiery trials, testings and sufferings. All of this has a purpose to it. Through it all the Church will come forth as pure gold, and it will conform to the Divine pattern that God has fore-ordained (Isaiah 52:14; 53:4-5; Job 23:10; I Peter 1:7 and II Peter 1:4).

(4) His shaft, and His branches, His bowls, His knops, and His flowers, shall be of the same. And six branches shall come out of the sides of it: three branches of the Candlestick out of the one side, and three branches of the Candlestick out of the other side: three bowls made like unto almonds, with a knop and a flower in one branch; and three bowls made like almonds in the other branch, with a knop and a flower: so in the six branches that come out of the Candlestick. And in the Candlestick shall be four bowls, made like unto almonds, with their knops and their flowers. And there shall be a knop under two branches of the same, and a knop under two branches of the same, and a knop under two branches of the same, according to the six branches that proceed out of the Candlestick. Their knops and their branches shall be of the same. Exodus 25:31-36.

The Golden Candlestick was fashioned out of one piece of Gold. It had a central shaft (Mainshaft, "His thigh") from which proceeded six branches, three on either side of the mainshaft. Counting the mainshaft, then, there were seven branches in all. Under each pair of branches there was a knop or knob upholding them. There were a total of three such knops. Upon the seven branches were seven lighted lamps, burning continually before the Lord.

The *Shaft* and the *Branches* are the first things that we notice. We see that they are spoken of as "His" shaft and "His" Branches. Who is He other than the Lord Jesus Christ (Jeremiah 23:5; Isaiah 4:2; 11:1-3; Hebrews 2:11-12 and Romans 11:17-24). Jesus said, "I am the Vine" (He is the shaft in which were the twelve) "and ye are the Branches" (the Church, John 15:5.) Just as the Branches abide in the shaft and the Branches abide in the Vine, so the Church in mystical union is to abide in Christ, the Head of all things. Just as the branches proceed from the side of the Shaft and Eve proceeded out of the side of Adam, so the Church proceeds out of the pierced side of Christ (Genesis 2:21 and John 19:34).

When we consider the *ornamentation* of the Candlestick we want to recognize that there are differences of opinion and understanding as to the exact nature of the "Knops," "Flowers" and "Bowls made like unto Almonds." Some suggest that the Knops were a pomegranate or an opening bud, the Bowls or calyses were as the leaf-like envelope of the flower or almond-shaped bowls, and the Flowers were like lilies. It is unfortunate that we no longer have the actual candlestick from which to draw understanding. However, if we draw from other Scriptures of like illustration, perhaps we can come to a fuller understanding of the actual ornamentation. Whatever we do, we want to be consistent with the total revelation found in God's Word.

When we look at the terminology used in regard to the ornamentation on the Candlestick, we are immediately struck by the similarity of language used in regard to *Aaron's Rod that Budded.* For we see that Aaron's Rod budded, flowered and brought forth almond fruit, (Numbers 17:8 and Jeremiah 1:11-12). In the almond tree we have the symbol of resurrection life. Since it is the fruit that comes from the Rod of Aaron, we can see plainly that Christ is typified in the Rod (Jeremiah 23:5; Zechariah 3:8 and 6:12). He becomes the measuring rod for the Church.

In these two prophetic pictures we see the stamp of the Godhead, as follows:

Aaron's Rod	The Candlestick	Symbolism-Interpreted
Budded	Knop (or bud)	Source — the Father
Flowered	Flowers	Begotten — the Son
Almond Fruit	Almond Bowl	Proceeding — the Holy Spirit

1. The **Knop** or round, unopened bud is a *type of the Father God* who is the source and beginning of everything.
2. The **Central Flower** is a *type of the Son of God* who was crushed as a flower emitting a sweet smelling savor.
3. The **Almond Bowl** is a *type of the Holy Spirit* who proceeds from the Father and produces fruitfulness in the people of God. Thus we see the fulness of the Godhead typified in this tri-unity.

The almond tree is the first of all trees to bud in Palestine Jeremiah 1:11-12. Therefore each year it carries the message of life out of death. In the Rod of Aaron we get the same message. It was once alive, then dead and finally came to resurrection life, bearing a bud, flowers and almond fruit. This tri-unity in Aaron's Rod attested to his Divinely-anointed and appointed priestly ministry on behalf of Israel. This ornamentation of Aaron's Rod is now taken by God as ornamentation for the Candlestick in the Holy Place speaking the same truth of the Lord Jesus Christ. All is significant of the fact that the **Church** (the Candlestick) is to measure up to the Divine standard of **Jesus Christ** (the Rod of God,) our HIgh Priest (Isaiah 11:1; Revelation 1:16-17 and 11:1-2).

Another interesting feature of the Candlestick is the truth revealed through the combination of numbers involved with it. All numbers in Scripture have significance, and the Candlestick is full of numbers. Let us briefly look at some of the numbers involved:

1. **One piece of gold** — The number one is significant of unity, oneness, one accord, or one Church (Hebrews 2:11-13; John 17).

2. **Three knops** — The number three is significant of the Godhead — Father, Son and Holy Spirit. These three knops upheld all of the seven branches as the very foundation. This is typical of the truth that the Godhead is the foundation and upholder of the Church (Matthew 28:19-20).

3. **Seven Lamps** — The number seven is significant fulness, completeness and perfection. Upon the seven branches were seven lighted lamps of fire. These seven lamps are significant of the seven Spirits upon Messiah, the Lord Jesus Christ. These are also to be revealed in the Church, His Body (See: Revelation 1:4; 3:1; 4:5; 5:6 and Isaiah 11:1-4. There were seven lamps. yet one Light. There are seven Spirits, yet one Spirit.)

   Seven has important significance in many other Scriptures. We submit the following:

   a. There is a seven-fold unity expressed·in (Ephesians 4:4-6).
   b. There are seven principles of the Doctrine of Christ (Hebrews 6:1-2).

4. **Nine ornaments** — In the branches the number nine is stamped. In each of the six branches proceeding out of the Candlestick were three Bowls, three Knops and three Flowers. Each branch had nine ornaments in all. The number nine is the number of the Holy Spirit in the Church. There are nine fruits of the Spirit (Galatians 5:22-24) and nine gifts of the Spirit (I Corinthians 12:1-2).

5. **Twelve symbols** — In the mainshaft of the Candlestick there were four groups of Bowls, Knops and Flowers making a total of twelve. The number twelve speaks of Apostolic Fulness and Government. There are many other twelves in the Scripture that complete this thought. Some of them include the following: the twelve loaves on the Table of Shewbread, the twelve foundations in the City of God, the twelve stones on the Breastplate of the High Priest, the twelve Tribes of Israel and the twelve Apostles of the Lamb.

6. **Sixty-six** — When the Bowls, the Knops and the Flowers on the shaft and the six branches are totalled we have a beautiful picture of the Books of the Bible. There were three groups of Bowls, Knops and Flowers in the three branches on one side. If we add the twelve in the mainshaft we have a total of 39 which speaks to us of the Books of the Old Testament (3 x 9 = 27 + 12 = 39). Then the remaining branches total 27 corresponding to the 27 Books of the New Testament. The complete total is 66. It has pleased God to give us His Book containing 66 Books yet one Bible (Psalms 119:105).The Candlestick reminds us that it takes the light of the Holy Spirit to illumine these 66 Books to the Church.

   The number six is also significant of *man*. It was on the sixth day that man was created. The 66 Books constitute God's Book which is the only Book of Divine light for *man!* The Bible is God's Word to fallen man. There were not 66 separate parts, but there were 66 ornaments fashioned out of one piece or talent of gold. Likewise, the Bible is 66 Books unified by the One Spirit and mind of God into **One Book**. The whole Bible is the essential Work of God. Jesus taught the unity of the Scriptures in their testimony to Him (Luke 24:27, 44-46; Hebrews 10:5-9; John 5:39-47; Luke 4:21 and Matthew 22:29).

(5) All of it shall be one beaten work of pure gold. Exodus 25:36

The Candlestick was made of *one* piece of gold. The thought of oneness or unity is stamped throughout the Tabernacle. There was only ever *one* Tabernacle of Moses, *one* Tabernacle of David and *one* Temple of Solomon because all these structures point to the way of approach to God. There is only **One Way** of approach to God provided for all mankind. "There is **One** God, and **One** Mediator between God and man, the man Christ Jesus" (I Timothy 2:5). There is but **One** great High Priest (Numbers 7:89; John 14:1-6). There is but **One** sacrifice for sins (John 3:16; Hebrews 10:7-12). This oneness in Christ carries over to oneness in His Body, the Church. Jesus prayed that they might be one that the world may believe John 17. In God's mind the Church is one (Hebrews 2:11).They are one Tabernacle, one Temple, one Bread, one Body and one Church(I Corinthians 10:17, 12:13 and Ephesians 2:20-22).

(6) And thou shalt make the seven lamps thereof: and they shall light the lamps thereof, that they may give light over against it. Exodus 25:37

Though there were seven lamps with seven lights (James 1:17 — God is the Father of Lights,) yet they are spoken of as **One** Lamp or **One** Light (I John 1:5 — God is light). The seven lamps gave forth **One** light or **One** witness. In the very light we have the continued thought of the unity of witness (Leviticus 24:1-2; Exodus 25:6; 35:14, 28). As we look at the Candlestick we are reminded of the Rainbow. The Rainbow has the manifestation of seven colors in one bow.

The purpose of the Candlestick was to give **light.** It was a light-bearer (Leviticus 24:2; Numbers 8:2-3; I John 1:5; John 1:4, 9; Job 33:30 and Ephesians 5:8).   This purpose involved the following aspects:

1. The Candlestick was to illumine the *Holy Place.* The Candlestick was the only light in the Holy Place. The Holy Place, as we will cover later, measured 10 x 10 x 20 cubits giving it a cubical content of 2000 (Exodus 40:24).So Christ and His Church are the only light in this 2000 years Dispensation or Age of the Spirit   (Matthew 5:14; Luke 1:78; John 8:12; II Corinthians 4:16; Philippians 2:15-16 and I John 1:5-7).   There was no natural light in the Sanctuary (John 9:5 and 12:35-36).

2. The Candlestick was to give light *before the Lord* (Leviticus 24:1-4; Exodus 40:25; 27:21 and Revelation 4:5). We are to shine before the Lord as we shine before the world (Matthew 5:15-16).

3. The Golden Candlestick was to give light on the *Table of Shewbread* and the *Altar of Incense* (Exodus 40:24-25 and Psalms 27:1).

4. The Golden Candlestick was to give light over against *itself* (Exodus 25:37 and Numbers 8:2-3). In other words it was to illumine itself or its own ornamentation. In the same way the Spirit illuminates the 66 Books of the Bible. It takes the light of the Spirit to illumine the Word (Psalms 36:9; 119:130; John 14:26; 16:13-14 and II Corinthians 3:18).

All priestly ministry unto the Lord was in the light of the Candlestick (Revelation 1:6; 5:9-10 and I Peter 2:5, 9).

The Candlestick was Divinely lit (Divine Sovereignty), but was kept alight by the supply of the Olive Oil daily (Human Responsibility).

This is seen in the fact that when the Cloudy Pillar of Fire left Mt. Sinai and came and dwelt on the Blood-stained Mercy Seat, **Divine fire** came out from the **Glory** and burnt the sacrifice on the Brazen Altar, thus lighting the Fire which was to burn continually and never to go out, (Leviticus 9:22-24). From this Divinely-lit fire were taken the coals of fire for the Golden Altar of Incense, and the fire to light the Golden Candlestick.

The Church, as God's Candlestick was Divinely and Sovereignly lit on the Day of Pentecost when the "Tongues like as of **Fire**" appeared in visible display upon the 120 Disciples in the Upper Room(Acts 2:1-4).

It is the responsibility of the believer to receive a continual supply of the Divine Oil, the Holy Spirit, to keep his Lamp burning before the Lord.

(7) Bring . . . pure oil olive beaten for the light, to cause the lamps to burn continually . . . Leviticus 24:2

They were instructed by God to use pure Olive Oil beaten for the light (Exodus 25:6; 27:20; 35:14, 28 and Leviticus 24:1-4). Jesus fulfills this symbol in His pre-cross sufferings. "Gethsemane" means "oil" or "olive press." Jesus became the fruit of the olive tree (Romans 11) who was pressed and beaten in the sufferings of Gethsemane and Calvary that we might have the pure Olive Oil, that is, the Holy Spirit as an Anointing and Oil for light and witness. The Holy Spirit is the Pure Olive Oil.

The Greek word for "oil" is "*Chrisma*" (Y.C.) which is also translated "*anointing*"(I John 2:20, 27).Christ is the Anointed One, and the followers of Christ are the Anointed Ones! Even as the Candlestick was anointed prior to its witness, so must the people of God be anointed to be a witness (Exodus 30:27 and Acts 1:8).

We notice also that the Lamps were to *burn continually.* They were never to go out . (Exodus 27:20; I Samuel 3:1-6 and Psalms 119:105). In order to burn continually there must be a continual supply of oil. In order for there to be light manifest, there must be a continual inflow of oil. This is especially true of the Church of the end times. It must be a Church with an abundant supply of oil (Matthew 25:1-13). The Church of this day is challenged to be a light in the midst of a perverse generation (Philippians 2:15-16). The ministry of the Holy Spirit as the Oil has never been so important.

(8) And Aaron . . . when he dresseth the lamps . . . lighteth the lamps at even . . . Exodus 30:7, 8

The ministry of Aaron the High Priest was to (1) trim the wicks by taking away the burnt part and (2) to supply oil in the morning and evening as he ministered at the Altar of Incense (Exodus 27:21; Leviticus 24:3 and Numbers 8:1-3). So Jesus Christ, as our Great High Priest performs His ministry of trimming the wicks of the believers taking away the burnt-out areas and supplying oil for further light-bearing (Philippians 1:19; Matthew 25:1-13 and Revelation 1:12, 20). This is done in connection with His ministry of Intercession (Hebrews 7:25; John 17). Unless the wicks are properly trimmed there will be an abundance of smoke and improper light. God wants a pure light and faithful witness to go forth.

Aaron used the tongs and the snuffdishes for this ministry (Exodus 37:23-24). These represent the instruments that the Lord uses to trim us and cleanse us to cause us to shine brighter for His glory (Hebrews 12:6 and John 15:2).

(9) And look that thou make them after their pattern, which was shewed thee in the mount. Exodus 25:40

The Candlestick was to be made according to the Divine pattern. It was made by the Spirit and wisdom of God as seen in the builders. This speaks to us of the Church which is God's True Candlestick. It, too, must be built according to the Heavenly Blueprint and Divine Pattern (Hebrews 8:1-5). God has only *one pattern* for His Church and He will only fully bless that which measures up to the Divine Standard.

(10) The Candlestick in transit. Numbers 4:9-10

In transit the Golden Candlestick was covered with the following cloths:

1. A Cloth of *Blue*—Here we see a type of the Holy Spirit. It is also representative of Him who is the **Lord from Heaven** (I Corinthians 15:47). Blue is the color of the heavens.

2. Wrapped in *Badgers' Skin* — This is typical of the Father God and it also speaks of Him in whom the world sees no natural beauty (Isaiah 52:14 and 53:1-2).

3. Carried on a *Bar* — This is significant of a pilgrimage and corresponds to the truth set forth in the staves on the furniture.

All of this speaks of the fact that Christ and His Church are of heavenly origin, and that there is no beauty in Christ of His Church to the natural, unregenerate man in the wilderness and pilgrimage wanderings of this world. The beauty is in its witness and function in the Sanctuary.

(11) Additional Thoughts for the Student.

What follows is not meant to be an exhaustive study, but rather a series of "seed thoughts" intended to inspire the student to further study.

1. *In Solomon's Temple* there were 10 Golden Candlesticks (I Chronicles 28:15; I Kings 7:49 and Jeremiah 52:19). The Church is God's Temple (I Corinthians 3:16; II Corinthians 6:16 and Ephesians 2:20-22), and the fulness of Light will be manifest in His Temple.

2. *In Solomon's Temple* there were Candlesticks of Silver in the Priests' Chambers around the walls of the Temple (I Chronicles 28:15 and I Kings 7:49). Silver always carries the thought of redemption. Thus, the Priests stood in the light of redemption before ministering in the Temple at the Golden Candlesticks.

3. *In Babylon* God used the Golden Candlestick to bring about the fall of Babylon (Daniel 5:1-5). So in the Last Days, Babylon (I Peter 5:13) will fall by the revelation and ministry of the true Church, God's Candlestick.

4. *Golden Candlestick(s)* are seen in relation to the vision of restoration times and are typical of the end times (Zechariah 4:1-14 and Revelation 11:1-4).

5. *The Seven Local Churches* in the Book of Revelation are symbolized by the seven Golden Candlesticks, each bearing light in the local city in which God has placed them (Revelation 1:12-20). Notice the sense of responsibility upon each Candlesticks for each local Church is also a universal Church (Revelation 2:5).

"I am the Light of the world" (John 8:12).
"Ye are the Light of the world" (Matthew 5:14-16).
"Light that shines more and more unto the perfect day" (Proverbs 4:18).
"Walk as children of Light" (Ephesians 5:13, 14).
"His Light is the Light of men" (John 1:4).

Thus the Church is to let the Light of God shine forth in the darkness of this world, giving the light of the knowledge of the Glory of God as seen in the face of Jesus Christ (II Corinthians 4:6).

The believer's life should be the light of men, for, **Light** is the very nature and character of God in Christ.

Altar of Incense and High Priest

Read the following: Exodus 30:1-10, 34-38; 37:25-29; 40:5, 9 and Numbers 4:11.

The Golden Altar of Incense

(1) And thou shalt make an altar . . . Exodus 30:1

There were two altars in the Tabernacle of Moses, The Brazen Altar and the Golden Altar. The Brazen Altar was for the Burnt Offering and was located in the Outer Court at the Door of the Tabernacle. The Golden Altar was for the burning of Incense and was positioned in the Holy Place before the veil. The Golden Altar is given several names throughout Scripture. It is called:

1. The Altar of Incense (Exodus 30:27 and 31:8).
2. The Incense Altar (Exodus 35:15 and 37:25).
3. The Altar of Gold (Exodus 40:5).
4. The Golden Altar (Exodus 39:38 and 40:26).
5. The Golden Altar which is before the Throne (Revelation 8:3).
6. The Whole Altar that is by the Oracle (I Kings 6:22).
7. The Altar before the Lord (Leviticus 16:12, 18).
8. The Altar to Burn Incense (Exodus 30:1).
9. The Altar of Sweet Incense before the Lord (Leviticus 4:7).

(2) To burn incense upon . . . Exodus 30:1

The Golden Altar was for the burning of Incense unto the Lord. Incense always speaks to us of the prayers and intercession of the saints which ascend unto God (Psalms 141:1-2 and Revelation 8:2-6). Incense begins on the Altar with man, and as it burns, it ascends upward to God. Likewise, our prayers begin in the heart of man and ascend heavenward unto God.

The burning of Incense also has significance when seen in relation to the ministry of the Lord Jesus Christ, our Great High Priest. The Bible says, "He ever liveth to make intercession **for us**" (Hebrews 7:25; 9:24 and I John 2:1-2).Christ appears before the Throne of God in our behalf. What a comforting thought to know that we have such as He pleading our case!

The ministry of the Holy Spirit can also be seen in connection with the incense. The Holy Spirit, we are told, makes intercession *in* us according to the will of God (Romans 8:26, 34).

Thus, we see that the Golden Altar is significant of Christ Jesus in His ministry of prayer and intercession *for* us and of the prayers and intercessions of the Holy Spirit *in* the Church.

(3) of shittim wood shalt thou make it . . .Exodus 30:1

The wood that was used in the construction of this piece of furniture again speaks to us of the truth that Jesus is the righteous **Branch** (Zechariah 6:10-12; Isaiah 11:1-4; 53:1-2 and Jeremiah 23:5). It is significant of His incorruptible and sinless humanity (Psalms 16:10; Acts 2:25-28; 13:35 and I Peter 1:23). The Lord Jesus Christ was incorruptible in thought, word and deed. He saw no corruption even when He was placed in the tomb.

(4) A cubit shall be the length thereof, and a cubit the breadth thereof . . . and two cubits shall be the height thereof . . . Exodus 30:2

When we look at the Altar of Gold in relation to the other pieces of furniture, we see that the Altar is the highest piece in the actual tent. This speaks of the fact that Christ's ministry of intercession is His highest ministry now in behalf of the Church in the 2000 years of the Church Age or the Dispensation of the Spirit.

(5) Foursquare shall it be . . .Exodus 30:2

The Golden Altar was to be foursquare, just as the Brazen Altar and the Most Holy Place were to be. Whenever the thought of foursquareness is alluded to, it immediately brings to mind the Foursquare City of God mentioned in the Book of Revelation (chapters 21-22). This is the New Jerusalem.

Another thought contained in the number four is the four corners of the world. Four is the number of earth, creation and the universe. We are told by Jesus to preach the Gospel to all the world (Matthew 28:19-20; Mark 16:15-20; Acts 1:8 and Revelation 5:9-10). This is a message that is to be world-wide in its effect.

In connection with the Altar of Incense we see the specific thought that the power of Christ's prayer and intercessory ministry reaches into all the world, to the four corners of the earth. Even so the prayers of the saints are to ascend to Heaven from the four corners of the world. Prayer is not something that is only for the select of the elect, but it is to be world-wide.

(6) The horns thereof shall be of the same . . . Exodus 30:2

The Altar of Incense had four horns in the four corners. Horns in the Scripture are always significant of power, authority and kingship. In (Habakkuk 3:4) we are told that God is seen as having "horns coming out of His hand: and there was the hiding of His power." The horns on the animals are their source of strength, power and their defense (Genesis 22:13).The fact that we have four horns here points to the truth that *all power* was given to Christ both in the heavens and the earth (Matthew 28:18-20).

The Horn was also used particularly by the prophets to anoint ministries. In order for the horn of oil (anointing of the Spirit) to be provided, a death had to take place. (See the following: I Samuel 16:1, 13; Psalms 92:10; 132:17 and Luke 1:69).

(7) And thou shalt overlay it with pure gold, the top thereof, and the sides thereof round about, and the horns thereof . . . Exodus 30:3

The Altar of Incense was completely overlaid with gold. In the wood of the Altar we see the incorruptible humanity of the Lord Jesus Christ. In the gold we see the divine nature of the Son of God. "The **Word** (gold) was made **Flesh** (wood)"(John 1:1-3, 14-18).Jesus had two natures in one person, for He was God manifest in the flesh (I Timothy 3:16). Jesus was the Son of God because His Father was God. Yet, He was the Son of Man because His mother was Mary. In Christ we have a New Creation, the **God-Man.** As there were *two* materials in *one* Altar, even so there are *two* natures in *one* Mediator between God and man (I Timothy 2:5-6).

Son of God (God the Father) — Deity

Becomes One God-Man

Son of Man (Virgin Mary) — Humanity

(8) And thou shalt make unto it a Crown of Gold round about . . . Exodus 30:3

The Altar of Incense had a golden crown on it just as we have seen was on the Table of Shewbread and the Ark of the Covenant. Crowns are symbolic of Christ as our **King** (Psalms 2:1-6 and 45:1-2).A crown in connection with the Altar of Incense reveals Christ as **King-Priest** (Psalms 110:1; Hebrews 7:1-4, 25 and 2:9). Jesus is now crowned with glory and honor as our King-Priest at the right hand of God.

Part of the function of this crown around about the Altar of Incense was to keep the burning coals of incense from falling to the ground. The ministry of Christ includes that which is described in Jude 24 where he says that Christ "is able to keep you from falling."

(9) And two Golden Rings shalt thou make to it under the Crown of it, by the two corners thereof, upon the two sides of it shalt thou make it . . .Exodus 30:4

The rings on the Altar of Incense convey the same thoughts as the rings pertaining to the Ark of the Covenant and the Table of Shewbread. However, there are differing opinions as to the number of rings involved here. Some expositors feel that there were two rings on each side making a total of four. If this is the case we can relate all of the thoughts covered under the four rings of the Ark and the Table. The other view, and perhaps the most widely accepted, is that the Altar of Incense has a total of two rings at opposite corners of the Altar. In case the two rings would be typical of the two persons involved in the ministry of intercession relative to the Church. As we have already seen, the Son and the Holy Spirit are involved in intercessory ministry, linking the Church in earth to the risen Lord in the heavenlies (Romans 8:26 and Hebrews 7:25).

If there were but two rings, as the Altar of Incense was being carried by the Levites, it would undoubtedly swing on the staves. This would give the effect of a huge censer, and thus, it would be functioning even in transit. Here, then, would be the truth of the continual sacrifice that we are to present to the Lord (Hebrews 13:15).

(10) And they shall be for places for the staves to bear it withal. And thou shalt make the staves of shittim wood, and overlay them with gold . . . Exodus 30:4-5

The two staves of "incorruptible" wood overlaid with gold were used for travelling in the wilderness wanderings and journeyings. This again speaks to us that we are strangers and pilgrims on this earth passing through, enroute to Eternity (John 16:33; Hebrews 7:25 and 11:10-16). The Lord Jesus prayed not that we should be taken out of the world, but that we would be kept from the evil that is in the world(John 17:14-16). The staves in connection with the Altar of Incense speak to us of the necessity of the ministry of Christ as intercessor and a personal prayer life in this earthly pilgrimage.

(11) And thou shalt put it before the veil that is by the Ark of the Testimony. Before the Mercy Seat that is over the Testimony, where I will meet with thee . . . Exodus 30:6

The Golden Altar of Incense was positioned immediately before the veil and directly in front of the Ark of the Covenant (Exodus 40:5) The only thing that separated these two pieces of furniture was the inwrought veil. In other words, this article was the nearest piece of furniture to the Ark of the Covenant and the Shekinah Glory of God. In the Book of Revelation we see a picture of "The Golden Altar which was before the Throne" (8:3).

The Golden Altar was at the very heart of the Tabernacle. We have already seen how the furniture was arranged in the outline of the Cross. The Altar is seen at the very *heart* in this picture. From all this we see that the ministry of intercession, prayer and praise are at the very heart of God. These are the nearest things to the Glory of God.

The Golden Altar was positioned in the Holy Place which measured 10 x 10 x 20 cubits. When this measurement is totalled we get the total of 2000. When we see this dispensationally these 2000 cubits speak to us of the 2000 years of the Church Age. The Altar of Incense is placed at the very end of this Holy Place or at the end of the 2000 cubits (years). This is symbolic of the fact that the Church at this end of the age is experiencing the Altar of Incense. The spirit of prayer, supplications and intercession will and must deepen in *all* the saints (Revelation 8:2-4).

(12) And Aaron shall burn thereon sweet incense every morning: when he dresseth the lamps, he shall burn incense upon it. And when Aaron lighteth the lamps at even, he shall burn incense upon it, a perpetual incense before the Lord throughout your generations . . . Exodus 30:7-8

We notice that Aaron the High Priest was to offer Incense every morning and at even as he attended and ministered to the Golden Candlestick (See II Chronicles 29:7). In the Old Testament we find that God always worked in connection with the morning and evening oblation and sacrifice (I Kings 18:36-38 and Daniel 9:21). David says, "Evening, and morning, and at noon, will I pray, and cry aloud" (Psalms 55:17). The Incense was to be continually arising, but morning and evening are especially set aside for "daily ministrations" unto the Lord (Malachi 1:11).

The ministry of Aaron before the Altar of Incense in connection with the Candlestick points to the ministry of our Great High Priest, the Lord Jesus Christ. As Christ ministers to the Church interceding for His own, He trims the wicks of the lamps and supplies the oil of the Spirit.

Only the High Priest and the priests could minister at the Altar of Incense (Numbers 4:16; Deuteronomy 33:10; I Samuel 2:28; I Chronicles 6:49; II Chronicles 2:4 and 13:11). King Uzziah presumed to unite the offices of King and Priest and was smitten with leprosy (II Chronicles 26:16-19). In Christ Jesus, however, these two offices are permanently united. He is the Great High Priest after the order of Melchisedec (Hebrews 7:1-4). Therefore, as we stand in Christ we become kings and priests unto God after the same order (Revelation 1:6). In Christ we have access unto the Father. We are believer-priests, and as such we have the joy and privilege of presenting our incense (prayers) to God by Jesus Christ (Revelation 1:5-6 and 5:9-10). We are "built up a spiritual house, an holy priesthood, to offer up spiritual sacrifices, acceptable to God by Christ Jesus" (I Peter 2:5; Ephesians 2:18).

(13) Ye shall offer no strange incense thereon . . . Exodus 30:9

There was to be no strange fire or strange incense on the Golden Altar of Incense. The first fire on the Altar was Divinely or Sovereignly lit. On the day of the dedication of the Tabernacle, God showed His approval by lighting the Brazen Altar in the Outer Court with Divine Fire coming out from the Glory of God. When the fire on the Brazen Altar was lit, the coals were taken from off the Brazen Altar and used to light the Golden Altar and the Candlestick. Hence, the fire was a divine fire. Any other fire was 'strange fire.' Any incense other than the prescribed Incense was 'strange incense.' Anyone who attempted to offer such an offering on the Golden Altar would be punished by being cut off from the Presence of God.

There are a couple of examples of men who offered strange fire and incense. Nadab and Abihu offered strange fire and incense and were smitten by the Lord (Leviticus 10:1-3). Korah and his company offered strange incense and were also plagued (Numbers 16).

This strange fire and incense is typical of all *false worship*. God is not interested in worship that is excited by mere religious feelings as is found in many of the heathen religions and false cults that are around today, both inside and outside of Christendom. There is much strange fire and incense going up today in the substitute religions and witchcraft (Deuteronomy 18:9-14). which are an abomination to God and will come under Divine judgment in due time.

God only accepts that Fire which originates with Himself on the basis of Blood Atonement (Leviticus 16:12). God lit the fire in the Church on the Day of Pentecost (Acts 2:4) It is the fire of the Holy Spirit which causes the fragrance to arise and ascend within the veil (Hebrews 12:29). God is only interested in worship that is in **Spirit** and in **Truth** (John 4:24).

God only accepts incense that He has prescribed. Jesus Christ is the only mediator between God and man. No man can approach God the Father except through His Son, Jesus Christ. Incense (prayer) apart from the **Name of Jesus Christ** is an abomination to the Father. Jesus said, **"I am the way, the truth, and the life: No Man cometh unto the Father, but by me"** (John 14:6). Paul testified by the Spirit within him, **"Wherefore He is able also to save them to the uttermost that come unto God by Him, seeing He ever liveth to make intercession for them"** (Hebrews 7:25).

(14) Nor burnt sacrifice, nor meat offering; neither shall ye pour drink offering thereon . . .
Exodus 30:9

There was to be no Burnt Offering, Meal Offering or Drink Offering upon this Altar. There were no sacrifices of blood here. Incense is all that was to be burned upon the Golden Altar in the Holy Place. This is because the Outer Court was the place of sacrifice. All the animal sacrifices took place in relation to the Brazen Altar. There was never blood sacrifice in the Holy Place, in the 2000 cubits, or in the Church Age. Jesus Christ shed His Blood at the close of the Law Age and became our "once for all" sacrifice at Calvary. He now lives in the power of an endless life to make intercession for us. Christ has died once unto and for sin, and He dieth no more! Death has no more dominion over Him (Romans 6:9-10).

(15) And Aaron shall make an atonement upon the horns of it once a year with the blood of the sin offering of atonement: once in the year shall he make atonement upon it throughout your generations: it is most Holy unto the Lord . . . Exodus 30:10

Once a year on the Great Day of Atonement, the Blood of the Sin Offerings which had been shed at the Brazen Altar was brought in and placed on the Golden Altar. The Blood was applied particularly to the horns of the Altar and was sprinkled seven times (Leviticus 16:17-19). See also Leviticus 4:7, 18.

It is Christ's Blood (our Sin Offering) that was shed on Calvary (Brazen Altar) which is the basis and foundation of His ministry of Intercession (Golden Altar) in behalf of the saints and the Church at the right hand of the Majesty on High (Hebrews 8:1-2). Only the Blood of Jesus gives power to the incense of prayer. It is only the Blood of Jesus that enables us to stand before a holy God (Hebrews 9:12-14 and I John 1:6-7).

As already pointed out, the blood of the Sin Offering was to be sprinkled on the Horns of the Golden Altar seven times. Seven is the number of fulness, completeness and perfection. Christ's ministry of Intercession is full, complete and perfect. It reaches to the Seven Times Prophecy at the end of this present age.

Christ intercedes for us because His Blood was shed for us.

(16) And the Lord said unto Moses, take unto thee sweet spices, stacte, and onycha, and galbanum; these sweet spices with pure frankincense: of each shall there be a like weight: and thou shalt make it a perfume, a confection after the Art of the Apothecary, tempered together, pure and holy . . . Exodus 30:34-35

As we have already seen, Incense speaks to us of the prayers, worship and the ministry of Intercession of Christ and the Church. If this is indeed the meaning of this symbol, then the ingredients of the incense must point to the various aspects of this ministry unto God. We notice that there were *five* ingredients involved in the sweet Incense. There were three specific spices, there was frankincense, and there was salt (the thought of tempering refers to salting the incense). All of these ingredients were to be of equal weight. We cannot help but notice the perfect balance in all these ingredients. God is interested in balance. Each ingredient is important, and in God's mind each ingredient is absolutely necessary. If this is the case, it is important to see the significance of these ingredients.

1. **Stacte**—Stacte is a fragrant sap of gum from a tree. The word itself means "to drop" or "to distil." In order to be used in this mixture it had to be *crushed fine.* (Connect Deuteronomy 32:1-2).

2. **Onycha**—Onycha was a ground shell-fish taken from the Red Sea. It received its fragrance from the things upon which it fed (See Matthew 4:4). It too had to be *crushed fine* before it could be any use in Incense.

3. **Galbanum**—Galbanum was also a sap or gum that came from a plant or tree-like shrub. It was a bitter gum used to drive away insects (Isaiah 53; Hebrews 5:7). As with the other ingredients it had to lose its identity by being *crushed fine.*

4. **Frankincense**—Frankincense is white in color and comes from the sap of a tree. White speaks to us of purity and righteousness. What a fitting gift to lay before the **Sun of Righteousness** (Matthew 2:11). See also (Song of Solomon 4:6 and John 19:39).

5. **Salt**—Salt acts as both a seasoning and a preservative. Salt speaks to us of speech that is pure, tasty and full of grace (Colossians 4:6). Salt has an enduring quality. God gave David a Covenant of Salt (II Chronicles 13:5). All this is included in the **New** Covenant in Christ (Matthew 26:26-28). See also (Leviticus 2:13; Matthew 5:13 and Mark 9:49-50).

As we come before the Lord with our incense we want to come in humility before Him. We want to come having tasted of the Bread of Life. We want to come in the Name that is above every name. We want to come having lost our identify in the Lord Jesus Christ, standing in His righteousness before the Holy God. We want all our prayer and worship to be seasoned with salt.

There were several other things that were to characterize this Incense. We notice that the Incense was to be:

1. **Sweet**—Christ's ministry was filled with sweetness (Song of Solomon 5:16).
2. **Pure**—Christ was absolutely pure (Hebrews 7:26).
3. **Holy**—Christ ministered in absolute holiness and sinlessness (I John 2:1 and Hebrews 7:26).
4. **Perpetual**—Jesus ministers in the power of an endless life. He ever lives to make intercession for us (Hebrews 7:25; Ephesians 6:18; Colossians 4:2 and Revelation 8:3).
5. **Perfume**—Jesus was fragrant in His whole being (Ephesians 5:2).

(17) And thou shalt beat some of it very small, and put it before the testimony in the Tabernacle of the Congregation, where I will meet with thee: it shall be unto you most holy . . . Exodus 30:36

All of these spices (the sweet and the bitter) were crushed fine, beaten very small and blended together with frankincense. They were tempered with salt as a final procedure. When all this was done, a very fragrant perfume was produced. This was to be placed on the coals of fire on the Altar of Incense before the veil. As the Incense burned upon the Altar, the fragrance would ascend within the veil into the Most Holy Place. Eventually the whole sanctuary would be permeated with the sweetness of the Incense.

In like manner our Lord Jesus Christ was crushed fine and beaten small in His whole being; spirit, soul and body. He was beaten and crushed in trials, testings, temptations and sufferings. He experienced the bitter and the sweet. Just as the incense was placed on the coals, even so Jesus experienced the fire. When He did, He came forth as sweet incense unto the Father. His whole life was saturated with prayer and incense to the Father (I Thessalonians 5:23). *The fragrance of Christ's life permeated Heaven's Holiest of All.* The fragrance was pleasing to the Father because in Christ there was a perfect balance of the spices of grace, love, truth, mercy, holiness and righteousness. In Christ all these things were in perfect balance and of equal weight. Christ alone, then, becomes the only Mediator between God and man. He is that Great Intercessor.

Even as Christ's life was in perfect balance and was pleasing in the nostrils of the Father, so is the life of the Church to be. These same spices of Divine character so manifest in Christ are to be manifest in Christ's Body, the Church. The Church is the Garden of the Lord from which spices are to flow out (Song of Solomon 4:12-16).

(18) **And as for the perfume which thou shalt make, ye shall not make to yourselves according to the composition thereof: it shall be unto thee holy for the Lord. Whosoever shall make like unto that, to smell thereto, shall even be cut off from his people . . .** Exodus 30:37-38

God is very emphatic here. He does not want any substitutes to be made of this Incense. God is not interested in imitation. To violate this meant that God would cut that person off from Israel (Leviticus 10:1-7). There is no substitute for true worship in **Spirit** and in **Truth** (John 4:24). There is no substitute or imitation of the prayer-life that God will or can accept. Everything must measure up to the Standard of the Sanctuary. Everything must be according to the pattern.

(19) The Golden Altar in Transit Numbers 4:11

When the Golden Altar was in transit it was covered with two coverings. When these are placed in connection with the Altar we see a picture of the Fulness of the Godhead Bodily. The covering of Blue points to the Lord from heaven. The Badgers' skins speak of the Word made flesh. And the Altar itself emphasizes the ministry of Christ as the anointed One who ever lives to make intercession for us.

Thus:— 1. The Golden Altar — Christ our Heavenly Intercessor
2. Cloth of Blue — Christ the Lord from Heaven
3. Badgers' skins — Christ in His Humanity, having no natural beauty to the unregenerate

The Golden Altar was carried upon the staves wrapped in the above cloths or coverings. In the wilderness wanderings all the articles were covered with their appointed coverings. The human eye would only behold these 'bundles' which would not be very attractive to the natural man. The beauty of all these things would only be seen when in function and operation. So it is for the things pertaining to Christ and the Church.

(20) The Golden Censer

The Golden Censer was especially used on the Great Day of Atonement when the High Priest went into the Holiest of All with the Blood. It is significant of Christ taking the prayers (incense) of the saints within the veil and presenting them before the Father on the basis of Who He is, what He has done, and what He said (Study the following: Hebrews 9:1-4; Revelation 8:1-6 and Leviticus 16:1-10). The Censer was to be a Censer of gold; a Censer of brass was not acceptable to the Lord.

Note—Numbers, the 16th chapter, and the *Censers of Brass* which brought *judgment* on those who used them in rebellion against Aaron.

(21) What God Thinks About Incense Now

In Isaiah 1:13 and 66:3 the Prophet foretold that the time would come when Incense would be an abomination unto the Lord. Since the coming of Christ, the Great Hight Priest, and the outpouring of the Holy Spirit, God is not interested in the natural shadow but only in the spiritual reality. The only true incense that God desires now is that which ascends from the heart. He is interested in prayers, worship, praise and intercession that comes from the spirit (John 4:24; Psalms 141:1-2).

(22) What is True Incense?

The Altar of Incense speaks to us of the ministry of prayer and Intercession. Prior to the first coming of

Christ, Zacharias received the revelation of the forerunner of Messiah while ministering at the Altar of Incense (Luke 1:1-23). In the same way, the Church will be made ready for Messiah's second coming as it enters into full ministry at this piece of furniture. If this is the case, we need to see just how important this piece of furniture is in God's mind. The very highest and closest ministry in the Church is the ministry of prayer, supplication and intercession, that worship which is in Spirit and in Truth.

The Bible teaches that the Saints are to pray *in* the Spirit (Jude 20), and they are to pray *by* the Spirit (Romans 8:26). The true incense is that which arises from the believer's heart, ascending within the Heavenly Sanctuary. It is that incense that comes by way of our Great High Priest, Jesus Christ (Psalms 141:2; Revelation 5:8).

When we send up Incense to the Lord, our whole nature and being must be involved (I Thessalonians 5:23). We must be saturated and permeated with the fragrance of prayerlife, and the fire of the Spirit will cause our Incense to ascend. God places a high premium on prayer.

Note the following Scriptures:

"And they continued steadfastly in the apostles' doctrine . . . and in **prayers**" (Acts 2:42).

"**Praying** always with all prayer and supplication in the Spirit" (Ephesians 6:18).

"Continue in **prayer**, and watch in the same with thanksgiving" (Colossians 4:2).

"Continuing instant in **prayer**" (Romans 12:12).

"My house is the house of **prayer**" (Luke 19:46).

Tabernacle Framework

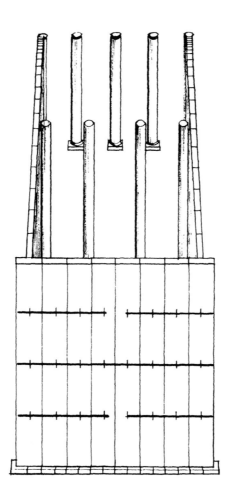

D. Strausser

Read the following: Exodus 26:1-37 and 36:8-38.

The Tabernacle Framework

(1) General Description of the Tabernacle.

In our study thus far we have dealt with all of the furniture in the Tabernacle itself. It, therefore, is fitting that we turn to a consideration of the actual Tabernacle itself. The Tabernacle consisted of a framework of 48 boards overlaid with gold. These 48 boards stood in 96 sockets of silver and were braced by five bars on each of its three closed sides. At the entrance or open side of the Tabernacle there was a hanging called "the Door of the Tabernacle." The Door was made of fine linen and was upheld by five pillars. This Door gave access into the Holy Place. At the end of the Holy Place there was another hanging curtain. This was the veil which was upheld by four pillars and guarded the entrance to the Most Holy Place or the Holiest of All. This curtain is often referred to as the "second veil." Over this whole structure there were other Curtains and Coverings which were the ceiling and roof of the Tabernacle. (These will be dealt with in the following chapter).

(2) And thou shalt make boards for the Tabernacle of shittim wood . . . Exodus 26:15

These Boards were to be made of Shittim wood. Here we see the same truth portrayed as we have seen all the way along. The wood speaks to us of Christ who is the **"Branch"**(Isaiah 11:1-4; Zechariah 3:8; 6:12-13)who was cut off from the land of the living(Isaiah 53:8).Before this wood could be shaped into boards, it had to be cut off from the land of the living. Christ is that **Root** out of the dry ground(Isaiah 53:1-2)who was cut off to become God's Tabernacle — the one and only meeting place between God and man.

Incorruptible wood points us to the sinless, perfect and incorruptible humanity of Christ. He was "holy, harmless, undefiled, separate from sinners"(Hebrews 7:26).His manhood was untainted by sin. As He became flesh and tabernacled among us, He did not sin, neither did the Father allow Him to see corruption in the grave(Psalms 16:9-10).He was uncorrupted by sin, Satan and the world of evil men in His life and was therefore incorruptible in death. He is the sinless, incorruptible, uncorrupted God-Man(I Timothy 2:5; Hebrews 2:14, 17).

In relation to the Church, the Boards of Shittim wood represent our redeemed humanity. When God found us, we were knarled, knotted and twisted like this desert wood growing in a parched land. In Christ we are taken through the process that these Boards experienced. The sinner is cut off from the former old life of the world, and he is shaped into Boards (stones) that fit together into **One** Tabernacle (building) to become the habitation of God by the Spirit (I Peter 2:5, 9).

(3) Standing Up. Exodus 26:15

Each Board was to be standing up or upright before the Lord. The Bible promises that "the upright shall dwell in the Presence"(Psalms 140:13; 64:10 and 112:4).Paul also tells us that having done all we are to stand (Ephesians 6:13 and Galatians 5:1).This is all we are told to do against Satan. Christ has given us a position of victory, we merely need to stand.

(4) Ten cubits shall be the length of a board, and a cubit and a half shall be the breadth of one board . . . Exodus 26:16

Each of the 48 Boards measured 10 cubits in height 1 ½ cubits in width. Each of these Boards was to be overlaid with gold. All of the Boards were to measure up to this Divine Standard in order to qualify as a Board in God's Tabernacle. There was only one standard for all of the 48 Boards. God has but one standard for every member of His Church. Every Board must measure up. Every Christian must measure up to the Standard of the pattern Son, the Lord Jesus Christ. The Church is to "all come . . . unto a perfect Man, unto the measure of the stature of the fulness of Christ"(Ephesians 4:11-16).We are never told to measure ourselves by one another or even by ourselves, but we are to measure up to God's Standard man, the Man Christ Jesus(II Corinthians 10:12. See also Ezekiel 43:10 and Revelation 11:1-2).

The Boards were to be ten cubits high. The number ten speaks to us of trial, testing, law, order and responsibility. We can see this pictured in the Ten Commandments, the Ten Talents, and the Ten Virgins and their responsibility before God. The Lord will have a building made up of those who are tried and tested, who have submitted to His Divine law and order and who are not afraid to take their responsibility before Him.

In addition, the Boards were to be 1 ½ cubits wide. As we have already seen, the Grate of the Brazen Altar, the Table of Shewbread and the Mercy Seat on the Ark of the Covenant were all 1 ½ cubits high. As we connect these four uses of this measurement, we see that the believer must have met Christ at the Brazen Altar (The Cross,) he must have been to the Mercy Seat (the Throne of Grace,) and he must be in fellowship at the Shewbread Table (Communion) to find his proper place in the structure of the Tabernacle (the Local Church).

(5) Two tenons shall there be in one board . . . Exodus 26:17

The Hebrew word used here for "tenons" is literally "hands." These tenons were instrumental in holding the structure together. Each Board had its two tenons. The two tenons speak of those two foundational facts that hold us together in fellowship. These are the same two facts found in all Apostolic preaching in the Book of Acts. They include the **death** and the **resurrection** of the Lord Jesus Christ(I Corinthians 15:3-4).Every Board (believer) must see that Christ **died** for us and that He also **lives** for us(Romans 5:6-10).All believers need to have these two hands (or feet) to keep a balance in his life. He needs to stand firm upon both of these foundational truths in the desert of this world. Both go hand in hand. Both are needed to keep the believer balanced in his walk in the structure of the Church. To emphasize the death of Christ apart from the resurrection of Christ produces death. Both tenons are needed. We are saved by His **Saving Death** and **His Saving Life!**

(6) Set in order one against the other: Thus shalt thou make for all the boards of the Tabernacle . . . Exodus 26:18

The Boards were to stand upright on their own and yet they were to stand collectively to make up a dwelling place for the Lord. No individual Board standing on its own could fulfill this tremendous goal. No single Board could make up a fit dwelling for the Lord God. It was only as the many Boards came together and, as we will see, were held together by the bars that the structure became stable and functional. When every Board was in its place the Tabernacle was complete and the Glory of God could dwell within.

As we apply this to the Church, the present-day dwelling place of the Most High, we find that it is made up of many individuals. A believer on his own is useless in the eternal purpose of God, but as the believers come together, stand together, stay together and are held together by the bars (see Section #10) they are able to fulfil their high calling. Then they can be called One Body or **One** Tabernacle. This is Church Structure as God intended it to be. It is this kind of Structure that the Glory of God is sure to inhabit. God respects the assembly of believers when they dwell together in **One** accord and in **One** place(Acts 2:1).God finds it a very pleasant thing to see brethren dwelling together in unity (Psalms 133:1).See also: (Ephesians 2:21-22; 4:3, 13; I Corinthians 12:12-18).

Christ is building His Church, His House, His Tabernacle Matthew 16:16-19.

(7) And thou shalt make the boards for the Tabernacle, twenty boards on the south side southward . . . and for the second side of the Tabernacle on the north side there shall be twenty boards . . . and for the sides of the Tabernacle westward thou shalt make six boards and two boards shalt thou make for the corners of the Tabernacle in the two sides. And they shall be coupled together beneath, and they shall be coupled together above the head of it unto one ring: thus shall it be for them both; they shall be for the two corners . . . Exodus 26:18, 20, 22, 23, 24

In the actual Framework of the Tabernacle there were 48 Boards. There were:

20 Boards for the South Side
20 Boards for the North Side
 6 Boards for the West Side
 2 Boards for the corners on the West end, giving a total of
48 Boards.

These 48 Boards formed **One** Tabernacle. In the number 48 we have the factors 4 x 12. **Four** is the number of earth. It expresses the thought of a universal or world-wide message (i. e. the four corners of the earth.) The Gospel is to be preached in all the *world* for a witness to every living creature (Mark 16:15-20; Matthew 28:19-20 and Acts 1:8). All power is given unto Christ both in heaven and the earth. The Church is to be both local and universal (world-wide.) It reaches to the four corners of the earth.

The number twelve is the number of Divine Government and the Apostolic Fulness (Refer to the Number 12 as covered in the Table of Shewbread.) The Church is built on the foundation of the Twelve Apostles of the Lamb (Revelation 21:12-14 and Ephesians 2:20). These first Twelve Apostles were symbolic of Apostolic Government. The Church is to continue stedfastly in the Apostles' Doctrine (Acts 2:42).

As we look at the combined thought in the number four and the number twelve we see that the Church universal and local is to be built upon the Apostolic revelation of the Church of God.

There is an additional thought seen in relation to the two corner Boards. These Boards were probably mitred. They speak to us of Christ who is the Corner Stone (Psalms 118:22; Isaiah 28:16). They were to give stability and structure to the Tabernacle. They were instrumental in squaring off the building and giving it its alignment. Even so Christ and His Apostles were that which gave that initial stability to the Early Church. They laid the foundation and got the building off the ground on the proper alignment being firmly laid in God's Word. As we continue or abide in Christ and in the Apostles' Doctrine we can be sure that our building will be properly aligned.

The Corner Boards were supported by coupling rings which were to be beneath and above the Corner Boards (See Diagram). These rings would give added rigidity to the Framework and would be instrumental in keeping the Boards from leaning. These rings were very important to the overall strength of the Framework, and yet, they were virtually unseen when the Tabenacle was fully erected. A ring always speaks to us of the eternal nature of God. The unseen binding ring would best apply to the ministry of the Holy Spirit who is unseen and yet binds all believers (Boards) together to make up the one Bread, the one Body, and the one Building, the present Tabernacle of God.

Note: The number 48 can also be seen in connection with the 48 cities given to the Levites for priestly ministry (Joshua 21).

(8) And thou shalt overlay the boards with gold . . . Exodus 26:29

These Boards were to be overlaid with pure gold. Again we have the thought of deity in connection with gold. In the Boards, gold (Deity) and wood (Humanity) again come together, speaking to us first of Christ and then the Church. In Christ we see this union between the Divine and Human natures. Jesus is the **God**-Man. He receives the wood or human nature from His mother Mary, making Him the Son of Man. He receives the gold or Divine nature from His Father God, making Him the Son of God. He is therefore the only true Mediator between God and man (I Timothy 2:5). For in Him, Deity and Humanity have come together to form the New Creation in Christ Jesus.

As this truth is seen in Christ, so it is to flow into the experience of the Church. The Boards point to the believer who is standing in Christ. The believer is cut off from the old desert life of sin, his natural glory is stripped off, he is planed, shaped and fashioned to God's pattern and measurements. In Christ we are born again of the incorruptible seed of the Word of God (I Peter 1:4, 23). We become partakers of the Divine Nature (II Peter 1:4).

(9) And thou shalt make forty sockets of silver under the twenty boards; two sockets under one board for His two tenons, and two sockets under another board for His two tenons. And for the second side . . . their forty sockets of silver; two sockets under one board; and two sockets under another board. And for the sides of the Tabernacle westward . . . shall be eight boards, and their sockets of silver, sixteen sockets; two sockets under one board and two sockets under another board . . . Exodus 26:19, 20, 21, 22, 25

For each of the 48 Boards, there were two Sockets of silver. There were:

40 Sockets for the 20 Boards on the South Side,
40 Sockets for the 20 Boards on the North Side and
16 Sockets for the 8 Boards on the West Side totalling
96 Sockets in all.

The first thing that we notice about the Sockets is that they were to be made of silver. It is appropriate to ask, where did this silver come from? The answer is found in Exodus 30:11-16. Here we see that Moses was instructed to number the children of Israel. Every man that was twenty years old and above was to be counted. As they were numbered they were required to bring a half a shekel unto the Lord. This half shekel was to be after the shekel of the sanctuary which was 20 gerahs (Numbers 3:46-51; 18:16).This meant that each half shekel was 10 gerahs. This was God's standard and points to the 10 Commandments, God's Divine Standard of the Law. This money was to be atonement money for the souls of the people. The poor as well as the rich were to pay this same amount. God's standard is the same for all; He is no respecter of persons. Every man had to pay for himself. None could pay for another (Psalms 49:7-8).The soul had to be redeemed with silver, and as it was, God promised to prevent plagues from coming upon them.

The spiritual significance of all this is evident. As we have seen, silver speaks to us of atonement, redemption, ransom money and the price of a soul. Peter interprets this symbol for us when he says, "Forasmuch as ye know that ye were not redeemed with corruptible things, as **silver and gold,** from your vain conversation received by tradition from your fathers; But with the precious **Blood of Christ,** as of a Lamb without spot: who verily was foreordained before the foundation of the world, but was manifest in these last times for you"(I Peter 1:18-21).Jesus was sold for silver (Matthew 26:15).

The silver atonement of the Old Testament becomes the Blood Atonement of the New Testament (I John 1:6-7).The Blood of our Lord Jesus Christ under the New Covenant takes the place of the "ransom money" that was established in the Mosaic Covenant. His Blood is our atonement, our ransom, our redemption and the price of our soul. This is the price by which we are bought (I Corinthians 6:20).This is the standard that God has set for our redemption. The Bible tells us that the Son of Man came to "minister, and to give His life **a ransom** for many" (Mark 10:45)."**There is one God, and one Mediator between God and man, the man Christ Jesus; who gave Himself a ransom** for all"(I Timothy 2:5-6; Job 33:24; Isaiah 35:10).This is God's standard and all must meet this standard. None can pay for another to get into the Kingdom of His dear Son. No one can be numbered in the True Church unless they are redeemed with this price. Calvary is the mine (vein) of silver to which we all have access that we might obtain the price of atonement (Job 28:1). As we find our place in the Church, God prevents plagues from coming nigh unto us.

Another thought seen here in the silver is found in relation to the result of the numbering. In this numbering there were found to be 603,550 persons. This means that there would have been a total of 301,775 shekels of silver that were collected from the people. Each of the Sockets were to be made of one talent of silver. There were 3000 shekels in a talent. Thus, we see that each of the 96 Sockets was composed of one talent or 3000 shekels of silver. In addition there were four Sockets needed for the four pillars that upheld the veil. When we subtract the amount of silver needed for these 100 Sockets we are left with 1,775 shekels to be used for the hooks, chapiters and the connecting rods in the pillars of the Outer Court. (Exodus 30:11-16 compare with (Numbers 1:45-46 and Exodus 38:25-28).

If each Socket was comprised of 3000 shekels, then each Socket represented the redemption price of 6000 souls. Each Board had two such Sockets. Each Board was, therefore, typically upheld by 12,000 redeemed Israelites. The Church is now the true and spiritual Israel of God (Galatians 6:16). In the Book of Revelation, 12,000 of each of the Tribes of Israel of God are sealed with the seal of the living God(7:1-8).God knows the number of His redeemed out of every kindred, every tongue, every tribe and every nation (Revelation 5:9-10).

These Sockets were the very foundation of the Tabernacle. As we have seen, the Boards each had two tenons (two hands or feet) by which they stood in the silver Sockets. The Sockets of silver were the foundation or standing place for these Boards. No Board had its feet in the desert sands of this world, but each stood in redemption metal (compare Matthew 7:24-29). No believer is to stand on the sinking sands of earth's interpretation of life, but they are to stand firm and upright in the truth of Blood Atonement and the Word of God. "**Other foundation** can no man lay than that is laid, which is Christ Jesus"(I Corinthians 3:9-14). It is absolutely essential to have the proper foundation laid. Even as Moses laid the foundation of silver and atonement for the Tabernacle in the Old Testament, so Paul in Apostolic ministry lays the proper foundation of Blood Atonement for the Church of the New Testament (For other Scriptures relating to our foundation see: Psalms 11:3; Isaiah 28:16; Luke 6:46-49 and Hebrews 6:1-2).

(10) And thou shalt make bars of shittim wood; five for the boards of the one side of the

Tabernacle, and five for the boards of the other side of the Tabernacle, and five bars for the boards of the side of the Tabernacle, for the two sides westward. And the middle bar in the midst of the boards shall reach from end to end . . . and thou shalt overlay the bars with gold . . . Exodus 26:26-28, 29

On each side of the structure there were positioned five bars of Shittim wood overlaid with gold. These bars were placed through rings of gold attached to the Boards. As they were inserted, they would act as brace-bars to hold the entire structure in a firm position. Without these brace-bars the structure would be susceptible to every desert wind that came up. As the bars fulfilled their ministry the Tabernacle would stand sure.

Exactly how these bars were positioned on each side we are not told. Much speculation has been made in this regard. Some diagrams show two bars across the top parallel to two bars across the bottom with the central bar running the full length of the side. Others suggest that the bars were at diagonals forming a large "X" with the central bar again running the length of the side (See diagrams).

The most interesting of these five bars is the central bar. In speaking of the bar, the Scripture says that "the middle bar in the midst of the Boards shall reach from end to end" (Exodus 26:28). And again we are told that "he made the middle bar to shoot through the boards from one end to the other" (Exodus 36:33). Perhaps this bar ran through a hole in the middle of each Board. If this was the case, it would have been in the midst and shooting through the Boards.

In this case the central bar, when viewed alone, speaks to us of the Lord Jesus Christ who is in the midst of His redeemed people (Matthew 18:20; John 19:18 and Revelation 1:8). In speaking of Jesus, Paul says, "For of Him, and through Him, and to Him are all things: to whom be glory for ever. Amen" (Romans 11:36).

When we view the five bars collectively we get quite another picture. Five is the number of the grace of God. God's grace is manifest to the Church in many ways. One way by which God deals with His people to stabilize them is through the five-fold ministry. Just as these five bars were to stabilize the whole structure, bracing the Tabernacle from being shaken to and fro by whatever winds would come against it, even so God has placed five ministries in His Church (Tabernacle) to keep the Church from being swayed by every wind of doctrine. These five ministries include the Apostle, Prophet, Pastor, Evangelist and Teacher Ephesians 4:11-16. Just as the bars were responsible for keeping the Boards compacted together, even so these ministries keep the Church united in their goal. Without the five-fold ministry of the Ascended Lord, the Church lacks stability, solidity and proper structure.

The five bars are seen in relation to each side of the framework. This truth as seen in the five-fold ministry is to be realized in the Church all over the world. It is not something characteristic of one geographical area, but it is meant to become a part of every New Testament Local Church. The Church is the household of God, built upon the foundation laid by the Apostles and Prophets, "Jesus Christ Himself being the Chief Cornerstone in whom all the building fitly framed together groweth unto an Holy Temple in the Lord: in whom ye also are builded together for an habitation of God through the Spirit" (Ephesians 2:20-22, also I Peter 2:5; Colossians 2:2, 2:19).

(11) And make their rings of gold for the places for the bars . . . Exodus 26:29

The symbol of the ring speaks to us of endlessness, eternity, having neither beginning nor end. God has established His Everlasting Covenant of love with His redeemed Hebrews 13:20. It is the love of God that links all believers together (I Corinthians 13). If each of the 48 Boards had three rings, as most suggest, through which the five bars passed, they could point to the "abiding three" — Faith, Hope and Love (I Corinthians 13:13). It is these three that bind God and all believers together eternally.

In the whole of the Structure of the Tabernacle there were the golden Boards, the silver Sockets of redemption, the five stabilizing bars and the gold rings linking it all together. The Church, God's building is united together by the redemption that is in Christ Jesus, the Everlasting Covenant of God's love and the five-fold ministries of the Risen and Ascended Lord. When all this is together we have One Church!!

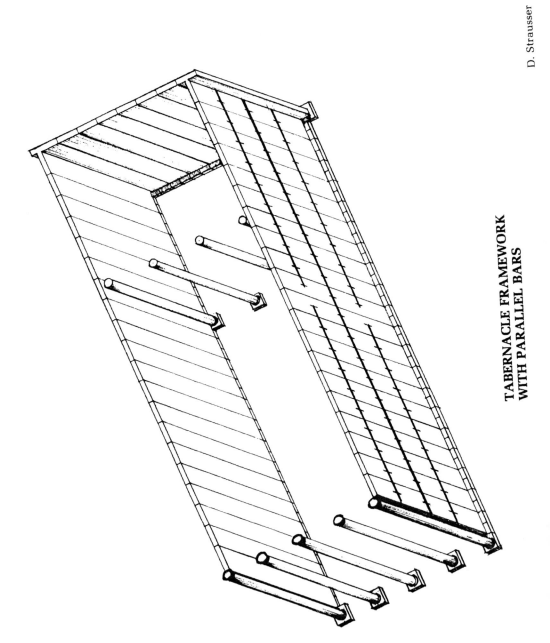

**TABERNACLE FRAMEWORK
WITH PARALLEL BARS**

D. Strausser

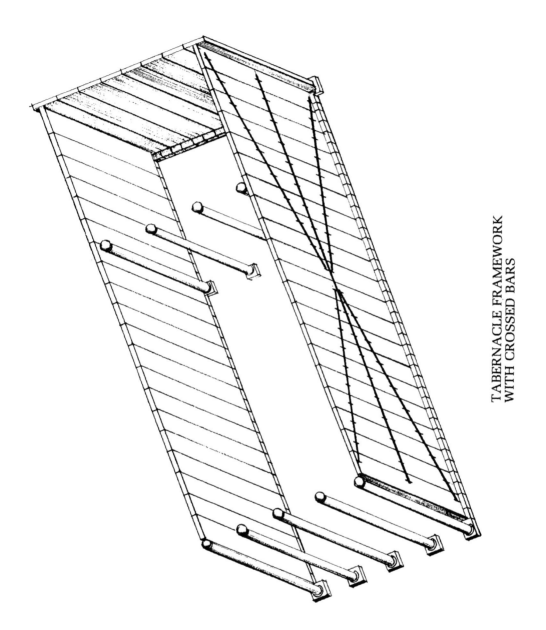

TABERNACLE FRAMEWORK
WITH CROSSED BARS

D. Strausser

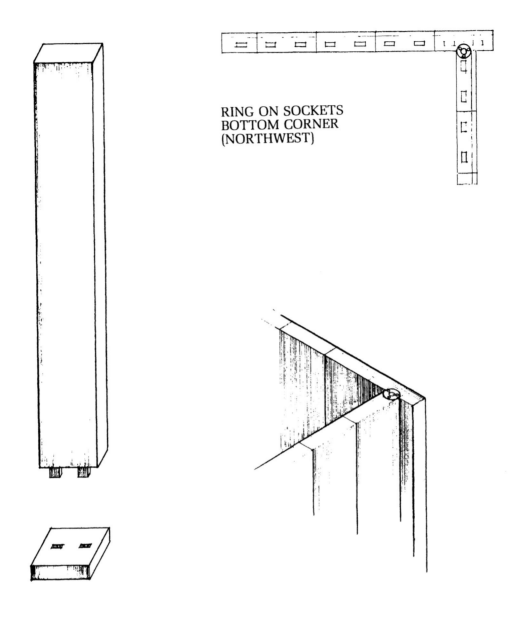

RING ON SOCKETS
BOTTOM CORNER
(NORTHWEST)

BOARD & SOCKET

THE CORNER BOARDS

D. Strausser

Read the following: Exodus 26:1-14 and 36:8-19.

The Curtains and the Coverings

(1) The Curtains and Coverings in General

There were various curtains and coverings involved in the Tabernacle. These Curtains and Coverings were hung or draped over the Framework. Some diagrams suggest that the final Coverings were placed in a tent position over tent poles. As to the specific arrangement of these Coverings we are not told. God has, however, given the order in which these Coverings were to be placed over the Framework and the materials from which they were to be made. These facts themselves give us a great field of study.

The Curtains and Coverings for the Tabernacle are laid out in the following order:

1. **The Curtains of Fine Linen** (Exodus 26:1-6 and 36:8-13) — These Curtains were placed directly over the Framework and comprised the actual roof or ceiling of the Sanctuary.

2. **The Curtains of Goats' Hair** (Exodus 26:7-13 and 36:14-18)— This curtain which is referred to as the 'tent' was placed over the Curtains of Fine Linen.

3. **The Rams' Skin Dyed Red** (Exodus 26:14 and 36:19)— This is referred to as a Covering and was next in order.

4. **The Covering of Badgers' Skins** (Exodus 26:14 and 36:19) — This was the final Covering and was that which was seen to all who were outside the Tabernacle.

It is suggested that the first two were Curtains and that the next two were the Coverings. "And they shall bear the **curtains** of the Tabernacle, and the **Tabernacle** of the Congregation, his coverings, and the covering of Badgers' skins that is above it . . . ." (Numbers 4:25).

(2) Moreover thou shalt make the Tabernacle with ten curtains . . . Exodus 26:1

The first thing we are told is that there were to be *ten* curtains. Ten is the number of the Ten Commandments and representative of the Law Covenant. It is significant here of the fact that our Lord Jesus Christ is the Perfect and Righteous Man. He is the only Man who ever kept the Law Covenant and the Commandments of God. The entire Law, the Moral, the Civil and the Ceremonial Law, was fulfilled in Him, for as the Spirit of Christ testified, "Thy Law is within My heart" (Psalms 40:6-8).

(3) of fine twined linen . . . Exodus 26:1

These ten Curtains of fine linen were referred to at times as "the Tabernacle." In Exodus 36:13, we are told in regard to these ten Curtains, "so it become **One Tabernacle**" (See also Exodus 26:1 and Numbers 3:25).

This Tabernacle was to be comprised of ten Curtains of fine twined linen. Clean, fine, white linen is perhaps one of the clearest symbols in the entire Scripture. Fine linen is always a symbol of righteousness. It speaks first of the righteousness of Christ as the pattern Son, and second, it points to the righteousness of the saints who are in Christ (Revelation 19:7-8). This is not self-righteousness. Self-righteousness is pictured for us by Isaiah as filthy rags(64:6).Clean, white, fine linen speaks of faith-righteousness. Fine linen is the clothing and garment of the Priests (Exodus 28:39-43). As we come in faith before the Lord we are ordained to be Kings and Priests before God and will wear the same garments. "He that overcometh, the same shall be clothed in white raiment" (Revelation 3:5). This is not something that we put on on the basis of our own merit, but "He hath clothed me with the Garments of Salvation, He hath covered me with the Robe of Righteousness" (Isaiah 61:3, 10 and Revelation 7:14).

(4) and blue, and purple, and scarlet . . . Exodus 26:1

As we have seen, *Blue* is the color of heaven. It speaks to us of the Lord Jesus Christ as the Second Man, the **Lord** from heaven (I Corinthians 15:47; John 1:1-3, 14-18). It is interesting that the Children of Israel were to have a Ribbon of Blue upon the border of their garment as a constant reminder of the Heavenly Commandments and the fact that their citizenship was not an earthly one (Numbers 15:32-41).

62

Purple is the color of royalty and kingship. Jesus Christ is the Royal Man who is our King of Kings and Lord of Lords. Purple is produced by a blending of blue and scarlet. In Christ there is a blending of the Human and Divine natures in **One** person. He is both Son of God and Son of Man (Luke 1:30-33 and Revelation 19:11-6). This qualifies Him to be the only Mediator between God and man, because being God (blue), He partook of flesh (scarlet).

Scarlet is the color of Blood and speaks to us of sacrifice and humanity (Matthew 27:28). All through the Old Testament the Israelites were to find atonement on the basis of the sacrifice of animal blood. All of their offerings point to the coming of the **Lamb** of God. This is the one and only sacrifice for sin. Animal blood only pointed to His Blood. Only His Blood has the power of atonement.

These four colors that we see prescribed for the ten curtains are no accidental choice. In fact the very order of these colors is not arbitrary. This same order for these same colors is repeated about 24 times in the Book of Exodus. These four colors are typical of the four Gospels which present Jesus Christ as the **True** Tabernacle. In relation to the Gospels we see the following:

1. White —Gospel of Luke—Son of Adam (The Sinless Man)
2. Blue —Gospel of John — Son of God (The Heavenly Man)
3. Purple —Gospel of Matthew—Son of David (The Royal Man)
4. Scarlet —Gospel of Mark—Son of Man (The Servant Man)

(5) With Cherubims of cunning work shalt thou make them . . . Exodus 26:1

These Cherubim were to be inwrought into the linen of "cunning" work. We have already seen that the Cherubim do not represent angels, nor do they speak of any human. The inwrought Cherubim speak to us of the gloriously manifested, intricate workings and operations of the Holy Spirit and the Father in the birth, life, ministry, death, burial and resurrection of the Lord Jesus Christ. Since the fine linen speaks first of all of the righteousness of Christ, the inwrought Cherubim manifest Christ as the fulness of the Godhead Bodily (Colossians 1:19; 2:9).

This linen with the inwrought Cherubim would then comprise the ceiling for the Sanctuary. As we know, from the description of the Mercy Seat, these Cherubim had wings. Putting these things all together we get a precious picture of the *Wings of the Almighty*. The Cherubim inwrought within the Linen Curtains would stretch forth their wings above the Sanctuary under which the Priest ministered. The Priest would in effect be walking, ministering and enjoying fellowship under the shadow of the wings of the Cherubim. It is to this truth that Scripture often alludes, **"In the shadow of Thy wings** will I rejoice" (Psalms 63:7). **"Under His wings** shalt thou trust"** (Psalms 91:1-2, 4). **"Under whose** wings thou art come to trust" (Ruth 2:12). "They that wait upon the Lord . . . shall mount up with wings as eagles" (Isaiah 40:30-31). Compare Psalms 61:4; 17:8; 36:7; 57:1; Ezekiel 1:24; Matthew 17:37; 23:37; Revelation 12:6, 14.

(6) The length of one curtain shall be eight and twenty cubits, and the breadth of one curtain four cubits: and every one of the curtains shall have one measure. The five curtains shall be coupled one to another. And thou shalt make loops of blue upon the edge of the one curtain from the selvedge in the coupling; and likewise shalt thou make in the uttermost edge of another curtain, in the coupling of the second. Fifty loops shalt thou make in the one curtain, and fifty loops shalt thou make in the edge of the curtain that is in the coupling of the second; that the loops may take hold one of another, and thou shalt make fifty taches of gold, and couple the curtains together with the taches: and it shall be one Tabernacle . . . Exodus 26:2-6

There were ten Curtains which were arranged in two groups of five. These two sets of five curtains were joined together by *fifty* clasps (taches) of *gold* and fifty loops of *blue*. When all was thus joined together, it formed **One** Tabernacle.

Each of these 10 curtains were 28 cubits in length and 4 cubits in breadth. When these were all joined together as we have just described, they formed a covering 28 cubits wide and 40(4 x 10) cubits long. This was placed over the Framework that was outlined in the last chapter. The Board Structure was ten cubits in height, ten cubits in width and thirty cubits in length. When the Curtains were placed over the framework with the gold taches directly over the veil, the curtains would cover the entire frame-work. Since the North side (10 cubits), the South side (10 cubits) and the ceiling (10 cubits across) totaled 30 cubits, we see that the Curtains were suspended one cubit above the ground on either side of the Framework.

With the Curtains so arranged, they would cover the full length of the Framework with an overhang on the West end of ten cubits. The full length of the joined Curtains was 40 cubits while the length of the Tabernacle was 30 cubits. Since there was a door for the East end of the Tabernacle, the Curtains undoubtedly covered the ten cubits of the West wall.

In the very couplings used in these ten curtains we have at least three important symbols:

1. The loops were to be of **Blue.** As we have seen, Blue speaks of the Lord Jesus Christ as the Second Man who is the **Lord** from heaven (I Corinthians 15:47).

2. The taches were to be made of **Gold.** Gold is typical of the Divine nature. Jesus was the Divine Man.

3. There were to be **Fifty** loops and **Fifty** taches. In connection with the number fifty we notice that every fifty years was to be a year of Jubilee (Leviticus 25:8-12). The Feast of Pentecost was celebrated on the fiftieth day (Leviticus 23:15-16). In fact, the word 'Pentecost' means "fifty." The number fifty is therefore significant of freedom, liberty, Pentecost and Jubilee. When we apply this truth to the Lord Jesus Christ, the God-man, it speaks of His freedom from the slavery of sin and His complete liberty walking in the will of His Father. Through Christ, the Church experiences the Feast of Pentecost for He is the Baptizer with the Holy Spirit. In Christ, the Church experiences the Jubilee joys and reality of life in the Spirit. Because of Christ, the Church will enter into her full possession!

   Note: For the student who finds this to be an area of great interest, it would do well for him to examine the Scriptures in regard to the fifty names and titles of Christ which reveal His Deity (fifty golden taches.)

(7) And thou shalt make curtains of goats' hair to be a covering upon the Tabernacle: eleven curtains shalt thou make. The length of one curtain shall be thirty cubits, and the breadth of one curtain four cubits: and the eleven curtains shall be all of one measure. And thou shalt couple five curtains by themselves, and six curtains by themselves, and shalt double the sixth curtain in the forefront of the Tabernacle. And thou shalt make fifty loops on the edge of the one curtain that is outmost in the coupling, and the fifty loops in the edge of the curtain which coupleth the second. And thou shalt make fifty taches of brass, and put the taches into the loops, and couple the tent together, that it may be one. And the remnant that remaineth, shall hang over the backside of the Tabernacle. And a cubit on the one side, and a cubit on the other side of that which remaineth in the length of the curtains of the tent, it shall hang over the sides of the Tabernacle on this side and on that side, to cover it . . . Exodus 26:7-13

Over the ten Curtains of fine linen were placed eleven Curtains of Goats' Hair. These Curtains are referred to many times in Scripture as the "tent" (Exodus 35:11; 36:14; 40:19; 26:7, 11, 13 and Numbers 3:25) as well as a Covering. It is the second covering over the Framework of the Tabernacle. The Goat Hair used here was most likely black in color as is characteristic of most goats in that region (Song of Solomon 1:5).

There were to be eleven curtains making up this Goats' Hair Covering. Eleven is the number of lawlessness and disorder and is associated with sin and rebellion. Eleven is one beyond ten which speaks of law and order (i. e. the Ten Commandments), and yet is one short of twelve which speaks of Apostolic Government (i. e. the Twelve Apostles of the Lamb. There were eleven Disciples after Judas fell. This symbol is brought together in the Tabernacle with the Goats' Hair.

The Goat was one of the animals used in Israel for sacrifice. It was used primarily in connection with the **Sin** Offering on the Day of Atonement and the cleansing of the Sanctuary (Leviticus 5:6; 9:3; 16:5-11, 20-26). The Goat was used in connection with the three Feasts in Israel. It was used in the Feast of Passover (Numbers 28:16-25),Pentecost (Leviticus 23:15-21) and Tabernacles (Numbers 29:1-11). On the Day of Atonement, two Goats were to be taken. One was to be killed as a sin offering, and one was to be preserved alive to be used as the scapegoat (Leviticus 16:5-11, 20-26). In connection with the Feast of Passover, the Israelites were instructed to offer "one Goat for a Sin Offering to make an Atonement for you" (Numbers 28:22). The Goat is used in connection with the Sin Offering (Leviticus 4:23).

1. For the common people (Leviticus 4:27-28),
2. For the Consecration of the Priesthood (Leviticus 9:2-3),
3. For the dedication of the Altar (Numbers 7),
4. For the sins of ignorance (Numbers 15:24, 27, and
5. For each new month (Numbers 28:11-15).

That the Goat speaks to us of sin is confirmed in the New Testament. Jesus gives us a picture of the Day of the Lord and likens the unrepentant sinners to goats at His left hand (Matthew 25:31-32).

In the number of Curtains and the material of this Covering we have the thought of sin. These Goats' Hair Curtains speak to us of the Lord Jesus Christ who became our Sin Offering and received for us the wages of sin — Death "He hath made Him to be sin for us, who knew no sin, that we might be made the righteousness of God in Him" (II Corinthians 5:21 and Romans 8:3). The Sun of Righteousness was made sin for us! What a contrast this load of sin that Christ took upon Himself was to that perfect life that He walked before God! What a contrast these Black Goats' Hair Curtains were to the White Linen Curtains below (See: Isaiah 53:10; Hebrews 9:26-28; 10:11, 14).

These eleven Curtains of Goats' Hair speak to us further of our Lord Jesus Christ who was "once offered to bear the Sins of many" (Hebrews 9:28). We notice that when this curtain was placed over the Tabernacle Framework, five of the curtains covered the Most Holy Place and the West wall, while the remaining set of six curtains covered the Holy Place to the Door. In this position with the taches directly over the veil, the eleventh Curtain would extend beyond the Door of the Sanctuary. It was this eleventh Curtain that was then folded or doubled over the forefront of the Tabernacle. This all sounds quite meaningless. However, we see that it was this eleventh Curtain only that the outside observer saw as he looked upon the Tabernacle. The other ten curtains remained unseen and hidden from view.

How does all of this apply to Christ? In the eleven Curtains we have a picture of the 33 years of Christ's earthly walk when He did indeed become Sin for us. Just as one/eleventh of the Goats' Hair Covering was all that was visible to the outside observer, even so one/eleventh of the life of Christ was manifest in public ministry (3 ½ years.) Just as ten of the eleven Curtains were concealed from public view, even so about thirty years in Christ's life are hidden from general view. As each of the eleven curtains (seen and unseen) measured exactly the same, even so the hidden and open years were the same in the eyes of His Father.

The length of these Curtains were to be thirty cubits. Thirty is the number of consecration to the Priesthood. Each Priest had to be thirty years of age before he could minister Numbers 4:3. Jesus was thirty years of age when He began His Priestly ministry (Luke 3:23),which consummated with His being offered as a Sin Offering for us at Calvary. Jesus was consecrated to the Father's will, even to the death of the Cross. He was both Priest and Offering.

The width of these Curtains was to be four cubits. The number four here speaks to us of the expanse of the ministry of Christ to the four corners of the earth. The ministry of Christ is a world-wide ministry. He is the Priest, Saviour and Sin Offering for the whole world. "God so loved the world, that He gave His Only Begotten Son" (John 3:16; Acts 1:8; Matthew 28:19-20).

The eleven Curtains were to be in two sets, a set of five and a set of six. These two sets were joined by fifty loops and fifty taches of Brass. As we have seen, fifty is the number of liberty, freedom, Pentecost and Jubilee release (See section #6.) Since there were fifty taches of gold in connection with the previous covering, this means there is a total of 100 taches in all. This number is suggestive of the many names and titles of Christ Jesus in the Old and New Testament.

These taches (clasps) were to be of Brass. As we have already seen, Brass is characteristic of Judgment against sin. How fitting that Brass taches be used in this black Covering. Brass is linked with the Sin Offering. Sin must be judged, and the wages of sin is death (Romans 6:23).

(8) And thou shalt make a covering for the Tent of Rams' Skins dyed red . . . Exodus 26:14

This next Covering was made of Rams' Skins and is spoken of expressly as a "Covering" (Numbers 3:25 and 4:25). The Ram was used in the Trespass Offering (Leviticus 5:15), Burnt Offerings (Leviticus 8:18) and Peace

Offerings (Leviticus 9:4). It is also called the **"Ram of Consecration"** (Exodus 29:15-22).The Ram was used in the *consecration* of the Priests to minister (Leviticus 8:22). The first place we see the ram in the Bible it is used as a *substitute* and offered *instead of* Isaac, the Only Begotten Son, on Mt. Moriah (Genesis 22:8-13).

This is all prophetic of the Son of God, Jesus Christ who became the Lamb of God to take away the sin of the world (John 1:29, 36).It reveals Christ as

1. The *Sacrificial One* who was offered to God (Hebrews 9:26-28),
2. The *Substitute One* who died in our stead (I Corithians 15:4; Galatians 1:4) and
3. The *Consecrated One* who was committed to God's will (Hebrews 7:25-28).

This is the Covering that Christ has provided for the Church that we may partake of His nature and Spirit (Romans 12:1-2; Romans 4:25). We are to give ourselves.

These Rams' Skins were to be dyed red. *Red* is the color of sacrificial blood and is identified in the cleansing from sin. The Rams' Skins dyed red were the central covering of the Tabernacle pointing to the central figure of the Godhead, the Lord Jesus Christ. They are typical of the Sacrifice of the Lord Jesus and His shed Blood for our sin. He is our Redeemer and that Ram of Consecration who was sold out to the Will of the Father and brought to us the Everlasting Covenant of Salvation (Hebrews 13:20). "Though your sins be as scarlet, they shall be white as snow: though they be red like crimson, they shall be as wool" (Isaiah 1:18).

In our Lord's First Advent, His Garments were *dyed red* in the Blood of Atonement. In His Second Advent, His Garments are also *dyed red* in the blood of His enemies. Here the dyed red Garments of the Lord speak not of Atonement, but they are associated with Jesus Christ in judgment upon sinners. "Who is this that cometh from Edom (red), with dyed garments from Bozrah? This that is glorious in his apparel, travelling in the greatness of His strength? . . . Wherefore art Thou red in Thine apparel, and Thy garments like him that treadeth in the winefat?" (Isaiah 63:1-3).In the final scene in the Book of Revelation we see a rider on a *white* horse whose vesture is dipped in Blood (19:11-14).

(9) And a covering above of Badgers' Skins . . . Exodus 26:14

The outer and final Covering, over all and above all, was the Covering of Badgers' Skins. Even as the Rams' Skins had no recorded measurements, so also we are given no measurements for this Covering. It is suggested that these skins were seal or porpoise skins of a bluish-gray color. In fact, the Septuagint translates from "skins of a blue color." Whatever the case, these skins acted as the final *protection* from the storms, weather and heat of the desert and wilderness life. Badgers' Skins were used as a covering for all of the vessels of the Tabernacle when they were in transit.

Badgers' Skins were not a precious fur or skin. There was, therefore, no natural beauty to the human eye in gazing upon the Tabernacle. Only the Priests who experienced the inside of the Tabernacle found out where the real beauty was.

This is the same that is true of Christ. Isaiah declares that "when we shall see Him, there is no beauty that we should desire Him"(Isaiah 53:1-3),because "His visage was . . . marred more than any man, and His form more than the sons of men" (Isaiah 52:14).To the natural and unregenerate man, there is nothing attractive about Christ, but to those who are in Christ, He is seen in great glory and beauty (Hebrews 1:3 and Colossians 1:19). To those who are in Christ, "He is altogether lovely" (Song of Solomon 5:16), but to those outside of Christ, He is nothing to be desired. For "the natural man receiveth not the things of the Spirit of God: for they are foolishness unto him: neither can he know them, because they are spiritually discerned."

These are the four Curtains and Coverings of the Tabernacle of Moses. The thought of the Coverings is not unique to the Tabernacle. The Ark of Noah had its Covering (Genesis 8:13). All of the Coverings in the Bible point to *The Covering* for the Church as seen in the Lord Jesus Christ. Christ is our

1. Linen Curtain — Righteousness
2. Goats' Hair Curtain — Sin Offering
3. Rams' Skin dyed red — Subtitution
4. Badgers' Skin — Protection and Covering.

Christ is the Covering for the Church, His Tabernacle. The Covering includes all that He is, all that He says and all that He does! "He hath **covered** me with the **Robe of Righteousness**" (Isaiah 61:10).

Read the following: Exodus 26:31-37 and 36:35-38.

The Tabernacle Entrances

Relative to the Sanctuary itself, there were two entrances. These were spoken of as 'The Vail' and 'The Door' and we will consider them in this order.

(1) And thou shalt make a vail . . . Exodus 26:31

The first entrance to be described is the 'second veil' (Hebrews 9:3).As with the furniture, God begins with that entrance that is closest to Himself. It was through this veil that the Priest entered once a year into the very Presence or Shekinah Glory of God. This was the way into the Holiest of All or the Most Holy Place. This entrance is given several titles throughout the Scriptures. These titles include the following:

1. **The Vail** (or Veil as we find it in the New Testament) (Exodus 26:31; Hebrews 6:19)—A veil is a divider or a separation curtain that is used to hide something. All this can be seen here in connection with this Veil.

2. **The Second Veil** (Hebrews 9:3) — The Door to the Sanctuary is considered here to be the first veil by which entry into the Holy Place is gained. In man's approach, the Veil before the Most Holy Place is the Second Veil he experiences.

3. **The Covering Vail** (Numbers 4:5) — This Veil was used to cover the Ark of the Covenant while it was in transit. The Ark was never seen by the people.

4. **The Vail of the Covering** (Exodus 35:12; 39:34; 40:21) — Again, this veil was a covering for the Ark.

5. **The Vail of the Testimony** (Leviticus 24:3) — As the Veil covered the Ark, it also covered the Tables of the Law that were in the Ark.

6. **The Vail of the Sanctuary** (Leviticus 4:6) — Once inside the Sanctuary, this was the only veil or divider between the Priest and the Most Holy Place.

(2) Of blue, and purple, and scarlet, and fine twined linen of cunning work . . . Exodus 26:31

This Veil was much like the Curtains of Fine Linen that were to be placed over the Tabernacle Framework (Refer to Curtains and Coverings #12). It, too, was made of Fine Linen with needlework of like colors. We see therefore the same truths symbolized in each.

1. **Fine Twined Linen** points us to the "Lord our Righteousness," the Lord Jesus Christ (Jeremiah 23:6; I Corinthians 1:30; II Corinthians 5:21; Revelation 19:7-8).   He is that Righteous Man who is pictured in the Gospel of Luke.

2. **Blue** is the color of heaven, and Jesus is the "Second Man . . . the Lord from Heaven" · (I Corinthians 15:47 and John 3:13, 31). He is the Heavenly Man revealed in the Gospel of John.

3. **Purple** is a royal color that is often associated with kingship. Jesus is the King of Kings and Lord of Lords. He is the only rightful Heir to the Throne of David (Luke 1:30-33).

    The blending of blue (Heavenly) and scarlet (earthly sacrifice) together produces purple (kingly). He is the Royal Man to whom the Gospel of Matthew bears record.

4. **Scarlet** is the color of sacrificial blood. Jesus is the Lamb of God, our Sacrifice (John 1:29; Matthew 20:28). He came to minister to man. Mark's Gospel demonstrates Jesus' Ministry as the Servant-Son.

All these colors were to be inwrought in the Veil. The Veil was to be of cunning work and inwrought by the wisdom and Spirit of God. It was to be according to the Divine pattern. This speaks to us of the marvelous design and the intricate detail worked out in the person, the life, and the ministry of **The** Lord Jesus Christ, the **Word** made **Flesh,** by the Holy Spirit.

(3) With Cherubims shall it be made . . . Exodus 26:31

Just as the Fine Linen Curtains had inwrought Cherubim, even so this Veil separating the Most Holy Place from the rest of the Sanctuary was to have Cherubim. This was the only difference between the Veil and the Door of the Sanctuary. Cherubim are not merely angels, as we have already seen. They are seen throughout the Scriptures in relation to types of the Godhead. We note that it was Cherubim that guarded the way to the Tree of Life (Genesis 3:24). Here they took their place with the Flaming Sword. On the lid of the Ark of the Covenant, Cherubim were seen watching over or gazing with satisfaction upon the Blood-Sprinkled Mercy Seat (Exodus 25:18-22). And so here, the Cherubim are inwrought into the Veil, which Paul tells us was Christ's flesh, guarding the Most Holy Place against any presumptuous entry.

The Veil was made of *cunning work* and *inwrought* by the wisdom and Spirit of God to the Divine Pattern; speaking of the marvellous design and intricate detail worked out in the Person, Life and Ministry of the Lord Jesus Christ, **The Word** made **Flesh,** by the Holy Spirit.

As the Cherubim were inwrought within the Veil, even so the Son of God was inwrought or indwelt by the Father and the Holy Spirit, *"for in Him dwelleth all the fulness of the Godhead Bodily"* (Colossians 1:19; 2:9, John 4:34; 14:10).

(4) And thou shalt hang it upon four pillars of shittim wood overlaid with gold: their hooks shall be of gold . . . Exodus 26:32

This Veil was to be hung by hooks upon four Pillars of Shittim Wood overlaid with Gold. Again, we have the thought of two natures in **One** Person (Pillar). It is interesting that there were *four* Pillars upholding this Veil which Paul interprets as **His Flesh** (Hebrews 10:20). The Door to the Sanctuary was upheld by *five* Pillars. The four Pillars are seen upholding Christ's flesh or, could we say, Christ's ministry after the flesh. These four Pillars can be likened to the four Gospels. These are the only four books in the New Testament which present Jesus Christ in His *earthly* Ministry; His death, burial and resurrection. The Book of Acts and the Epistles present Him in His *heavenly* ministry. Therefore, as the four Pillars upheld the Veil, so the four Gospels uphold the revelation of the "Christ after the flesh" (II Corinthians 5:16-17). They show forth "God manifest in the Flesh" (I Timothy 3:16).

Note: The student might find it a rewarding study to compare the *Four* living Creatures found in Ezekiel 1 and Revelation 4:6-8, in regard to the four Pillars.

(5) Upon the four sockets of silver . . . Exodus 26:32

As we shall see, the five Pillars of the Door were founded in Sockets of Brass. But here the four Pillars are upheld or founded in Sockets of Silver. These four Sockets came from the "Redemption Money" of the numbered Israelites (Refer to Framework, #9). These Pillars stood in redemption metal. These four Sockets would be representative of the price of 24,000 redeemed souls. Twenty-four is the number of Priestly Courses as seen in the Tabernacle of David and the Temple of Solomon. In the Book of Revelation we see twenty-four elders representing the thousands of the Redeemed out of every kindred, nation, tongue and tribe (Revelation 4:4; 5:9-10).

(6) And thou shalt hang up the vail under the taches, that thou mayest bring in thither within the vail the Ark of the Testimony: and the vail shall divide unto you between the Holy Place and the Most Holy . . . Exodus 26:33

Here we have the purpose of the Veil revealed. The Veil was to be a divider or a partition between the Holy Place and the Most Holy Place. The word "veil" actually means **"a separation, a curtain"** or **"that which hides."** This Veil was to hide the Shekinah Glory from the eyes of men. It acted as a partition to separate sinful man from the Most Holy God.

The Veil measured ten cubits square giving us a picture of the Ten Commandments. Any man who presumed to come into the presence of the Holy One of Israel had to face that Law. The keeping of the Law would have brought one to a place of fellowship with God, but no one has ever kept the Law. No one, that is, but the Lord Jesus Christ. He is the only one who kept the Law perfectly. He was the only sinless Man who fulfilled the conditions of the Mosaic Covenant. He alone merited all that this Covenant provided (Psalms 40:7-8).

This Veil points to much more than the Law for the New Testament believer. Paul, the Apostle, expressly interprets the significance of the dividing Veil. "But into the second (veil) went the High Priest alone once every year, not without blood which He offered for himself, and for the errors of the people: the Holy Ghost this signifying (speaking by the sign,) that the way into the Holiest of All was not yet made manifest, while the first Tabernacle was yet standing: which was a figure for the time then present . . ." (Hebrews 9:7-9).

This Veil speaks to every man of the "middle wall of partition" (Ephesians 2:14).that separates God and man. Before anyone can experience Atonement, he must see his condition as it naturally is before our Holy God. As long as the Veil stands, it speaks an emphatic "Keep Out!" Only once a year, on the Great Day of Atonement, did Aaron the High Priest enter within the Veil making Atonement for the sins of the people.

When the Lord Jesus Christ died on the cross, shedding His Blood, as both sacrifice and Priest, Offering and Offerer, God, by a miracle, rent the dividing Veil of the Temple in twain. "And, behold, the Veil of the Temple was rent in twain from the top to the bottom" (Matthew 27:51; Mark 15:38 and Luke 23:45). This was an act of God, for the Veil was rent from top to bottom! This was nothing man did, but a Divine act of God. This was in fact the **Grace** of God. Grace is God approaching man, and not man approaching God. If God had not made the way open by rending that Veil when Christ's flesh was rent on the Cross, then that separation and division brought about by man's sin would have remained forever. When God rent the Veil in the Temple it was a symbolic act declaring to the entire nation what God had done in His Son. Some of the Priests of the Aaronic Order accepted the miracle of the rent Veil, (Acts 6:7) but an overwhelming majority rejected what God had done.

The rent Veil signified the fulfillment and abolishment of the Old Covenant, the Mosaic Economy and the Ceremonials pertaining to animal sacrifices and ritualism. In making the Mosaic Covenant old, it marked the ushering in of the New Covenant to which all of the external form in the Mosaic Covenant pointed. It ushered in the spiritual realities which had been hidden in the external form (Romans 2:20).

The rent Veil speaks to us of the fact that the **Way** into the Holiest of All is now open to men. When man fell into sin he lost the **Way**. In Christ the **Way** is restored. The Veil no longer stands as a separation between God and man. The middle wall of partition has been removed once and for all. God will never go back to that old form which was fulfilled and abolished in His Son. God has opened the Way. In Christ we have access into the very Presence of God, and we may enter "within the Veil" to behold the Glory of the Lord that we might be changed from Glory to Glory. "Having therefore, brethren, boldness to enter into the Holiest by the Blood of Jesus, by a new and living way, which He hath consecrated for us, through the Veil, that is to say, His flesh; and having an High Priest over the house of God; let us draw near . . ." (Hebrews 10:19-22).

Jesus is our High Priest who has passed within the Veil and stands as our hope of entry. Jesus is the fore-runner who was made High Priest forever after the Order of Melchisedec (Hebrews 6:20. See: John 20:17; Acts 1:8-11; I John 2:1). A Forerunner implies that there will be runners following Him. He is the File-leader. He made the way for us to follow!

On the Mount of Transfiguration the Shekinah Glory shone out through the Veil of His flesh (Matthew 17:1-5; John 1:14-18).

The truths in connection with the Veil can be summed up in the following:

1. **The Inwrought Veil** — The beauty of this inwrought veil speaks of the Incarnation and the beauty and perfections of the life of the Lord Jesus. As long as He lived, as long as the Veil of His flesh stood, His perfect, sinless life condemned us. As long as He lived there was no full access to the Father.

2. **The Dividing Veil** — The veil standing as a curtain speaks of the great wall of division and separation between God and man as a result of sin. There would be no access into His Presence until sin had been dealt with. "The Way" was not yet manifest for man to approach God.

3. **The Rent Veil** — This rent veil symbolizes the Broken Body of the Son of God at Calvary. The Veil must be rent. Christ must die. The rent Veil points to His rent flesh through which the **Way** to the Father is restored. "**I am the Way, the Truth, and the Life: no man cometh unto the Father but by Me**" (John 14:6).In the rent Veil we behold His Body which was broken for us. In the Mercy Seat we behold His Blood which was shed for us.

In Christ we have an abundant entrance into the Everlasting Kingdom of our Lord and Saviour Jesus Christ (II Peter 1:10-12).

70

(7) For Further Study

The subject of the "Veil" throughout Scripture is a rich field of study. The serious student will want to examine the following:

1. The Veil of the Tabernacle (Exodus 26:31-35),
2. The Veil of the Temple (II Chronicles 3:14),
3. The Veil upon Moses' face (Exodus 34:33-35),
4. The Veil of Christ's Flesh (Hebrews 10:19-20),
5. The Veil of Blindness on Natural Israel (II Corinthians 3:13-16),
6. The Veil upon the Nations (Isaiah 25:6-9)

The time is coming when every Veil will be abolished, and we shall behold him face to face Revelations 22:4.

(8) And thou shalt make an hanging for the door of the tent, of blue, and purple, and scarlet, and fine twined linen, wrought with needlework . . . Exodus 26:36

At the entrance to the Holy Place there was a Door hanging. The Door was much like the Veil just described, but it lacked the inwrought Cherubim. Throughout the Scripture this hanging is referred to in several ways:

1. The Hanging for the Door of the Tent (Exodus 26:36),
2. The Hanging (Exodus 26:37),
3. The Hanging for the Tabernacle Door (Exodus 36:37),
4. The Door of the Tabernacle of the Congregation (Leviticus 1:3).

The Holy Place measured 10 x 10 x 20 = 2000 cubits. The Holy Place speaks to us of the 2000 years of the Church Age (See Prophetic Significance of the Tabernacle Measurements.) This Door was the *one and only* entrance into the 2000 cubits. The Holy Place was exclusively reserved for Priestly ministry. The Lord Jesus says, **"I am the Door: by Me if any man enter, he shall be saved"** (John 10:9). The Lord Jesus is the *one and only* Way to God and into the Church. The Church is the place of Priestly ministry, for we who are in Christ are made Kings and Priests unto God. The believer has access as a King-Priest to offer up spiritual sacrifices, in the spiritual Priesthood, in a spiritual House (I Peter 2:1-9; Revelation 1:6).

The Door, therefore, speaks of the Lord Jesus Christ. The materials themselves bear out this truth. The materials are the same as we have seen in the Veil (Refer to section #2).

In Christ there was a perfect balance of these four colors. He was the Righteous Man (fine linen, I Corinthians 1:30), the Heavenly Man (I Corinthians 15:47), the Royal Man (Luke 1:30-33), and the Sacrificed Man (Matthew 26:28). The four Gospels present Him typically in these colors.

(9) And thou shalt make for the hanging five pillars of shittim wood, and overlay them with gold, and their hooks shall be of gold . . . Exodus 26:37

The Hanging for the Door of the Tabernacle was placed upon gold hooks which were on five Pillars of Shittim Wood overlaid with gold. Again, we have the two elements of wood (perfect humanity) and gold (absolute Deity). These two are brought together in Christ, the **Word** (Deity) made flesh (humanity).

Upholding this Door there were to be *five* Pillars. Five is the number of the Grace of God. In the Lord Jesus Christ we have the Grace of God personified, for **"the Law was given by Moses, but Grace and Truth came by Jesus Christ"** (John 1:17). These five Pillars can be viewed in several ways. We offer the following:

1. To the Old Testament saints, the number five surely spoke of the *five Books of the Law* given to Moses or the Penteteuch.
2. Isaiah receives a revelation of a glorious *five*-fold name of Christ. "His Name shall be called Wonderful, Counsellor, The Mighty God, The Everlasting Father, The Prince of Peace" (Isaiah 9:6).
3. To the New Testament Church the number five also has special meaning. The New Testament Church is given the *five*-fold ministries of Apostle, Prophet, Pastor, Evangelist and Teacher (Ephesians 4:9-16). It is their responsibility to uphold the Lord Jesus as the Grace of God.

4. Five is also the number of the New Testament *writers of the Epistles* — Peter, James, John, Jude and Paul. These were indeed Pillars in the Early Church, upholding the glorious person of the Son of God and the revelation of truth as it pertains to the New Testament Church (Galatians 2:8-9).

These five Pillars at the Door of the Tabernacle had Capitols (crowns) and Fillets (connecting rods). Jesus Christ and His Saints will be crowned with glory and honour (Hebrews 2:9-10). They will be connected by the plan of redemption.

(10) And thou shalt cast five sockets of brass for them . . . Exodus 26:37

In contrast to all the Boards of the Tabernacle and the Pillars that upheld the Veil, these five Pillars for the Door stood in Sockets of Brass. As we will see, Brass is particularly characteristic of the Outer Court and its furnishings for it was here that sin was judged. Brass is a symbol of judgment against sin and disobedience. God threatened Israel in their disobedience that He would make the heavens as Brass over them (Deuteronomy 28:23). In the Holy Place and the Most Holy Place everything is overlaid with Gold. The Door stands at the shutting off of the Outer Court and the entering of the Holy Place. So we see the coming together of the Sockets of Brass and the Pillars overlaid with Gold.

All this speaks to us of Jesus who was judged for our sins. He stands at the end of the **Law** Dispensation (Brass) and is the **Door** into the Church and the present Dispensation of the Holy Spirit (Gold). We are told that His feet were as Pillars of Brass (Revelation 1:15; 10:1; Daniel 10:6).

In the same way, the Pillar ministries of the Early Church stood at the close of the Old Covenant Dispensation. But as the Old passed away, they are instrumental in ushering in the New Covenant Dispensation in which Jew and Gentile become **One Body** in Christ.

(11) For the Student

The subject of the Door in the Bible is also a rewarding study. All of the Doors are types of Him who is **The Door.** Note the following:

1. The Blood-sprinkled Door (Exodus 12:22-23),
2. The Door of the Tabernacle (Exodus 26:36),
3. The Door of the Marriage (Matthew 25:10)
4. The Door set for the Church (Revelation 3:7-8),
5. **The** Door HImself, Jesus Christ (John 10:8-9).

(12) The Entrances Compared

In summarizing the two entrances of the Tabernacle we offer the following comparison:

The Door	The Veil
Called "the Door"	Called "the Veil"
Entrance to Holy Place	Entrance to Most Holy Place
Shut out Israelites	Shut out Priests
Let in the Priests	Let in the High Priest only
Had Five Pillars of Gold	Had Four Pillars of Gold
Had Five Sockets of Brass	Had Four Sockets of Silver
Had Four Colors: Blue, Purple Scarlet and Fine Linen	Had Four Colors: Blue, Purple Scarlet and Fine Linen
No Inwrought Cherubim	Inwrought Cherubim
Crowns and Fillets	No mention
Faced the East	Faced the East

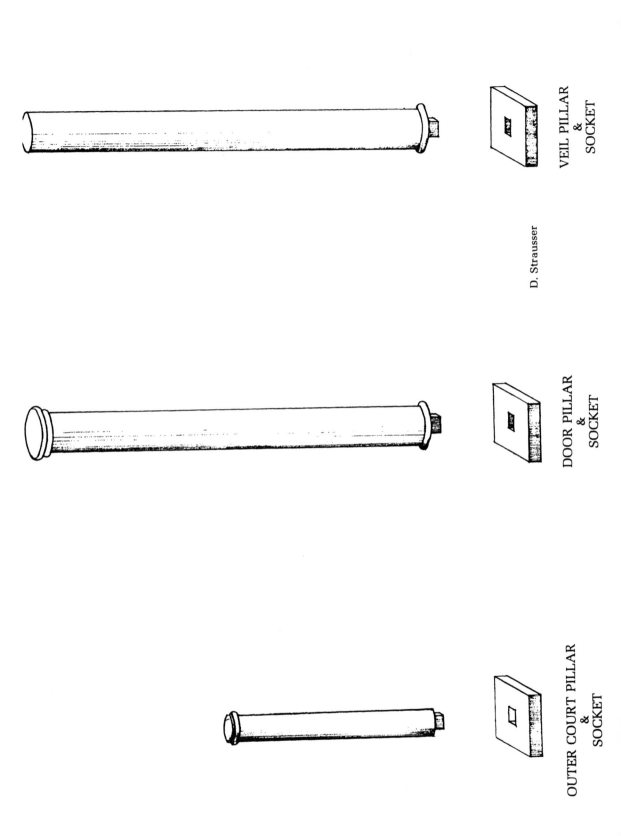

OUTER COURT PILLAR
&
SOCKET

DOOR PILLAR
&
SOCKET

D. Strausser

VEIL PILLAR
&
SOCKET

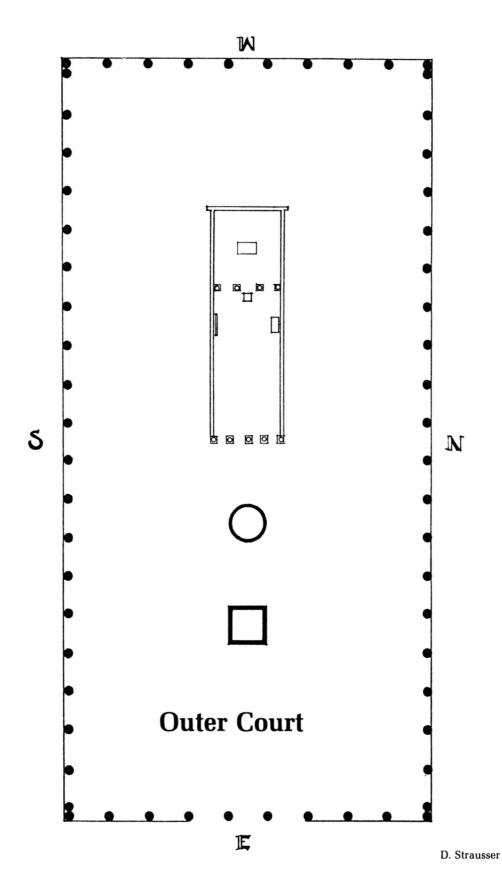

W

S

N

Outer Court

E

D. Strausser

The Outer Court

(1) And thou shalt make the court of the Tabernacle . . . Exodus 27:9

Surrounding the Tabernacle, as we have described, there was to be an Outer Court consisting of a high Linen wall. When one approached the Tabernacle from the outside, this Linen wall would be the first thing to appear. The Linen wall was to be five cubits in height and was to be hung upon 60 Pillars of Brass in Sockets of Brass. These Pillars were to have Silver connecting rods and crowns on top of them. The wall of Linen went all around the circumference of the Outer Court which was 100 cubits by 50 cubits except at the East end where there was a gate. This Fine Linen acted as a dividing wall between God in the Tabernacle and man outside. Hence, the purpose of the Court was to prevent any wrongful approach to the Tabernacle of God. The Court itself was open to all Israelites to worship. It was opened to all those who had been redeemed. It was the largest area seen in connection with the Tabernacle. But there was still a proper way of approach. Even though the Court was uncovered, there was a prescribed way in which one was to enter.

The Outer Court is the place where man began his approach to God. As we view the plan of redemption from man's point of view, we see that man begins at the Brazen Altar in the Outer Court. He begins at the place of sacrifice where sin is dealt with. From the Brazen Altar we pass on until we reach the Holiest of All where the very Presence of God dwells. This is redemption from man's point of view. Man can only approach God on the basis of Atonement.

As we have already seen in the discussion of the Ark, this approach is opposite to the approach of God. When we look at the plan of redemption as God sees it, we begin at the Holiest of All. God, who dwells in perfect holiness, always begins with Himself. The Grace of God is seen in the fact that God proceeded out from this Most Holy Place to meet man in the Outer Court. This is redemption from God's point of view. God coming in grace out to fallen man.

At the East end of the Court was the Gate of the Court. This was the **One** and **Only** entrance to that within the wall of Fine Linen. Everyone who wanted to experience the truths of the furniture had to approach the same way. They had to come through the Gate. It did not matter what Tribe the individual was from or who he was. All of the people had to face the Fine Twined Linen Curtains and all had to go through the Gate to enter into what God was doing in their midst (Leviticus 17:8-9; 22:18; Numbers 15:14-16). It meant certain death for a stranger to presume to approach the Tabernacle (Numbers 1:51; 3:38). The Linen Curtains were designed to keep out those who would not enter at the Gate. The Linen curtains directed the seeker to the way of entry, the Gate of the Court.

The Court, therefore, served a two-fold purpose. To those on the outside, it acted as a barrier and a wall of separation. The wall of the Fine Linen spoke an emphatic "Keep out!" to all who would approach unto them. It acted as a *separation* between the outside world and God's habitation or Sanctuary. But to the man who was truly drawn to the Tabernacle these curtains pointed to the Gate or the way of approach by which he could enter in faith. The Tabernacle was absolutely limited to the Redeemed of Israel and those who came to God by faith in His Word and Order of approach.

Once on the inside, however, the wall of Curtains acted as a surrounding or shield from the outside world. To all those who found their place inside it became a place of *protection* and stability. Once on the inside, the message of the Linen changed to "Stay In!" This indeed was the place where one could meet with the Living God. The Court therefore was exclusive as well as inclusive!

Many times throughout the Scripture, the Outer Court is referred to, directly or indirectly. In the following Scriptures from the Psalms, we find reference to the Court of Moses' Tabernacle or the Courts of the Temple of Solomon:

"Blessed is the man whom Thou choosest, and causest to approach unto thee, that he may dwell in **Thy Courts**" (Psalms 65:4).

"Come into His **Courts**" (Psalms 96:8).

"Those that be planted in the House of the Lord shall flouirsh in the **Courts** of our God" (Psalms 92:13).

"My soul longeth, yea, even fainteth for the **Courts** of the Lord . . . For a day in Thy **Courts** is better than a thousand" (Psalms 84:2, 10).

"Enter into His **Gates** with thanksgiving and into His **Courts** with praise" (Psalms 100:4).

Israel came and stood in the Courts of the Lord. They were to enter with praise and thanksgiving by way of the Gate. This is the proper way that God had ordained for the believer to come before the presence of God. Praise and Worship are not only pleasing before the Lord, but they help to purify the worshipper. It is important that we come before the Lord with clean hands and a pure heart. Isaiah says that the Courts are the Courts of God's holiness (Isaiah 62:9). He further interprets the wall of Linen and the Gates when he says, "Thou shalt call Thy walls Salvation, and Thy Gates praise."

Note: In the Book of Revelation we see that the Outer Court is not measured but trodden under foot (Revelation 11:1-3). God desires His people to measure up to His standards.

(2) There shall be hangings for the Court of fine twined linen . . . Exodus 27:9

The Hangings of the Court walls were to be made of Fine Twined Linen as we have already seen. From all that we have said before, it is clear that Fine Linen speaks to us of righteousness and holiness (Leviticus 11:43-45) As one approached the Tabernacle, all he would see would be this white hanging. What a contrast to the black curtains of Goats' Hair. The White Linen points first of all to the perfect righteousness of Christ (Jeremiah 33:15; I Timothy 2:5; I John 4:17 and I Corinthians 1:30). Christ is the Righteous Branch, the Righteousness of God. The Fine Linen is symbolic of that spotless purity of Christ. His sinless and righteous humanity. He is the only righteous man born of the entire human race, for He is "The Lord our Righteousness." When Christ stood before the Pharisees, the Sanhedrin, Pilate, and Herod, and when He hung before the Centurian, they all had to declare that He was a righteous man in whom no fault could be found.

To the unregenerate man who approaches unto God, this is the first thing that He must see. He must face the white linen of the hanging. All the four corners of the earth (the camp) must see Him as He now is before God. If anyone desires to draw nigh unto God, he must first face the absolute holiness of God. When he sees this, when he sees Christ exalted at the right hand of God, when he sees the Son of God dwelling in perfect holiness, he can but come on his face before a holy God.

God is interested in a people, a holy people, for God wants a Church to enter into His holiness. The righteousness of Christ is to become the righteousness of the Church. God is not interested in our own fleshly works of righteousness, for they are as "filthy rags" in His sight (Isaiah 64:6). God is not interested in the legal righteousness of the Law, for that is self-righteousness (Romans 10:1-6 and Philippians 3:7-9). God is looking for a people who are standing by faith in the righteousness of Christ. It is the righteousness of Christ that God accepts, and as we put on Christ we become righteous. Those that have put on Christ are the Body of Christ or the Church. These are the saints who are mentioned in reference to righteousness (Revelation 19:7-9; II Corinthians 5:17-21; Hebrews 2:11; Psalms 132:9, 16-17 and Romans 8:4). It is the Body to whom the righteousness of Christ is imputed and in whom His righteousness is inwrought and outworked (I Corinthians 1:30 and Isaiah 61:10). He is the Lord our Righteousness (Jeremiah 23:6; Revelation 3:4).

(3) The length of the Court shall be an hundred cubits, and the breadth fifty every where, and the height five cubits of fine twined linen . . . Exodus 27:18. See also Verses 9, 11, 12, 13

The measurements of the Tabernacle Outer Court area were to be 100 x 50. This meant that the perimeter of the Outer Court measured 300 cubits. The Fine Linen that made up the wall separation was five cubits in height. Thus, the Linen area of the Court Curtains was 1500 square cubits (5 x 300).

The number 1500 becomes significant and prophetic of the approximate period of the **Law Age**. The Law was given to Moses, and from Moses to Christ we have about 1500 years. This 1500 years was the Dispensation of the Law Covenant. The Outer Court, then, speaks to us of this Dispensation of the Law and all that it implies. The Outer Court (1500 years) had to be experienced before one came to the Tabernacle (**The** Tabernacle, the Word made flesh, (John 1:14-18).

When we look at the Outer Court in this way we see some important truths. First of all, we notice that all the Priests had to experience the Outer Court before they could move any further to enter the Sanctuary. If the Outer Court speaks of the **Law,** then it portrays the truth that the Law was a Schoolmaster to bring us to Christ (Galatians 3:24).

A second truth contained in this picture is that all the sacrificial blood that was shed took place in the Outer Court. There were no animal sacrifices or oblations in the Holy Place or the Most Holy Place. This is prophetic of the fact that all the sacrifices of blood took place in the *Law Age*. When Christ died on the Cross, He fulfilled and abolished all animal sacrifices and oblations. He "caused the sacrifice and oblation to cease" (Daniel 9:24-27 and Hebrews 10:1-2). The Blood of Christ, the perfect Lamb of God was brought into the Heavenly Sanctuary. This once-and-for-all, perfect sacrifice of Christ at Calvary absolutely and eternally closed off the 1500 years of the Law age and the Mosaic Covenant. This being the case, God will never turn back to that which He fulfilled and abolished at the Cross. He now has the Body and Blood of His Only Begotten Son to which all the Old Testament sacrifices pointed.

In regard to the measurements of the Hanging itself, we have the following significance:

1. **One Hundred** — This measurement is significant of Christ's 100% unconditional surrender to the will of the Father.
2. **Fifty**—Fifty is the number of Pentecost, liberty, freedom and release. All of these things can only be realized in the finished work of Christ.
3. **Five**—The height of the Hanging points us to the Grace of God. Our Lord Jesus Christ was the Grace of God personified (John 1:17).He alone brings the believer to the total commitment to God's will. He alone brings freedom by His grace.

(4) For the south side southward there shall be hangings for the court of fine twined linen of an hundred cubits long for one side: and the twenty pillars thereof and their twenty sockets shall be of brass; the hooks of the pillars and their fillets shall be of silver. And likewise for the north side in length there shall be hangings of an hundred cubits long, and his twenty pillars and their twenty sockets of brass: the hooks of the pillars and their fillets of silver. And for the breadth of the court on the west side shall be hangings of fifty cubits: their pillars ten, and their sockets ten. And the breadth of the court on the east side eastward shall be fifty cubits. The hangings of one side of the gate shall be fifteen cubits: their pillars three, and their sockets three. And on the other side shall be hangings fifteen cubits: their pillars three, and their sockets three . . .Exodus 27:10-15

Including the Pillars that were in the Gate (Exodus 27:16-17),there was a total of sixty Pillars around the Court upholding the Linen Curtains. They were

20 Pillars for the South Side,
20 Pillars for the North Side,
10 Pillars for the West side and
10 Pillars for the East side giving a total of
60 Pillars.

It is not expressly stated of what materials these Pillars were made. Some suggest that they were made of Shittim wood, others suggest that they were Pillars of Brass, while still others suggest that these were most likely of Shittim wood overlaid with Brass. Whatever the case, we do know that the Sockets for these Pillars were to be made of Brass. There is some question about how these Pillars were arranged about the Court. It is very likely that there were two Pillars in each of the corners. If this were so then it would account for 20 Pillars on each side and 10 Pillars on each end. Others suggest that there was but one Pillar in each corner, and if this were so then the Linen Curtains suspended between each of the Pillars would have the measurements of five cubits by five cubits. If this was so, then these are the same measurements that we will find in regard to the Brazen Altar in the Outer Court.

A *Pillar* speaks to us of stability, uprightness and solidarity in the work of the Lord. The opposite of this would be instability in the things of the Lord. As New Testament Christians, we are all to be Pillars in the building of God. A Pillar, therefore, speaks of faithful believers all throughout history. Just as the Pillars in the Tabernacle were to stand upright, and uphold the white Fine Linen Curtains from defilement by the earth, even so God's believers are to stand upright and uphold the righteousness of God and Christ for all the world to see. The believers are to stand as Pillars upholding God's standard, not allowing it to become defiled by lowering it to the dirt and defilements of this world (Psalms 33:1; 71:19).

The Pillar is seen throughout Scripture in the following ways:

1. The Lord Jesus is pictured as having legs as *Pillars* of marble (Song of Solomon 5:15).

2. Jeremiah was to be as an iron *Pillar* and a brazen wall (Jeremiah 1:18).
3. Peter, James and John were *Pillars* in the Early Church (Galatians 2:9).
4. The Church is the *Pillar* and ground of truth (I Timothy 3:15).
5. The Overcomer is likened to a *Pillar* in the Temple of God (Revelation 3:12).

In the entire Outer Court there were to be sixty of these Pillars. In relation to this number, it is significant to note that in the Geneology of Christ (Compare Matthew 1:1-16 and Luke 3:23-38) running through Joseph's side there are *sixty men* in the Blood-line from Adam to Christ (Note: There are 75 or 76 names in relation to the blood-line of Mary). All of these men were Covenant men, and faith-righteousness was seen in their lives. They had passed under the Rod of the Shepherd and were marked out as holy unto the Lord. "The tenth shall be holy unto the Lord" (Leviticus 27:32). Just as these Pillars were not visible to the man standing outside of the Tabernacle in that they held forth the Fine Linen Curtains, even so these Pillars of faith attracted no attention to themselves as they upheld the righteousness of God in their lives.

These sixty men were truly men of vision. They were Pillars in the Outer Court which speaks of the *"Brass Age."* They were living in the age when animal sacrifices were used in judgment for sin, and yet they looked ahead to the coming of their Messiah. They were Pillars indeed. As the Linen was that which pointed men to the Door and that within this natural Tabernacle, these men bring us to Him who is the Word made flesh, the true Tabernacle.

In connection with the sixty Pillars there are additional references that would be of interest to the eager student. One would do well to note the following:

1. Solomon's Temple had two great *Pillars* called "Jachin" and "Boaz." Jachin means "He shall strengthen," and Boaz means "He shall establish" (II Chronicles 4:12-13 and I Kings 7:15-22).
2. Solomon is seen in connection with *sixty* valiant men who are likened unto Pillars (Song of Solomon 3:6-7).

(5) All the pillars round about the court shall be filleted with silver . . . Exodus 27:17

The sixty Pillars were to be jointed together by "fillets" or connecting rods of silver. The fillets were either cords of silver or silver connecting rods. These acted as a stabilizing rod to keep all of the Pillars perfectly alligned and to keep them from swaying to the right or the left as they upheld the Linen Curtains. The remainder of the silver that was not used in the Sockets throughout the Tabernacle was used for the connecting rods, the hooks and the chapiters. The remainder of the silver from the price of the Firstborn and the Atonement money was 1,775 shekels of silver (Exodus 30:16 and 38:25-28).

As we have already seen, silver is representative of redemption, Atonement money, ransom and the price of a soul. All Israel had to pay ½ shekel of silver as a ransom for their soul. We remember that Joseph was sold for silver (Genesis 37:28). Silver was the price of a slave (Exodus 21:32). All of these pictures point to the **One** who was to be our ransom. They all point to the **One** who was to be sold for thirty pieces of silver to provide our Atonement (Matthew 27:1-5, 9 and Zechariah 11:12-13). We "were not redeemed with corruptible things, as silver and gold . . . but with the precious blood of Christ, as a lamb without blemish and without spot" (I Peter 1:18-19).

The silver connecting rods, therefore, speak of the fact that all believers (Pillars), though standing individually in the sockets of brass, are connected by the Atonement and redemptive Blood of Jesus Christ (silver rods). The silver rods point to the same truth that is seen in the "scarlet thread" in other scriptures. The "scarlet thread" also points to the thought that it is the Blood Atonement that links all believers of every age (Joshua 2:18).

In relation to the 60 men in the Blood line in Christ's geneology, it is their faith in the Blood as revealed by God in His Covenants to them that links them all together. These men who lived under the Brass Dispensation were all in Covenant relationship with God. And as they stood in Covenant relationship before God they were joined together in a common bond. These were men who had had their sins judged by a substitutionary death. They were faith-righteous men upholding the righteousness of God (Linen Curtains). They were men redeemed by the Blood of Atonement. It is these men who are all brought together in the godly line of Messiah.

Sixty combines the meaning of the Number of Man (6), and Law (10).

(6) Their hooks shall be of silver . . . Exodus 27:17

At the top of the 60 Pillars there were to be hooks of silver upon which the fine linen curtains were to be hung. These hooks were to uphold the fine linen from falling to the ground. They were to keep the curtains from the defilement of the earth. Antitypically, all believers must be as hooks upholding God's standard of righteousness in the earth. They must be the upholders of that righteousness which Christ manifested in His earth walk. This is the righteousness that is both imputed to and inwrought in the lives of the saints. This righteousness is to be upheld by the life we live and is sorely needed as a witness to this generation of the holiness of God (fine linen). This is the faith-righteousness that Paul deals with in Romans 4.

(7) And the overlaying of their Chapiters of silver . . . Exodus 38:17

Each Pillar was topped with a silver Chapiter. A Chapiter is the "cap" or the "head" of the Pillar. It was a type of crown atop the Pillar. It points to the fact that the Saints are crowned with the glory of redemption's plan. The saints are clothed with the *helmet of salvation* (Ephesians 6:17).

As we have seen, Jesus was crowned with thorns by the very men that He came to redeem (Mark 15:17). The thorns were a product of a cursed earth. Jesus, desiring to lift that curse, became a curse for us. As He humbled Himself and became obedient unto death, God highly exalted Him Philippians 2:9 and crowned Him with glory and honor (Hebrews 2:7-9). As Christ was crowned, He won for us a golden crown. In Christ the Old Testament saints have their crowning joy also, for they share in the fruit of the sacrifice of Christ. The Ark, The Table, The Incense Altar had *crowns of gold.* These Pillars are *crowned with silver.*

Throughout the Scripture there are many crowns mentioned. We find the following:

1. The Crown of Life (James 1:12; Revelation 2:10; 3:11),
2. The Soul-winner's Crown (Philippians 4:1),
3. The Crown of Rejoicing (I Thessalonians 2:19),
4. The Crown of Righteousness (II Timothy 4:8),
5. The Crown of Glory (I Peter 5:4).

Note: For further study refer to the following: Revelation 4:4, 10; 12:1 and 14:14.

(8) And their sockets of brass . . . Exodus 27:17

These 60 Pillars stood in Sockets of Brass. As we will see, Brass was the most prominent metal in the Outer Court. These Pillars stood in Sockets of *Brass*, the sockets of the Door were to be *Brass*, the pins of the Court were of *Brass*, the Altar of Sacrifice was overlaid with *Brass* and the Laver was made of *Brass*. The Brass had been brought to the Lord as a freewill offering (Exodus 25:3; 35:5, 16). Being used in the Outer Court, therefore, it was the first metal that the Israelite saw in his approach to God.

As we have seen, Brass is symbolic of *strength and judgment against sin and disobedience* (Deuteronomy 28:15-23; Leviticus 26:19). For the Israelite, this was the first truth with which he had to come to grips. Sin must be judged.

Brass is also associated with the Holy Spirit who is the Spirit of Judgment and the Spirit of Burning (Isaiah 4:4). It is the ministry of the Holy Spirit to convict us of sin, righteousness and judgment (John 16:8-11).

The Sockets of Brass here in the Pillars speak to us of *feet.* Christ Himself is seen by Ezekiel as a man whose appearance was like the appearance of brass (40:3). Christ is also pictured as having *feet of brass* (Daniel 10:6; Revelation 1:15; 2:18 and 10:1) for He stands to judge sin in His people, His Church.

As the Church stands "in Christ" it too is seen with feet of brass. The Church is spoken of as Zion which is to be given hoofs (feet or sockets) of brass (Micah 4:11-3). The Church is to be a place of judgment. Indeed, judgment begins in the House of the Lord. (I Peter 4:17).

(9) All the vessels of the Tabernacle in all the service thereof, and all the pins thereof, and all the pins of the court, shall be of brass . . . Exodus 27:19

Finally, we see that there were to be pins and cords of brass for the Tabernacle Curtains as well as the Outer Court Pillars and Curtains (Exodus 35:18; 38:20, 31). These pins and cords were also used in connection with the Gate (Exodus 39:40; Numbers 3:26, 37; 4:26, 32).

The cords themselves were probably made out of strong twined linen. It was their job to give stability to the Pillars. They were to aid in holding the Pillars upright in the midst of whatever desert storm might come up. In relation to the Lord Jesus Christ, the cords speak to us of His divine grace and love. In Hosea we are told that when Israel was a child God drew them with cords of a man, with bands of love. Thus, the cords speak of God's love and grace that hold the believer upright (Hosea 11:4).

The pins were much like tent stakes. This word in the Hebrew can also be translated "nail" (Judges 4:21-22; 5:26).In this regard it is prophetic of the Lord Jesus Christ who is spoken of in Scripture as a nail. "I will fasten Him as a Nail in a sure place . . . and they shall hang upon Him all the glory of His Father's house" (Isaiah 22:20-25). "Out of him (Judah) came forth the Corner, out of him the Nail" (Zechariah 10:3-4). Jesus was *nailed* to His Cross.

The cords and the pins, therefore, find their initial fulfillment in the Lord Jesus Christ who was nailed for us to become that nail in a sure place. It is His grace and love and security that upholds the believer (Pillar). It is His grace and love that gives strength, stability and uprightness in the midst of the storms of life. It is His grace and love that enables the believer to put forth a pure testimony of the righteousness of God in Christ.

As the cords and pins find fulfillment in Christ, they also find a measure of fulfillment in the Church. They speak particularly of the enlargment of the Church as God's habitation. The Lord says to His Church, "Enlarge the place of thy **tent**, and let them stretch forth the **curtains** of thine habitations: spare not, lengthen thy **cords**, and strengthen thy **stakes**; for thou shalt break forth on the right hand and on the left; and thy seed shall inherit the Gentiles, and make the desolate cities to be inhabited"(Isaiah 54:1-3). See also: Isaiah 33:20-22 and Jeremiah 10:20. The Church is instructed to enlarge her borders for the coming in of the Gentiles. How do we know this is referring to the Church? Paul, under the inspiration of the Holy Spirit, applies Isaiah 54:1 to the New Testament Church (Galatians 4:27).

As far as the Tabernacle of Moses was concerned, it was to be fixed for *one nation*. Its measurements were to be set for that nation only. In the Tabernacle of David there is a stretching forth for *all nations* to come into blessing through Christ Jesus. The New Testament Church is that Tabernacle that is to accommodate all nations.

(10) Summary on the Outer Court

The following are the main points demonstrated in the Outer Court:

1. The Outer Court fine linen points us to the standard of God's righteousness that all must face before coming to God.
2. The 60 Pillars in sockets of Brass upholding the standard of God speak of the 60 faith-righteous men in the godly line of Messiah or believers in Christ who are to uphold the righteousness of God.
3. The sockets of Brass indicate that judgment against sin has taken place.
4. The Silver fillets, hooks and chapiters connected, upheld and crowned these 60 Pillars with redemption's plan.
5. The measurements of the linen Curtains surrounding the Court being 1500 cubits in area point us to the Law Age from Moses to Christ, 1500 years.
6. There was but one entrance to the Court. There was but one prescribed way of approach for man to come to God.

Read the following: Exodus 27:16 and 38:18-19.

The Gate of the Court

(1) The Gate in General

The Gate of the Court is given at least three different titles throughout the Scripture. They include:

1. The Gate (Exodus 27:16),
2. The Curtain for the Door of the Court (Numbers 3:26),
3. The Door of the Court (Numbers 3:26)

This Gate marked the way of approach into the Tabernacle itself. All the way around the outside of the Tabernacle there was a high wall of fine linen. Everyone approaching the Tabernacle any place but the Gate would have to face that linen. These linen curtains told man to keep out, but if a man would follow the curtains he would in every case eventually come to the Gate. The Gate spoke quite a different message. The Gate said that man could enter, but only God's way. The Court Gate was the one and only way and entrance into the Court. Everyone had to come the same way. All Israel, whatever tribe they were from, and all strangers in Israel from all four corners of the camp, near or far, had to come the same way (Ephesians 2:11-18).

If any man tried to enter the Tabernacle another way, by climbing over the wall or sneaking under the curtains, the same would be a thief and a robber. God had only one Gate in the Tabernacle for there is only one way for man to approach God. He must enter at the Gate. Read John 10:1-10.

We notice four things about this Gate:

1. This was the **Only** entrance to the Court. Jesus said, "I am the **Way,** the Truth, and the Life: no man cometh unto the Father but by Me" (John 14:6). Just as there was one entrance, there is but one Savior, the **One** Mediator between God and man. "There is none other name under heaven given among men, whereby we must be saved" (Acts 4:12).

2. This Gate was a **Wide** Gate. It was wide enough to accommodate everyone that wanted to come. God would "have all men to be saved, and to come to the knowledge of the **Truth**" (I Timothy 2:4).

3. This Gate was a **Beautiful** Gate. It was inwrought with several colors that made it something that attracted those searching for something beautiful in the wilderness.

4. This was a distinctive Gate. No one seeing the Gate could mistake it for the rest of the wall. The colors in the Court Gate marked it out clearly for all to see, distinguishing it from the white linen Curtain wall of the Outer Court. There was no mistaking this **One** entrance. Jesus Christ is distinguished among men by Who He was, what He did and all that He said. He stands unique among the faith-righteous men. He alone stands out as the Sinless Man, the Redeemer whose righteousness is His very nature and essence. His was an underived and uninherited righteousness! He is righteousness personified, the Lord our Righteousness (I Corinthians 1:30; Jeremiah 23:5 and 33:15).

(2) And the hanging for the gate of the court was needlework, of blue, and purple, and scarlet, and fine twined linen . . . Exodus 38:18

The same materials that went into the construction of the Door of the Sanctuary and the Second Veil were used in the Gate of the Court (See The Tabernacle Entrances). We will merely mention the key thoughts in connection with each material.

1. **Fine Twined Linen** speaks to us of Christ as the Righteous One who is portrayed in the Gospel of Luke.

2. The inwrought **Blue** points to Christ as the Heavenly One of the Gospel of John.

3. The inwrought **Purple** foreshadows Christ as the Royal One or Kingly One of whom Matthew testified.

4. The inwrought **Scarlet** depicts Christ as the Sacrificed One who is central to the Gospel of Mark.

The Fine Linen was inwrought with these three colors. This speaks of the fact that the life of Christ was inwrought, inworked, outworked and indwelt by the Spirit of God. His character was a perfect example for us of the nature, character, operations, gifts, graces and virtues of the Eternal Godhead, for in Him dwelt all the Fulness of the Godhead bodily (Colossians 1:19;2:9 and John 3:34). His life was the most intricate in the work of the Holy Spirit.

(3) And twenty cubits was the length, and the height in the breadth was five cubits, answerable to the hangings of the court . . . Exodus 38:18

    The Gate of the Court was to be five cubits high and twenty cubits wide. This was certainly high enough and wide enough to accommodate the entry of all who would believe. This Gate was 100 square cubits. When this is seen alone it speaks of a total or 100% commitment to God. But when we see the measurements of this entrance with the other Tabernacle entrances we get another picture. Notice the following:

The *Gate* was   100 square cubits in area (5 x 20),
The *Door* was   100 square cubits in area (10 x 10) and
The *Veil* was   <u>100</u> square cubits in area (10 x 10) which yields a total of
               300 square cubits in the entrance areas.

    The number 300 is significant of several things, but primarily of the *faithful remnant*. In every generation God has preserved a group of people who were sold out 100% to the will of the Lord. Gideon's army is significant of this group of people who would not be discouraged from participating in the move of God no matter what the cost. Gideon had 300 faithful men whom he arranged in three groups of 100 (Judges 7:6). Enoch is another picture of a man faithful in a wicked generation. We are told that Enoch walked with God *after* he begat Methuselah 300 years, and then, he experienced translation into the glory of God (Genesis 5:21-24).

    In the entrances we have the thought of the three entrances totaling 300 square cubits. The 100 cubits of the Gate led the Priest to the 100 cubits of the Door to the Sanctuary. The 100 cubits of the Door led him to the 100 cubits of the Veil and into the very presence of the Glory of God.

    It is possible to stop before we reach that full 300. Some may be 30-fold, some may be 60-fold, but God wants us to be 100-fold (Matthew 13:23). The Lord Jesus wants His believer-priests to be 100% for Him and to go all the way. He wants them to experience each piece of furniture as we approach unto His full Glory.

(4) And their pillars were four, and their sockets of brass four: their hooks of silver, and the overlaying of their chapiters and their fillets of silver . . . Exodus 38:19

    The Gate of the Court was upheld by four Pillars in sockets of Brass. These four were part of the 60 Pillars that made up the entire Outer Court. The four Pillars are significant of the world-wide availability of the Gate. Whosoever will may come in at the Gate, but they must come by way of the Gate. Four also speaks to us of the four Gospels, Matthew, Mark, Luke and John. These are the first four books of the Bible that we see in our approach to God through Christ. These four Gospels are seen in the four colors in the Gate and thus present Christ as the Gate. They hold up Christ in His earth walk. No access can be given to the New Testament Church (Sanctuary) unless we come through the four Pillars, the Gate which point to the Lord Jesus Christ.

    The four Pillars, seen here in relation to the 60 Pillars overall, could also be significant of the fact that in the geneology of Christ as found in Matthew and Luke there are **Four Women** mentioned in connection with their husbands (Matthew 1:3, 5, 6). Thamar, Rahab, Ruth and Bathsheba are all included in the geneology. We have here a mixture of Hebrew and Gentile who all become part of the Chosen Race through Divine Grace.

    All three of the entrances had their Pillars. The *Gate* of the Court had four Pillars (Exodus 27:16). The *Door* of the Tabernacle have five Pillars overlaid with gold (Exodus 26:36-37). The *Veil* also had four Pillars overlaid with gold (Exodus 26:31-33). These three entrances together typified the Lord Jesus Christ who said,

I am . . .

1. **The Way**   —The Gate of the Court is seen as the Way of approach and there is no other. It was open to all Israelites. This Curtain hid the Outer Court furniture.

2. **The Truth**   —This speaks to us of the Door of the Tabernacle. The Door hid the furniture in the Holy Place. It was open to all the Priests to minister.

3. **The Life** —This speaks of the 2nd Veil which hid the one piece of furniture in the Holiest of All. It was open to only the High Priest (John 14:1, 6 and Hebrews 7:25-26).

Note these Scriptures also pertaining to "Gates" and entering into the Presence of the Lord.

"Open to me the **Gates of Righteousness** . . . this **Gate** of the Lord" (Psalms 118:19-20).

"Open ye the **Gates,** that the Righteous Nation which keepeth the truth may enter in" (Isaiah 26:1-4).

"Enter into His **Gates** with thanksgiving, and into His Courts with praise" (Psalms 110:4).

"The Lord loveth the **Gates** of Zion" (Psalms 87:2; 122:2; 24:7).

Refer also to the following: Isaiah 60:11, 18; Genesis 28:17; Revelation 21:21, 25; 22:14.

Brazen Altar

Read the following: Exodus 27:1-8; 30:28-29; 38:1-7; Leviticus 6:10-14; 8:10-11; 16:18-19; Numbers 3:30-31; 16:36-40 and 19.

The Brazen Altar

(1) The Brazen Altar in General

The Brazen Altar is by no means the first altar mentioned in the Scripture. Indeed, throughout the Old Testament there is a progressive revelation of the altar. Many of the early men of faith were men of sacrifice. We see this in the following examples:

1. There is an altar at least implied in the first sacrifice for man's sin made by God Himself in the Garden of Eden (Genesis 3:21-24).
2. An altar is also implied in Abel's offering at the Gate of Eden (Genesis 4:1-4 and Hebrews 11:4).
3. Noah built an altar unto the Lord. This is the first specific use of the word "altar" (Genesis 8:20).
4. Abraham built an altar in connection with the Covenant God gave him (Genesis 12:7).
5. Isaac also built an altar in connection with the Covenant being renewed in his ears (Genesis 26:25).
6. Jacob also built an altar at the command of the Lord (Genesis 35:1).

God's revelation is always progressive. All of these altars add line upon line and are forerunners of that which is to come in the Brazen Altar.

God permitted altars to be made to Him. Yet we see in Scripture that He gives instructions as to just what type of an altar can be made. In (Exodus 20:24-26).God outlines the following:

1. The Children of Israel were permitted to build an altar of *earth*. This is where He recorded His Name. Perhaps this was the type of altar found in the first two cases above (See also II Kings 5:17).
2. They were allowed to build an altar of stone providing that it was of unhewn *stone*. It was to have nothing tooled of man that would pollute it (See I Kings 18:31.)
3. We see in Exodus 17:1 that God prescribed an altar of *Brass*. God's altars were to have no steps (Exodus 20:26) and this Brazen Altar was to be no exception.

   It is suggested that there was a sloping ascent or ramp to this high Altar, because steps were forbidden. God forbad the use of steps because He wanted no flesh to be seen when the priest carried out his ministrations. Flesh was always characteristic of pagan feasts and ceremonies. The heathen nations round about Israel were all involved in fleshy worship to their idols. Israel was to be a people set apart. There is no place for "the flesh" at God's Altar (Exodus 20:25-26; 28:43 and Leviticus 9:22).

(2) And thou shalt make an altar . . . Exodus 27:1

As we have already indicated, there were two Altars in the Tabernacle, the Golden Altar of Incense and the Brazen Altar. Sometimes there is confusion in Scripture as to which is being referred to in a given passage, and yet, if we remember two things in regard to the Golden Altar of Incense, we will have no problem. First of all, no Blood sacrifice was to be offered on the Altar of Incense. Secondly, only the Priests were allowed to enter into the Holy Place wherein the Golden Altar was placed. Throughout the Scriptures, the Brazen Altar is referred to in the following ways:

1. The Altar of Shittim Wood (Exodus 27:1)
2. The Altar of Burnt Offering (Exodus 30:28; 31:9; 35:16; 38:1; 40:6)
3. The Braen Altar (Exodus 38:30; 39:39)
4. The Altar of God (Exodus 43:3, 4)
5. The Altar (Exodus 29:36-44; Leviticus 1:5; 8:11)
6. The Table of the Lord (Malachi 1:7, 12)
7. The Altar at the Door of the Tabernacle (Leviticus 1:5).

The word "Altar" itself has primarily two meanings. It means "lifted up", "high" or "ascending" (See John 3:14; 8:28; 12:32-34). Jesus Christ was *lifted up* on the Cross, His Altar. Since then He has *ascended* up and is *high* above all (Acts 2:30-36). It also means "slaughter place" to the Hebrew understanding. In the Greek it carries the thought of being a place "for the slaying and burning of victims." Calvary was indeed the *slaughter place*.

Christ was led as a Lamb to the slaughter and flayed alive for us (Acts 8:32; Isaiah 53). Hence the Altar pointed to Calvary's Cross where all that the Brazen Altar foreshadowed was fulfilled.

(3) of shittim wood . . . Exodus 27:1

The same wood that was used in the Ark of the Covenant, the Table of Shewbread, the Altar of Incense, the Boards and the Pillars was to be used in the Brazen Altar. The same truth that was related to all the other pieces of furniture applies here. Shittim wood is white, durable, "incorruptible" wood. It speaks of Christ's sinless and incorruptible humanity. He was uncorrupted by sin, Satan or the world of fallen men. Neither did His Body see corruption when it was laid in the tomb (Hebrews 7:25-27; Psalms 16:10; Acts 2:31 and I Peter 1:23). He is the Righteous Branch who was cut off (Jeremiah 23:6; 33:15; Isaiah 11:1-3). His Life was the only perfect life ever lived here on earth. In the Son of Man there was sinless, deathless and incorruptible humanity, for He was the very Son of God.

Wood is an integral part of the message of Christ. He died on a *wooden* Cross. Even as Isaac, the only begotten son of the Old Testament carried the *wood* for his own typical sacrifice, even so Jesus carried His *wooden* Cross upon which He was to be sacrificed (Genesis 22:6-8 and John 19:17). The wooden Cross was His and our "Altar" (Hebrews 13:10).

(4) Five cubits long, and five cubits broad . . . the height thereof shall be three cubits . . . Exodus 27:1

We see two particular numbers in connection with the measurements of the Brazen Altar. The Altar was to be *three* cubits high. Three is the number of the Godhead. In connection with this altar which was instrumental in providing the Blood of the Atonement, it points out to us that the Godhead; Father, Son and Holy Spirit was involved in the three days and three nights of the Atonement (Matthew 12:39-40; 28:18-20 and I John 5:6-8).

The other prominent number in connection with the Brazen Altar is the number *five*. The Brazen Altar was to be five cubits long and five cubits broad. The number five is typical of the *Grace of God* in the Atonement. The Brazen Altar was the place of the shedding of that precious Blood that brought Atonement to the People, just as the Cross of Calvary was the place where the precious Blood of Christ was poured out for us. On the Cross, Christ suffered five wounds; His feet, His hands and His side. These five wounds of Christ are God's answer to the five "I wills" of Satan when he crossed God's will in Heaven.

The number five is seen all throughout the Tabernacle. In fact it is the most prominent number in the whole of the Tabernacle. How fitting that the number of Grace should be the dominating number in the place of God's dwelling among His people. If not for the Grace of God there would be no such dwelling. Because of the prominence of this number, we offer the following summary of the number five and multiples of five throughout the Tabernacle.

In the Court:

1. There were 60 (12x5) Pillars, Chapiters and Sockets.
2. There were probably 120 (24x5) Pins.
3. The Outer Court measured 100 (20x5) x 50 (10x5) x 5 cubits.
4. If the Pillars were evenly spaced, there were 5 square cubits of Linen upheld by each Pillar.

In the Tabernacle:

5. There was a total of 100 (20x5) Sockets of Silver.
6. There were 15 (3x5) Bars passing through the Boards.
7. There were 10 (2x5) Linen Curtains.
8. There were 50 (10x5) taches of Gold for the Curtains.
9. There were 50 (10x5) taches of Brass in the Goats' Hair Curtain.
10. There was a total of 100 (20x5) loops of blue.
11. The whole structure measured 30 (6x5) x 10 (2x5) x 10 (2x5) cubits which was equal to 3000 (600x5) square cubits.
12. The Holy Place measured 20 (4x5) x 10 (2x5) x 10 (2x5) cubits which was equal to 2000 (400x5) square cubits.

13. The Most Holy Place measured 10 (2x5) x 10 (2x5) x 10 (2x5) cubits which was equal to 1000 (200x5) square cubits.

In the Entrances:

14. The Outer Court Gate was 20 (4x5) x 5 cubits which was equal to a Linen area of 100 (20x5) square cubits.
15. The Door to the Holy Place was 10 (2x5) x 10 (2x5) giving it an area of 100 (20x5) square cubits.
16. The Pillars for the Door were 5 in number.
17. The Veil before the Holiest of All was also 10 (2x5) x 10 (2x5) cubits making it also 100 (20x5) square cubits.

The Grace of God is stamped throughout this structure. Even in regard to the Two Tables of the Law found in the Ark of the Covenant we see Grace. For there were 10 (2x5) Commandments on these two Tables of Stone.

(5) The Altar shall be foursquare . . . Exodus 27:1

The thought of foursquareness is not new to the Brazen Altar. We have seen that the Golden Altar was foursqaure; the Most Holy Place was foursquare; the Veil was foursquare and the Door was foursquare. The Breastplate of the High Priest was foursquare and the Court could be equally divided into two foursquares. The number four points us to the fact that this message of Atonement is a world-wide message. The Gospel is to be preached to the four corners of the earth. The Gospel is the power of God unto salvation to all who believe (Romans 1:16). The Gospel is for all (Acts 1:8; Matthew 28:18-20).

In spite of this emphasis of foursquareness we can not help but remember that the furniture, yes, even the very camp was ordered in the form of a cross. In this we have a double type. The four Gospels point us *first* to the Cross. Once we have experienced the Cross, we are directed *last* to the *Foursquare* City of God in the Book of Revelation (21-22). The only way into the Foursquare City of God is through the Cross!

(6) And thou shalt make the horns of it upon the four corners thereof: his horns shall be of the same . . . Exodus 27:2

There were to be four horns on the Brazen Altar. Here we find another link between the Golden Altar and the Brazen Altar. Horns, as we have already seen, are always typical of the power and strength of the animal (Psalms 92:10; 132:17; Jeremiah 17:1; and Habakkuk 3:4). Horns speak of salvation, strength and power (Luke 1:68-69; Romans 1:16 and I Samuel 17:40) which is to go into all the world, to every creature (Acts 1:8; Matthew 28:18-20; Mark 16:15-20 and Revelation 5:9-10).

Throughout the Scripture the horn is seen in connection with some important events. Note the following:

1. The Ram of substitution was caught in the thicket by its horns (Genesis 22:13).
2. Israel blew Rams' Horns at the fall of Jericho (Joshua 7).
3. Christ is seen as a Lamb with seven horns (Revelation 5:6).
4. There are horns on the symbolic Beast-Kingdoms (Daniel 7-8 and Revelation 13:1-2).
5. The horn was used in the anointing of Kings (I Samuel 16:13).

In connection with the Brazen Altar the horn has added significance. First of all they were a functional adornment. It was to these horns that the sacrificial animals were tied. The sacrifices of the Old Testament were *unwilling* sacrifices (Psalms 118:27). But Jesus Christ came as our New Testament once-and-for-all sacrifice. He was a *willing* sacrifice that did not have to be tied. He was only bound by a love to do His Father's will. No one took His life, but He laid it down on Calvary's Altar (Hebrews 10:7-10; John 3:16 and 10:15-18).

Another interesting and highly symbolic event took place in connection with these horns. In (Exodus 21:14) we are told that the horns of the Altar were to be a place of refuge. In this respect it speaks to us of the Cross which is our only place of *refuge* (Hebrews 6:18). In at least two cases in the Old testament we see that men fled to the Altar in obedience to this Scripture. In each case we have quite a different result:

1. In a time of rebellion Adonijah who was caught in his sin fled to the horns of the Altar seeking a place of refuge from the judgment of the King (I Kings 1:50-53). Solomon showed mercy and gave him a chance to prove himself.

2. In another case when Joab rebelled and fled to the horns of the Altar; he received no mercy (I Kings · 2:28-34).

To one man the Altar meant *life*. To the other the same Altar meant *death*. We see this points to the message of the Cross so vividly portrayed in the two thieves (Luke 23:32-34).The Gospel is a savour of life unto life or death unto death (II Corinthians 2:14-16). To those that are perishing it is foolishness, but to us that are being saved, it is the power and wisdom of God (I Corinthians 1:18).

The primary message of the Brazen Altar is the message of the Cross. The horns of the Altar are those which were touched by the blood on the Day of Atonement. In this regard four horns point us to the four central truths involved in the Cross and the Atonement. The four horns speak of:

1. Redemption
2. Ransom
3. Substitution
4. Reconciliation

(7) And thou shalt overlay it with brass . . . Exodus 27:2

The Brazen Altar was to be overlaid with Brass. This Brass was no doubt taken from the offerings which were brought before the Lord to build the Tabernacle (Exodus 25:3; 35:5, 16).Throughout the Scripture, Brass is generally seen in connection with evil, evil men or judgment upon sin (See Genesis 4:22; Judges 16:21; II Kings 5:27; I Samuel 17:5, 6, 35; Psalms 107:16; Isaiah 48:4; Jeremiah 1:18 and Revelation 1:15).Brass is the symbol of strength and judgment against sin. In the Tabernacle, Brass is particularly characteristic of the Outer Court and its furniture. Brass is seen in connection with the following: the fifty taches on the Goats' Hair Curtains, the five sockets for the Tabernacle Door, the Pillars, Pins, and Sockets in the Outer Court, the Brazen Altar and the Brazen Laver. All these were of Brass (or Copper as some translate).

It was the Outer Court in which sin was to be judged. There was the sacrificial cleansing by the Blood of the animal of sacrifice, and there were the ceremonial washings to wash away all defilement. Brass clearly speaks of this judgment on sin. In Deuteronomy we find that one of God's promises to His people was that if they were disobedient, the heaven would be as *Brass* over their heads (28:15-23).In other words their communication with God would be cut off, and worse than that, the heavens which are the place of God's Throne would be characterized with judgment against the sin of disobedience and a broken law. To the obedient, God's throne is a throne of *mercy*, but disobedience transforms it into a seat of *judgment* (Leviticus 26:19).

There is another clear example in the Old Testament which illustrates this thought of Brass being associated with judgment. When Israel murmured against God who had just delivered their enemies into their hands, God sent serpents to judge them for their sin. The serpents had a venomous bite which was deadly. The people soon came to repentence, and God provided a means whereby through the exercise of faith the people might be healed. Moses was to lift up the *Serpent of Brass* upon a pole. As the people looked upon this Serpent of Brass, they were healed from the judgment of sin in the fiery brazen serpents which bit them (Numbers 21:6-9).

All of this speaks of our Lord Jesus Christ who became that One who was lifted up on a pole (the Cross) and judged for our sins. He even prophesied, "**As Moses lifted up the Serpent in the Wilderness, even so must the Son of Man be lifted up: that whosoever believeth in Him should not perish, but have eternal life**"(John 3:14-16). At Calvary Jesus fulfilled all of this. He was judged for our sins. He judged Satan, the Serpent and with him all sin, sickness and death. He took upon Himself the punishment of all, for the wages of sin is death (Genesis 2:17; Leviticus 17:11; John 5:24; Romans 3:21-23). Sin must be punished or judged, and by God's own Word it must be by death. So Christ was made *sin* for us·(II Corinthians 5:21); He became a curse for us (Galatians 3:13),He was *judged* for us when He was lifted up as a *Serpent* on a pole.

As we look upon the entire Tabernacle as a picture of Christ, the Brazen Altar speaks of the feet of Christ. Jesus Christ was "the **Man** whose appearance was like the appearance of **Brass**"(Ezekiel 40:3).His feet were like unto Brass burning in a furnace (Revelation 1:15 and 2:18). As we come to Christ by the wooing of the Spirit of God, we must begin here, at the *feet* of Christ. We must experience all that the Brass of the Brazen Altar typifies.

The Brazen Altar was overlaid within and without with Brass. We saw this in connection with the Ark of

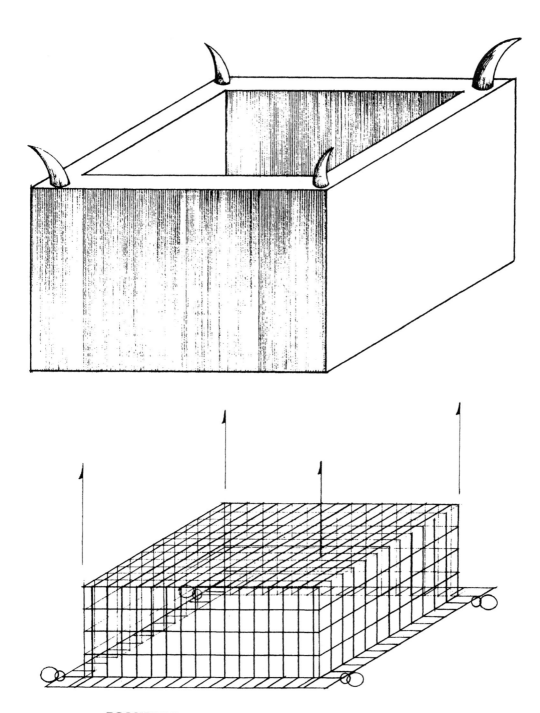

POSSIBLE RELATION OF GRATE TO ALTAR

D. Strausser

the Covenant. When this was accomplished, a cross-section of the Altar would reveal *three* layers. There would be three layers *in one* Altar. The truth here is evident:

1. Brass within is symbolic of the Holy Spirit who dwells within. It is His ministry as the Spirit of Judgment (Isaiah 4:4) to convict the world of sin, righteousness and judgment (John 16:8-11).
2. Wood in the midst reminds us of the *wooden Cross upon* which the central One of the Godhead, the Son, was judged for us (Isaiah 53; Micah 5:1-2).
3. Brass without points us to the Father who is judge of all. He judged His Son for our sin and sins.

   The number *three* points us to the Godhead. The Godhead was involved in what took place on Calvary. The number *one* reminds us that there is only *one* Cross, *one* Sacrifice, *one* Atonement, *one* Savior, *one* Way and a *once*-for-all Sacrifice for sin. In the Tabernacle we have, therefore, but **one** Altar of Sacrifice (John 14:1, 6; Hebrews 7:25-26; I Timothy 2:5-6).

(8) And thou shalt make his pans to receive his ashes, and his shovels, and his basons, and his fleshhooks, and his firepans: all the vessels thereof thou shalt make of brass . . .
Exodus 27:3

Again we see the number five in connection with this Altar. There were to be five vessels of ministry used in connection with this Altar. These include the following:

1. **Pans** — The Pans were used to carry forth ashes to clean place outside the camp (Leviticus 6:10-11). Ashes were also to be used in purification (Numbers 19:17).
2. **Shovels** — These shovels were used to pick up the ashes and for tending the fires.
3. **Basons** — The Basons or Bowls were used to pour the blood at the Altar and for spinkling the blood (Hebrews 9:12; 13:20; Matthew 26:28; Romans 5:9 and Revelation 12:11).
4. **Fleshhooks** — The Fleshhooks were used to arrange the sacrifices on the Altar. They were to put the sacrifice in order that it would be perfectly consumed.
5. **Firepans** — The Firepans or Censers were used to carry the coals of fire from the Brazen Altar to the Golden Altar. It was on the basis of the coals on the Brazen Altar that incense was caused to ascend unto God.

These are the vessels referred to by Isaiah who said, "Be ye clean, that bear the vessels of the Lord." All of these vessels were to be constructed out of Brass (Leviticus 10:1-2 and Numbers 16:46). They point to the Believer-priest who is to be standing in the Blood of Christ as a pure vessel before the Lord.

The *five* vessels point also to the *five*-fold ministry (Ephesians 4:11-6) which are again typified in Aaron and his four sons. *Five* is also seen in the number of Levitical Offerings that were burnt on this Altar: the Burnt Offering, the Meal Offering, the Peace Offering, the Sin Offering and the Trespass Offering (Leviticus 1-7).

All of these various fives point to the *Grace of God;* God coming out in Grace to man in redeeming power. Divine grace to sinful man flows from Calvary.

(9) And thou shalt make for it a grate of network of brass; and upon the net shalt thou make even four brazen rings in the four corners thereof. And thou shalt put it under the compass of the altar beneath, that the net may be even to the midst of the altar . . . Exodus 27:4-5

The Altar had a grate or network of interwoven strands of Brass which was to be positioned "in the midst" of the Altar. This would mean that it would be placed in the center of the three cubits of the height of the Altar. The Grate was, therefore, 1 ½ cubits high. It was the same height as the Table of Shewbread and the Ark of the Covenant or the Mercyseat. The width of the Boards was also to be 1½ cubits. The spiritual significance of this connecting height has already been considered (See Table of Shewbread).

Various diagrams show the grate of network in different positions. Some suggest that the whole of the Altar was surrounded by this grate from the ground to the midpoint of the Altar, or 1 ½ cubits high. Others show the grate in the center of the Altar on which the sacrifice was upheld while the fire beneath consumed it.

Whatever the case, the chief spiritual thought is that the grate upheld the body of the sacrificial victim, and this grate was *"in the midst"* of the Altar. This all pointed to the Cross which was the grate which upheld the

Body of Jesus Christ, the supreme sacrifice and victim for sin. Even as the grate was *"in the midst"* of the three cubits height of the Altar, so also was Jesus Christ crucified between two thieves placing His Cross or His Grate "in the midst" of the three Crosses (John 19:8). Jesus is always the one "in the midst" as the central figure or person of the Godhead (Matthew 18:20; Genesis 2:7; Revelation 1:12-17 and Daniel 9:24-27).

This grate can be seen as the Judgment Seat of the Tabernacle. This Seat which was 1 ½ cubits high which was made accessible on the basis of shed blood. In fact, the blood that was shed at the Brazen Altar on the Day of Atonement was taken to the other seat, the *Mercy* Seat by the High Priest. Judgment and mercy are linked up in these two pieces of furniture (Psalms 85:10; John 1:17; James 1:13 and Matthew 18:23-25); the first and the last pieces of furniture.

The Grate was to have four brazen rings in the four corners. These rings were to be instrumental in carrying not only the Grate but also the Altar itself. Just how these rings were positioned is not certain. It is possible that there were slits in the four corners of the Altar which would allow these rings to pass through to the outside. Whatever the case, the symbolism is not altered. These rings carry much the same message that was proclaimed by the four rings on the Table of Shewbread and the four rings on the Ark. They speak of endlessness, eternity and the eternal attributes of God.

In regard to the Ark and the Table we saw gold rings. These gold rings were seen in connection with the four descriptions of God in the New Testament. (1) God is Light(I John 1:5),(2) God is Love(I John 4:16),(3) God is a Consuming Fire(Hebrews 12:29) and (4) God is Spirit (John 4:24).When these descriptions of God are associated with the four brazen rings or the four rings of judgment against sin we note that the Light, Love, Fire and Spirit of God purify and cleanse us. They are instrumental in judgment on our sin that we might approach unto the presence of God.

The four rings of brass speak specifically of those eternal attributes of God that come together in His perfect judgment. They speak of (1) Mercy, (2) Truth, (3) Righteousness and (4) Peace (Psalms 85:10) which all meet together in perfect balance in the judgments of our Holy God.

(10) And thou shalt make staves for the altar, staves of shittim wood, and overlay them with brass. And the staves shall be put into the rings, and the staves shall be upon the two sides of the altar to bear it . . . Exodus 27:6-7

Again we see staves in connection with this piece of furniture. The staves are symbolic of pilgrimage, wanderings and journeyings in the Wilderness enroute to the Promised Land. They point us to the fact that Christ and His Church together are pilgrims and strangers in the earth having no continuing city, for they are seeking one that is to come (Hebrews 13:10-14; 11:10-16 and I Peter 2:11).

The staves were composed of shittim wood overlaid with Brass. The shittim wood as always points to Christ's perfect, incorruptible humanity. The wood (humanity) coupled with the Brass indicates the judgment that was to come upon the Man Christ Jesus. He was judged for our sin.

The fact that there were *two* staves points us to the two foundation facts of the Good News of Salvation. These include (1) the *Death* and (2) the *Resurrection* of the Lord Jesus Christ (I Corinthians 15:1-3). All the sermons in the Book of Acts are built upon these two fundamental truths. The message of the Apostles was a balanced message presenting both the Death and Resurrection of Christ. The Apostles used both of the staves when they preached Christ. We, too, need a balanced presentation of the Gospel. We need to see the importance of the two staves, for our salvation is on the basis of both. We are saved by His Death first, and then we are saved by His Saving Life (II Corinthians 4:10 and Romans 5:8-10). All the animals sacrificed in the Mosaic Economy stayed dead. Not one animal was able to give us a demonstration of the Resurrection. Christ, however, died once and for all, and He now is raised to live in the power of an endless life. His perfect life condemns us, even as the Law did. But the perfect life He lived enabled Him to die that perfect death, in order that we might be saved by His perfect Resurrection Life.

(11) Hollow with boards shalt thou make it . . . Exodus 27:8

The Altar of Sacrifice was to be hollow. This is understood to mean that it had no bottom plate in it. It was a hollow Brazen structure having a porous grate in the midst. This would put the fire on the earth beneath the Altar, and all the ashes would fall to the ground. If this was so, the Altar could be lifted up from the earth by means of the staves so that the ashes from the burnt sacrifices could be cleaned up and taken outside the camp to the clean place that was prescribed for purifications. This act itself points us to the Lord Jesus Christ who when He was taken down from the accursed tree, His Altar, He was placed in a clean place, in a tomb in which no man had ever laid. Just as the ashes were taken outside of the camp, Christ suffered outside of the camp of Judaism (Hebrews 13:11-13). The ashes cleaned out from under the grate indicated that the sacrifice had been made, and the work was finished. As Christ bowed His head His work was finished (John 19:30; 17:1-4).

Because of the size of this piece of furniture, every other piece that we have dimensions for was able to fit inside of the hollow area of the Brazen Altar. When we recognize that the Brazen Altar is typical of what Christ did for us on the Cross, the truth is evident. All that we receive from God in this life and in eternity is ours on the basis of the comprehensive work of Christ on the Cross. He paid it all. He defeated every evil adversary. His work on the Cross is the grounds for our claiming any and all of the promises of God.

The hollowness of the Altar declares another truth. Being hollow, this Altar was open to heaven and to earth. It speaks of the fact that Christ had an open ear to the will of His Father, and at the same time, He had an open heart to the needs of man on earth. He is the only Mediator. He was one with God and yet He *emptied* Himself of all but love (Philippians 2:8) that He might become our sympathetic High Priest.

(12) As it was shewed thee in the mount, so shall they make it . . . Exodus 27:8

The Brazen Altar was to be made by the Spirit and the Wisdom of God according to the Divine Pattern revealed to Moses. Nothing was to be left to the imagination of the mind of man (Exodus 31:1-6). The Brazen Altar represents God's grace, because it was His plan not man's. In relation to the Cross of Christ the same is true:

1. It was the Wisdom of God that planned man's redemption through the blood (I Corinthians 1-2).
2. It is the Spirit of God that effects and applies that work of the Cross (Zechariah 4:6; John 3:1-5).
3. Everything was to be conformed to the Divine Pattern.

God has His Blueprint that was conceived in the Godhead prior to the creation of man. The whole plan of redemption and salvation is the outworking of the Wisdom and Spirit of God in this Divine Blueprint.

God's pattern must be conformed to. No substitute means of salvation is accepted by Him. We must come His way. Satan tries to deceive us into believing that we can devise our own plan if we are sincere. Wicked King Ahaz thought he could approach God in his own way when he set aside God's Altar and established a counterfeit Altar (II Kings 16:10-18). All his idolatry did not help him (II Chronicles 28:5, 19, 21).

(13) And thou shalt set the altar of the burnt offering before the door of the Tabernacle of the congregation. And thou shalt set the laver between the tent of the congregation and the altar . . . Exodus 40:6-7

The Brazen Altar was set in the Tabernacle Court Yard between the Brazen Laver and the Court Gate. It was, therefore, the *first* piece of furniture that any Israelite had to face if he was desirous of meeting with God who was inside the Gate. There was no chance of missing this Altar because this was the largest piece of furniture. It loomed out with its message of repentance, and judgment against sin and death. There was no way you could get around this piece of furniture. Any such attempt would have been a sin of presumption which was always met with death. No one can come to a place of open fellowship with God unless they have come by way of the Brazen Altar (the Cross).

We can view the plan of Salvation in two ways. We can look at it from God's point of view, or we can look at it from man's point of view. God begins with the *Ark of the Covenant first* and then proceeds out to meet man in the Outer Court at the Brazen Altar. Hence, he arrives at the *Brazen Altar last*. This is God's approach to fallen man.

Man's approach unto God is exactly the reverse of God's approach. Man, who was born in sin and shapen in iniquity must begin at the *Brazen Altar first* to have his sin dealt with. From there he begins the walk to God until he reaches the *Ark of the Glory last*. For man, the Altar is first and foremost! Unless God had provided the Altar in His Grace, man would never be able to proceed to the Holy Place. But God in His infinite love provided such an Altar in the Cross of our Lord Jesus Christ. This Altar or Cross is the *first* and the *most* important thing to be experienced by man in his fallen and sinful state. It is here where he begins his approach to God.

This is the way of approach that God has declared to man through His Only Begotten Son. Salvation is of the **Lord!** It is not from the mind of man. Any other approach to God is presumption on man's part to be met with eternal death. There is only *one way* of approach unto God. We must come *God's way* as a fallen man. Taking up the Cross (Matthew 16:21-27) is the first step into God's Presence. This is the wisdom of God.

There was only **One** Altar, **One** Court Gate, **One** Tabernacle and **One Way.** These are all prophetic of that **One** Mediator between God and man, the Man Christ Jesus (John 14:1, 6; Hebrews 7:25-26 and I Timothy 2:5-6). None of these matters are open to private interpretation. No one could built a private Altar of his own. Everyone, individually and corporately had to come to God's Altar in unity and union through faith in the Blood Atonement.

(14) **The Covering for the Brazen Altar** Numbers 16:36-40; Jude 11

In the rebellion of Korah and company they made Brazen Censers. In doing so they invoked judgment upon themselves, for they presumed to go beyond Aaron who alone had the Golden Censer. Aaron was the only anointed and appointed High Priest of the Most High God (Hebrews 7:1-6).As a result the ground opened up and swallowed these "sinners against their own soul," as they are called. They had chosen to go their own way. Any man who presumes to do the same will meet the same end. The only thing Korah and his company gained was a quick trip to judgment.

When Korah had been dealt with by the judgment of God, their Brazen Censers were then made into a broad plate covering for the Brazen Altar. This was to be **a sign** to Israel that Divine Judgment befalls all who dare present their own incense and presume into the "Presence of God" apart from the High Priest, the Lord Jesus Christ (Acts 17:31; Hebrews 8:1-2; 7:1-25). As the Children of Israel would approach this Altar, the covering would be a sign and a reminder to them not to presume upon God or reject His Appointed Priest.

(15) **The Altar in Transit** Numbers 3:30-31; 4:13-14

This covering (above) of the Brazen Censers made into a broad plate would be the first covering upon the Altar in the wilderness wanderings. Upon this would be placed the cloth of Purple with the five vessels on it, and the Badgers' Skins would cover all. The Altar is a type of the Cross and speaks to us of Jesus Christ and Him crucified. It directs our eyes to the Lamb of God who suffered in our stead (I Peter 1:11 and Luke 21:26).

The Altar was the only article to be covered with Purple in transit. Perhaps it is because of the fact that it was at the Altar that the Blue and the Scarlet met. Purple is a kingly and royal color, but it is derived from a mingling of blue and scarlet. It was at this Altar which the Blood sacrifices were made pointing us to the shed Blood of the very Son of God at Calvary. Jesus Christ was **both** Divine and human, the **God-Man.** He was clothed in Purple at His crucifixion (Mark 15:17).In Him the Scarlet and the Blue come together.

As with the other articles of furniture, the Altar was covered finally with Badgers' skins. They speak of the fact that there is no external beauty to the Altar or the Cross. In fact, to the unregenerate man it is foolishness. In Christ there was no external beauty (as opposed to many representations of Him), but His beauty was on the inside (Isaiah 52:14; 53:1-3).

(16) **The Divine Fire** Leviticus 6:12-13; 9:24; Isaiah 4:4; Hebrews 12:29

In the dedication of the Brazen Altar and the Tabernacle itself, the *Glory of God* came down to the Ark in the Most Holy Place, and out from the Glory there came *Divine Fire* and kindled upon the sacrifices on the Altar. This Fire came out from the Glory! It was to burn continually. It was to never go out. This fire was sovereignly lit, but it was human responsibility to maintain this Fire by bringing wood daily to burn the morning and evening sacrifices. God is a consuming fire. Just as the Old Testament sacrifices were Divinely consumed, even so Christ was Divinely consumed. At the Cross the Fire came out from the Glory of God's Holiness, and Divine Wrath exercised judgment against sin in that sacrifice (John 3:16; Matthew 3:16).

God lit the Fire, man must maintain the fire. The believer must maintain that sovereignly lit flame by bringing wood daily and presenting himself a living sacrifice unto God (Romans 12:1; Ephesians 5:1   and Leviticus 1:9).

At Christ's Second Coming He comes in the Glory of His Father, in Flaming Fire. It is then that He will take vengeance on them that know not God and obey not the Gospel of Christ (II Thessalonians 1:7-10. Compare Leviticus 9:22-24; 10:1-7).

All throughout the Scripture we have examples of this Divine Fire falling in approval from God in certain sacrifices.

1. **Fire fell** (undoubtedly) at Abel's sacrifice of faith-righteousness (Hebrews 11:4; Genesis 4:1-6).
2. **Fire fell** at the dedication of the Altar in the Tabernacle of Moses (Leviticus 9:22-24).
3. **Fire fell** on David's Altar at the Temple site (II Samuel 24).
4. **Fire fell** at the Brazen Altar in Solomon's Temple at its dedication (II Chronicles 7:1-3).
5. **Fire fell** on Elijah's Altar on Mt. Carmel (I Kings 18:38-39).
6. **Fire fell** typically on Christ Jesus at Calvary as He died and was judged for all that we did and all that we are by nature (Hebrews 12:29). At the Cross He received a Baptism of Fire.

Once the fire was lit by God it was man's responsibility to take the fire and light the Candlestick and the Altar of Incense. Hence the Fire from the Glory becomes the foundation for all light and all incense that is to follow. God sovereignly lit the fire in the Church at Pentecost. Until the fire was lit we could not be lights. But now that He has lit the flame we have the responsibility to spread the flame and to be lights to the world.

The fire sent from God caused the sacrifices to *"ascend"* as a sweet savor unto the Lord God. So the fire of the Holy Spirit causes us (living sacrifices) to ascend unto God (Matthew 3:11-12, 15-16).

(17) The Anointing of the Altar Exodus 30:28-29; 40:10; Leviticus 8:10-11

The Brazen Altar was to be anointed. The oil of the anointing was to be sprinkled seven times. Seven is the number of fulness or perfection and it points us to the Lord Jesus Christ who was anointed of the Spirit (Hebrews 9:14; 1:9; Luke 4:18; Acts 10:38), Christ received the fulness of the anointing for He received not the Spirit by measure. He was anointed by the Spirit to enable Him to be offered up on the Cross.

The Altar was to be anointed because it was to be holy before the Lord. The Vessels and Altar were all anointed and sanctified. Whatever touched the Altar after that, with the sacrificial blood that was shed there, would be holy unto the Lord. The Altar sanctified the gift (Exodus 29:37; Matthew 23:19) and the giver.

As we present ourselves a living sacrifice unto God as a gift, He sanctifies and makes us holy. "He that sanctifieth, and they who are sanctified are all of one" (Hebrews 2:11).

(18) For the life of the flesh is in the blood; and I have given it to you upon the altar to make an atonement for your souls: for it is the blood that maketh an atonement for the soul . . .
Leviticus 17:11

Upon this Brazen Altar the five Levitical Offerings were presented (Leviticus 1-7). The main message and revelation of the Brazen Altar must therefore be seen in connection with *Blood Atonement* (Revelation 5:9-10). This Altar which is typical of the Cross was the one and only place of Blood Atonement and Sacrifice. No other place was revealed by God for the Israelites to Sacrifice. No other place was acceptable to God. All had to come by way of the Blood on the Altar. All had to recognize and accept "the slaughter place" at God's Altar.

On the Day of Dedication every other piece of furniture had to be sprinkled with the Blood taken from this Altar. The Golden Candlestick, the Golden Altar of Incense, the Table of Shewbread, the Laver, the Mercy Seat, the Tabernacle — all had Blood sprinkled upon them. It was only as the Blood was sprinkled upon them that they took on meaning and had a place of ministry in the Sanctuary. It was only as they were sprinkled by the Blood that God could seal the work with His Glory! God could only dwell there on the basis of the Blood. It was the Blood that changed things. It was the Blood that was given for the Atonement of the soul Leviticus 17:11-14. God promised "when I see the Blood, I will pass over you" (Exodus 12:12-13; Romans 5:9; 3:24-25).

There was nothing beautiful about the slaughter of animals. There was nothing photogenic about the body and blood of the slain victims. It was probably a smelly, ugly, repulsive sight. In fact, it was not meant to be pretty. It was the place of judgment. It was a scene of fire, smoke and the shedding of Blood.

This scene points us to Calvary. Calvary was the scene of sin, suffering, blood and death. There sin was dealt with by God. It was the slaughter place of the Lamb of God, and it is the only place in the universe where the Blood of Jesus was shed for sins. It was the scene of judgment against sin and the shedding of Blood. It was not a pretty sight. But without the shedding of Blood there is no forgiveness of sins. No Blood means no life! Man tries to make salvation so attractive to the pagan world by concealing the Cross. He even tries to make the Cross something attractive to the flesh, but the Cross was not attractive in the Bible days. The Cross was the instrument or place of **Death!**

Calvary was the place where Christ was judged for our sins. Because we were all born in sin and we have all participated in sin, we deserved the wages of sin. "The wages of sin is **Death**" (Romans 6:23; Genesis 2:17). Jesus Christ, the only Righteous Man chose to take our punishment. The Blood spilt on Calvary is the evidence that the Death has taken place. That Blood is now in Heaven. It was taken within the Veil of the Heavenly Sanctuary and presented to the Father. It now gives power in Heaven and earth to all who accept its power. It is that Blood that makes His present Earthly Sanctuary (the Church) possible.

For the Israelite the animal sacrifice was a matter of faith. God had promised to meet man at the Altar and to judge his sin. The sinner came with his sacrifice. It was an exercise of faith to believe God and to lay his hands of faith and identification on the sacrifice confessing his sins upon it. Without faith it is impossible to please God. This is true today, but it was also true in the Law Age. At the Brazen Altar the Israelite expressed and declared his faith in God through the substitutionary death of an innocent victim. They had faith in the Blood. They were coming God's way (John 14:1, 6; Hebrews 7:25-26).

God's way for the Israelite was first set forth in the Gate of the Court in the exercise of Repentance. The next step was to come to the Altar and receive **Justification by faith** in the Blood. The Old Testament spiritual condition in Israel was judged on the basis of the value they placed on this Altar and their attitude toward it. We are judged the same way.

Many outside Christendom reject the message of the Cross and the Blood Atonement as being a "bloody" or a "slaughter-house religion." Any one who rejects the Blood of Jesus Christ is missing the Wisdom of God. Any other religion which does not accept Christ's Blood is simply an abomination to God. They are following the "Way of Cain" as Blood-rejectors. God wants us all in the "Way of Abel" which is the Way of faith in the Atonement (Jude 11; Hebrews 11:4).

The culmination of that seen in connection with the Blood was the Great Day of Atonement. On the Great Day of Atonement the four horns of the Brazen Altar were sprinkled seven times with Blood Leviticus 16:18-19. On the Day of Atonement the sins of the entire nation were dealt with. There was a seven times sprinkling. Seven is the number of perfection. It was the Blood that brought the nation to a glimpse of sinless perfection as that shed Blood gave way to the High Priest entering into the very Throne Room of God.

The Lord Jesus Christ gave us a vast inheritance through the work of the Cross. It is the power of His Blood that will bring the Church unto perfection at the End of the Age. The Power of the Blood is Power to all the world.

(19) And the priest shall put on his linen garment, and his linen breeches shall he put upon his flesh, and take up the ashes which the fire hath consumed with the burnt offering on the altar, and he shall put them beside the altar. And he shall put off his garments, and put on other garments, and carry forth the ashes without the camp unto a clean place . . . Leviticus 6:10-11

The fact that there were ashes indicates that there was a finished work or a finished sacrifice. These ashes were to be carried outside the camp to a clean place for the purpose of purification (Leviticus 4:12; Numbers 19). All this points to the Lord Jesus Christ who suffered outside the Camp (Hebrews 13:11-13) and finished the work of redemption (John 19:30; 17:1-5). He was the burnt sacrifice that was turned to ashes (Psalms 20:3, Margin, "Turn to ashes Thy burnt sacrifice".

These ashes, as we have already stated, were to be carried outside the camp to a clean place. This would simply mean that there were both clean and unclean places outside the camp. Let us briefly examine these two places:

1. **Outside the camp — the clean place** — The Ashes of the Sacrifices were taken "outside the camp to a clean place" and used for the purifications and washings of separation (Leviticus 4:11-12 and Numbers 19:9).

   This aspect is significant of the fact that Jesus Christ went forth "Outside the Camp" of Judaism, suffering outside the city walls of Jerusalem at Calvary. Calvary became the clean place before God;

the only place of cleansing from sin and uncleanness; the only place and means of washing and purification and separation from the filthiness of sin's defilements (Hebrews 13:12-14).

We are to go unto Him "Outside the Camp," bearing His reproach, even as Levi went to Moses who took the Tabernacle of the Congregation "Outside the Camp" as they identified with God and Moses against the Golden Calf idolatrous worship (Exodus 32:26; 33:7-10).

2. **Outside the camp — the unclean place** — There were also places outside the camp that were associated with defilements. These include the following:

   a. The dead were buried outside the camp (Leviticus 10:5). No death or dead things were to remain inside the Camp of Israel, the Camp of the Lord.
   b. All lepers were put outside the Camp (Leviticus 13:46).
   c. All othe uncleanness was to be outside the Camp (Deuteronomy 23:10-13).
   d. Blasphemers were to be stoned outside the Camp (Leviticus 24:14).

   God was inside the Camp of Israel, and it was to be holy in order for Him to remain in their midst (Deuteronomy 23:14).

   This aspect speaks of the Ultimate New Jerusalem, the Holy City, the Eternal Habitation of God and the Saints, the Camp of the Lord. There is to be nothing unclean or defiled in that camp. All the unclean, the liars, the whoremongers, the murders and the sorcerers are "Outside the Camp" in that Unclean Place called Gehenna, the Lake of Fire (Revelation 21:27; 22:15).

It is better to be "Outside the Camp" of Apostate Religion, in the *Clean Place* called Calvary with Christ and His Church now, than to be "Outside the Camp" of the Lord in the *Unclean Place* called Hell or Gehenna with Satan and the Apostate and Unregenerate for all Eternity!

(20) Additional Thoughts for the Student

There is much food for thought in the following Scriptures pertaining to the theme of God's Altar. The student would do well in meditating upon the following:

1. **The Dedication of the Brazen Altar in the Tabernacle of Moses** Exodus 29:35-37; Numbers 7 — This dedication was in association with the 12 princes of Israel and their special offerings. The number of the offerings and sacrifices are especially in multiples of twelve and seven. At the Dedication of the Church Age (God's Sanctuary), we have the 12 Apostles of the Lamb (Revelation 21:14) and that Perfect, Sinless, Once-for-all Sacrifice of the Lord Jesus Christ.

2. **Solomon and the Congregation at the Altar** II Chronicles 1:1-13 — As Solomon and the whole congregation came to the Altar at Gibeon, God granted wisdom and knowledge (I Corinthians 1:30; 12:8; Colossians 3:3, 9-10).

3. **The Dedication of Solomon's Temple** II Chronicles 5:11-14 — There were 120 Priests with trumpets at the Dedication of the Temple. Then 120 gathered together in the Upper Room at the Dedication of the New Covenant Church (Acts 1-2). These stood at the *east* end of the Altar (Leviticus 1:6; 6:11; Psalms 20:3) where the ashes were poured out.

4. **The Brazen Altar in Solomon's Temple** II Chronicles 4:1 — This great Altar measured 20 x 20 x 10 cubits which was equal to 4000 cubicle cubits. This 4000 cubits was the only place of blood shed. This is typical of the 4000 years between the Fall of Adam to Christ whence all sacrificial Blood was shed.

5. **The Brazen Scaffold at the Dedication** II Chronicles 6:13 — Solomon knelt upon this Brazen Scaffold which measured 5 x 5 x 3 cubits (Exodus 27:1; Romans 12:1-2). It demonstrates that Solomon was presenting himself a living sacrifice, wholly, acceptable unto God.

6. **Isaiah at the Altar** Isaiah 6:1-7 — For Isaiah the Altar was a place of cleansing, purging and commission.

7. **Restoration of the Altar** Ezra 3:1-3 — In the restoration from the Babylonian Captivity, the *first* thing that was restored was the Altar (Blood Atonement). So in the Restoration of the Church from the Dark Ages, Justification by Faith in the Blood was the first message of Restoration.

8. **Judgment began at God's Sanctuary, at the Altar** Ezekiel 9:1-7, Compare I Peter 4:17.

9. **Counterfeit Altars:**

   a. The Altar of Ahaz (II Kings 16:10-16).

   b. The Altar of Jeroboam (I Kings 12:25-33; 13:1-5)— It was rent in judgment.

   c. The Altar to the Unknown God (Acts 17:23) — This represented the height of Greek wisdom and culture.

   d. The Altars to Baal and all false gods (I Kings 18) — These altars were built on every high hill, and groves were built under every green tree. These were an abomination to God, and an insult to God's Altar.

The 'high or low' altars made by the religions of men are an abomination to God and despise that Altar of Calvary. There is only **One** Altar in the universe and that was the Cross of Jesus. It fulfilled and abolished in itself all typical Old Testament Altars of earth, of stone and of brass. "**We have an altar, whereof they have no right to eat which serve the tabernacle**" (Hebrews 13:10).

May we honor the Cross of Jesus and the Blood of Atonement, giving it the place and importance that God does in His Word!

Brazen Laver

Read the following: Exodus 30:17-21 and 38:8.

The Brazen Laver

(1) Thou shalt also make a laver . . . Exodus 30:18

Moses was instructed to make a Laver which was to be set in the Court Yard between the Tent of the Congregation and the Brazen Altar (Exodus 40:7, 30). Of all the pieces of furniture, we have the least information in regard to the Laver. This piece is called:

1. A Laver of Brass (Exodus 30:18; 38:8)
2. A Laver (Exodus 30:28; 31:9; 35:16; 39:39; 40:7, 11, 30)

There are no specific measurements or pattern for the Laver recorded in Scripture. Most all we know about the Laver has been handed from tradition. The Laver is described as a Brazen Vessel containing water, standing on a pedestal or foot. It clearly consisted of two parts for it is referred to as "as Laver and His Foot (Exodus 30:18). The foot is literally "a base, basis or foot" (compare Leviticus 8:11.)

The Dictionary defines a Laver with three definitions:

1. "A washing vessel, basin or bowl for water which cleanses."
2. "A vessel in the Tabernacle of Moses for the Priests to wash therein."
3. "A Vessel in the Temple of Solomon for the sacrifices to be washed therein."

Others suggest that the Basin was a reservoir for water from which water was taken to supply the foot in which the feet of the Priests were washed. The Priests would wash their hands in the top or large basin. Whatever the case, the vessels' chief function was to supply the water for the cleansing of the Priests. The other pieces of furniture were used particularly in reference to God but the Laver was used especially for the Priests. The Brazen Altar was for sacrifice unto the Lord, the Ark of the Covenant was His Throne, the Table was His Table, but the Laver was for the cleansing of the Priest. "Kiyyor," which is the Hebrew for "Laver" literally means "Pot, pan or laver." It was this large pot or Laver that contained the water needed to cleanse the Priests for ministry.

(2) Of brass, and his foot of brass . . . Exodus 30:18

The Laver was placed in the Outer Court. The Outer Court was primarily seen in connection with Brass. The Pillars were probably Brass, the hooks and pins were of Brass, the Altar of Sacrifice was overlaid with Brass and the Laver as well was constructed with Brass. In this piece of furniture there was no wood. It was to be solid Brass.

The fact that it was solid Brass puts strong emphasis on the nature of the ministry (if we can call it that) of the Laver. Brass, we have said, is symbolic of strength, firmness, endurance and judgment against sin. We see Brass in connection with the following:

1. Gates of Brass (Psalms 107:16)
2. Bars of Brass (I Kings 4:13)
3. Fetters of Brass (Judges 16:21)
4. His Feet as Polished Brass (Daniel 10:6; Revelation 1:15)
5. The Serpent of Brass (Numbers 21:8-9)
6. The Censers of Brass (Numbers 16:36-40)
7. The Heavens as Brass (Deuteronomy 28:23)

The ministry of the Laver points us to the ministry of the Word of God in our lives. The Holy Spirit who is the Spirit of Judgment and Burning uses the Word of God to convict of sin, righteousness and judgment (Isaiah 4:4; John 16:6-12). Jesus Christ who was the Word made flesh was given authority to exercise judgment upon sin (John 5:27). The Laver speaks of this judgment upon sin operating through the Word of God. It speaks of that cleansing that comes as the Word exposes areas of our life that are not in conformity to the standard of God. It speaks of the washing of water by the Word (Ephesians 5:26).

Sin is to be judged itself.
Sin is to be judged in self

In the Brazen Altar there is judgment against **Sin,** our sin!
In the Brazen Laver there is judgment against **Self,** our self!

The Bible teaches that if we would judge ourselves, we would not be judged (I Corinthians 11:31-32). Had the Priests entered into the Holy Place without having cleansed themselves in the Laver they would have been judged by God upon entry. There is a time of judgment for all who are not already judged. (I Peter 1:7 and I (Corinthians 3:12-15). Judgment must begin at the House of God I Peter 4:17. This occurred for the Priest as he washed at the Laver. This happens for us when we submit to the Word and the Spirit as they convict us. As we submit and let the Word wash us, we experience a real cleansing. The desire of Christ is to have a cleansed people. The Lord Jesus Christ is our High Priest Judge who has the Breastplate of Judgment (Exodus 28-29).He wants a holy nation and a people set apart to offer up spiritual sacrifices unto God (I Peter 2:9).

(3) Of the looking glasses of the women assembling, which assembled at the door of the Tabernacle of the congregation . . . Exodus 38:8

The Altar was made of Brass, and we are told from where the Brass came. The Brass came from the looking-glasses of the women. These looking glasses were Brazen Mirrors or hand mirrors which the women gave over to the Lord for His service. Normally these mirrors were instruments of *vanity* and *pride* that the Lord was able to transform into an instrument of cleansing.

The thought of the mirror in connection with the Laver is quite appropriate. The whole design and purpose of a mirror is to reflect back an image of that which is in front of the mirror. Men and women use mirrors to observe or behold their 'natural beauty' or defilements. They use a mirror to take physical inventory of themselves before they leave the house. They use the mirror to help them adorn themselves. But mirrors can be used as a source of pride to display to our own eyes our natural beauty or defects. Its primary purpose is to expose ourselves to ourselves. It shows us what we are by nature and what we can be by cleansing ourselves.

Not all mirrors give a true picture. Mirrors can be distorted to produce nearly any desired effect. Mirrors that are used at amusement parks are examples of such. These mirrors do not give a true reflection. They distort what we are in our eyes and in the eyes of others. They give a lying or deceiving impression.

What an appropriate article the mirror was from which to construct a Laver. The figure or symbol of the mirror is used by James in the Word of God. He says, "For if any be a hear of the Word, and not a doer, he is like unto a man beholding his natural face in a glass . . ." (James 1:23).**The Word of God is a mirror!** It gives us a true and clear image of ourselves as we are, as God sees us. But it also gives us a view of what we can be through Christ. As we look into the Word of God, we see our need of cleansing. The Word reveals any defilements that need to be scrubbed off.

This is exactly how God changes us through His Word. He wants to move us from glory to glory, and He does it by giving us little glimpses of ourselves as we really are. With the glimpse, He gives us the strength and desire to change. Job saw himself as he was and it abhorred him (Job 42:5-6).Isaiah saw himself as he was before the Lord (Isaiah 6:5). Peter saw his own inner nature before Jesus (Luke 5:8).We all can see ourselves in Him. He — **The Living Word** — shows us what we are, what we ought to be, and all that we can be. Self-discovery is at first frightening because we see our own uncleanness. But self-discovery is the first step to cleansing. As Isaiah was made aware of his own uncleanness, he was made ready to be touched of God.

We, too, must be willing to recognize and accept that which the Mirror reveals, not to live a life of self-contemplation or self-condemnation, but to avail ourselves of the God-provided cleansing water.

The *mirrors* of the Brazen Laver simply point to the *water* of the Brazen Laver. The Word points us to the washing! The mirror of the Word is to be a corrective instrument not an instrument of condemnation. We need the *corrective Word* before we can experience the *cleansing Water.* The Word of God itself provides both of these aspects. The Word acts as a **mirror** (James 1:23-25) to give us a true reflection of what we are before God. The Word of God is also the **water** which also gives an image, but with the image it becomes the agent by which we receive cleansing (Proverbs 27:19 and Ephesians 5:26). The Priest saw his reflection in the polished Brass and the water.

(4) To wash withall . . . Exodus 30:18

As we have seen, the Laver had a twofold purpose. It was to reveal all uncleanness by the mirrors Hebrews 4:12-14, and it was to provide the cleansing by the water (Ephesians 5:26). When we are cleansed by the Mirror and the Water of the Word, we are beholding as in a glass the Glory of the Lord and may therefore reflect that same image (II Corinthians 3:18).

The primary purpose of the Laver is summed up in the three words "to wash with all." The Laver held the water that was to be used for the cleansing of the Priesthood. Just where this water came from is the object of much conjecture. It is very likely that they filled the Laver with the same water that they used for drinking. This we know came from the Smitten Rock that followed them (Exodus 17:6),and that Rock that followed them was Christ (I Corinthians 10:4). The Lord Jesus Christ is our Smitten Rock. He is the one who provides the Waters of refreshing. In His death, burial and resurrection He provided the needed cleansing (John 7:37-39; I Corinthians 10:1-4).

This experience of the Water was the second experience for the Priest in his approach to God. The Priest first went to the Brazen Altar to experience the cleansing by the Blood of the substitutionary death. From here the next step was the Brazen Laver where he was to experience the cleansing Water. This was the order in man's approach unto God —

First the *Blood* (Brazen Altar),
Second the *Water* (Brazen Laver).

At the Brazen Altar man receives *justification from sins,* and at the Brazen Laver man is *sanctified from self* unto the Lord.

All throughout the Scripture there is an emphasis on **Water** and **Blood.** These were the two main agents of cleansing in the ceremonial laws in the Old Testament for Israel, "the Church in the Wilderness"(Acts 7:38).

Blood was seen in relation to the thought of cleansing in the following examples:

1. The Blood of the Passover Lamb (Exodus 12)
2. The Blood of the Day of Atonement (Leviticus 16)
3. The Blood of the Offerings in the Feasts of the Lord (Leviticus 23)
4. The Five Levitical Offerings (Leviticus 1-7)
5. The Blood Atonement for the Soul (Leviticus 17:11-14)
6. The Blood (the Life) Crying unto God (Genesis 4; Hebrews 12:22-24)

Water was seen in connection with ceremonial cleansings in the following cases:

1. The Waters of Separation and the Ashes of the Red Heifer (Numbers 19)
2. Water in Consecration to Priestly Ministry (Leviticus 8:6)
3. Water in the Cleansing of the Leper (Leviticus 14:1-8)
4. The Divers Washings of the Law (Hebrews 9:10)
5. Israel Baptized into the Cloud and Red Sea (Exodus 13-14; I Corinthians 10:1, 2)
6. Israel's Experience of the Waters of Jordan (Joshua 4:19, 5:10)

The spiritual significance of all of this is seen in the New Testament where these two agents of cleansing meet at the Cross of Jesus. On the Cross when Jesus died, the soldiers pierced His side and forthwith there came out **Blood and Water!** And he that saw it bare record and his record is true (John 19:34-35).

John is the one who receives this vital truth and revelation and bears record of it both his Gospel and his Epistles. "This is he that came by water and blood, even Jesus Christ; not by water only, but by water and blood. And it is the Spirit that beareth witness, because the Spirit is truth" (I John 5:6).When Christ died on the Cross, and the Blood and Water flowed from His side in miraculous life, He fulfilled and abolished the Blood and the Water of the Old Testament. In Christ's perfect, once-for-all sacrifice and oblation all the typical animal blood and ceremonial waters converged. This Sacrifice of Christ was the antitype or the real sacrifice to which all animal sacrifices pointed. His shed Blood is the antitype of all animal blood that was shed under the Mosaic Covenant. The Water that flowed from the pierced side of Christ fulfilled all that was in the ceremonial washings of the Old Covenant. Because of this, the Blood and Water become a vital part of the New Covenant.

These same two cleansing agents remain for the New Testament Church. Not that same blood and water that was seen in connection with the children of Israel, but the spiritual reality, that which is eternal by the Spirit in the Lord Jesus Christ Himself. This is **not** animal blood and **not** Ceremonial washings!

It is the **Blood** *that cleanses us from sin.* As we wash in the Blood of Christ our garments are made white (Revelation 1:5; 7:14; 22:14), because the Blood of Jesus Christ cleanses us from all sin (I John 1:6-7, 9).

It is the **Water** *that cleanses us from self-defilement.* We are to be washed by the "washing (literal, Laver) of regeneration" (Titus 3:5), and we are to be cleansed by the "washing (literal, Laver) of Water by the Word" (Ephesians 5:26). This water is to cleanse, sanctify and perfect the Church.

Water can also be seen in relation to the various ministries of the Godhead in dealing with man.

1. **Water in Judgment** — The earth, being covered with water at the beginning of the Bible in (Genesis I). receives its second baptism by water in the great Flood in the days of Noah (Genesis 7-8). This water in both cases is seen in connection with judgment and is associated with *the Father God.*

2. **Water in Cleansing** — This Water speaks of the Son, the Lord Jesus Christ who was the Word made flesh. Jesus demonstrated this truth when He (the **Word)** washed the disciples' feet. They were washed of water by the Word (John 13; Titus 3:5; Ephesians 5:26).

3. **Water in Drinking** — The water that Jesus gives points to the *Holy Spirit.* He is the one who provides that artesian well within the believer (John 7:37-39).

(5) **And thou shalt put it between the Tabernacle of the congregation and the Altar, and thou shalt put water therein . . .** Exodus 30:18

Water was to be held in the Laver. Water points us to the washing of Water by the Word, but it also has added importance in the Church of the New Testament. We see water referred to in two areas.

1. **The Water in Regeneration** — This points us to the "washing of regeneration, and renewing of the Holy Ghost" (Titus 3:5). Jesus said, "Except a man be born of Water and of the Spirit, he cannot enter the Kingdom of God." Regeneration and renewal is being born again or born from above. This is the initial bath. It is a washing, a cleansing and a purification that takes place in regard to the former source of life (compare Acts 15:9; I Thessalonians 4:7; II Corinthians 5:17). It is this that makes us a new creature. Paul says, "But ye are washed, but ye are sanctified, but ye are justified in the Name of the Lord Jesus, and by the Spirit of our God" I Corinthians 6:11. Jesus said, "He that is washed . . . is clean every white and ye are clean"(John 13:10). All this refers to the believer's initial cleansing in Water when he is indeed born again.

2. **The Water in Baptism** — The believer is cleansed by the Blood of Jesus and the Water in and of Regeneration. The next step in God's order is Water Baptism. In the New Testament Baptism is not optional, it is a command (compare Acts 2:36-38, 41; Hebrews 6:1-2; Mark 16:16; Romans 6:1-4; Colossians 2:12-13 and Matthew 28:18-20). If we are going to be obedient to the words and command of Christ, then we will want to be baptized. We let the following Scriptures speak for themselves:

"Repent, and be baptized every one of you . . ." (Acts 2:36).

"And now why tarriest thou? Arise, and be baptized, and wash away thy sins, calling on the name of the Lord" (Acts 22:16).

We are "buried with Him in baptism" (Colossians 2:12).

"Eight souls were saved by water. The like figure whereunto even Baptism doth also now save us, (not the putting away of the filth of the flesh, but the answer of a good conscience toward God), by the resurrection of Jesus Christ" (I Peter 3:20-21).

(6) **For Aaron and his sons shall wash their hands and their feet thereat: when they go into the Tabernacle of the congregation, they shall wash with water, that they die not; or when they come near to the Altar to minister, to burn offering made by fire unto the Lord: so shall they wash their hands and their feet, that they die not . . .** Exodus 30:20-21

All the Priests were to wash at the Laver before any ministry. They could not enter the Sanctuary for any ministry or function before the Presence of the Lord until or unless they had been to this article of furniture. They could not minister at the Table of the Lord, the Altar of Incense, or the Candlestick which were all to be found in the Holy Place (Psalms 119:9; I Peter 1:22; Hebrews 10:22). In addition to this, they were not allowed to minister at the Brazen Altar in the Outer Court unless they had first washed. All must be clean who bear the vessels of the Lord (Isaiah 52:11).

The spiritual significance is evident. Absolutely no ministry was acceptable to the Lord without cleansing. Before there could be ministry the Priest had to submit to the Word of the Lord. So serious was any violation of this Divine Order that they would be struck dead if they came any other way.

How much 'spiritual death' comes into the Sanctuary of the New Testament Church today because the believer-priests fail to cleanse and prepare themselves at the Laver before entering into the Sanctuary worship. The Church at Corinth illustrates this truth (I Corinthians 11:23-31). "For this cause many are weak and sickly among you, and many sleep. For if we would judge ourselves, we should not be judged!" (I Corinthians 11:30-31).If we judge ourselves at the Brazen Laver, then *we will not be judged* at the Table of Shewbread!

We are called to be Priests unto the Lord in a Spiritual House. We need to be sure we are clean who bear the vessels of the Lord. We need Priestly cleansing continually as we serve in His Sanctuary.

(7) And it shall be a statute for ever to them, even to him and his seed throughout his generations . . . Exodus 30:21

Moses wholly bathed Aaron and his sons in the initial cleansing (Once-for-all). From that point on it was their responsibility to maintain that cleansing at the Laver by daily washing their hands and feet (Exodus 29:4; 40:12).Jesus Christ who is our Moses has ministered to us the initial bath of regeneration, but it is our personal responsibility to maintain the daily cleansing of our hands and feet (I Peter 1:22; II Corinthians 7:1; Ephesians 5:26; I Corinthians 6:11). Paul exhorts us to "cleanse ourselves from all filthiness of the flesh and spirit, perfecting holiness in the fear of God" (II Corinthians 7:1). He tells us that we are to draw near having "our bodies washed with pure water" (Hebrews 10:20-22).The responsibility for maintaining this condition is placed on us; in fact, we are to help maintain one another by washing one another's feet (John 13:1-4).

It did not matter if the Priests were aware of the principle or rules or not. Ignorance of such defilement was no excuse. God had provided the Laver and the Water and had made it available to the Priests. It was there, it was offered. If they refused to use it they would suffer the consequences. As the Priest ministered before the Lord he was to have clean *hands* and *clean* feet. Clean hands speak of their service before the Lord. They were to lift up holy hands (Psalms 24:3-4; I Timothy 2:1, 8; James 4:8 and Isaiah 1:16). Clean feet refer to the walk of the Priests before God (Hebrews 12:13; Ephesians 4:1-3 and John 13:1-8). The Priests were to have a straight and pure walk before the Lord. Had these washings not taken place, regardless of the ignorance of the Priest, judgment would have fallen. Redeemed people must be a clean people. Judas was a man who sat at the Table with unclean hands and unclean feet!

The Laver was to be used for the cleansing of the Priests as they ministered before the Lord, but it was also to be the site of the cleansing of the sacrifices that were made. All the animals offered had to be ceremonially bathed in water. We are Priests unto the Lord, but we are also to be the sacrifice. We are to present our bodies a living sacrifice, holy and acceptable unto God (Romans 12:1-2),compare Leviticus 1:9; I Peter 2:5-9; Revelation 1:5-6; 5:9-10; Acts 15:9 and I Thessalonians 4:7. We are both *Priest* and *Sacrifice*.

God has given us this wonderful type to direct us to a truth that operates in the Kingdom of God. He is telling us that there must be a holiness or separation from all the defilements of the flesh as we enter into His Presence. Just looking at the water never made anyone clean. The Water had to be applied. It is the application of the Water alone that cleanses. It is not sufficient to merely see the Word or to see a truth in the Word of God; that truth must be applied personally and practically to the life of every individual if it is going to have cleansing power.

This was to be a perpetual statute to Aaron and his Seed in all generations. This was the type. Aaron points us to Christ (Hebrews 5:1-5). Aaron's seed points us to the Church, the offspring of God and the Seed of the Royal Priesthood (Galatians 3:16, 27; Revelation 1:6; I Peter 2:5-9; Revelation 5:9-10). As long as the Aaronic Priesthood existed they were to wash in the Laver. They were to be clean as they ministered before the Lord. When Christ came He fulfilled and abolished the Aaronic Priesthood by bringing in a higher Priesthood, an eternal Priesthood after the Order of Melchizedek. The Aaronic Priesthood was only a shadow of that which was to come. The Brazen Laver was only a shadow of the cleansing power of the Word. In Christ these shadows are abolished because **The Word was made Flesh** (John 1:14).It now remains for Christ's Seed, the Church, the Kings and Priests after the Order of Melchizedek to maintain their cleanness by washing in the Spiritual or True Laver, the Word of God. This Seed must maintain the ordinances of a clean Priesthood unto the Lord unto all generations!

(8) The Three Witnesses

The Laver was sprinkled with *Blood,* anointed with *Oil* and it contained *Water* for cleansing (Exodus 40:11; Leviticus 8:10-11). So the *Water* of the Word for cleansing comes to us through the *Blood* of Jesus and by the Spirit (Oil) of God. These are the three witnesses that John speaks about, "For there are three that bear record in heaven, the Father, the Word, and the Holy Ghost: these three are one. And there are three that bear witness in the earth, the **Spirit,** and the **Water,** and the **Blood:** and these three agree in one" (I John 5:7-8).

As believer-priests we need to experience all three of these witnesses if we are to be complete in Him. We need to have our hearts sprinkled with the Blood. We need to have that continual washing by the Water of the Word. And we need that Holy Anointing Oil of the Holy Spirit to be poured over our head which will give us a place of service. One witness without the other two is incomplete. We all need to be complete in Him!

(9) The Laver in Transit

There is no record of the design or measurements of the Brazen Laver. There is no record of how it was carried in transit in the Wilderness, whether by staves or by a bar. There is no record of how or if it was covered in the journeyings of the Camp. In the Order of Marching and the list of the Coverings for the articles of furniture in Numbers 4, the Brazen Laver is not mentioned.

The possible significance of this is that the power of the cleansing Word of God cannot be measured in its function for the Church in the pilgrimage journeyings of this present world.

(10) Additional Thoughts for the Student

The sincere student of the Word would do well to examine the following seed thoughts in connection with the Laver:

1. **The Brazen Lavers in Solomon's Temple** II Chronicles 4:2-6 — There were ten Brazen Lavers in Solomon's Temple. These Lavers were for the washing of the sacrifices (compare Romans 12:1-2; I Peter 2:1-9).The Church is to be a living sacrifice unto God and is to come under the number ten which speaks of Divine Order.

2. **The Molten Sea in Solomon's Temple** I Kings 7:23-26, 44; II Chronicles 4:2-6. The Molten Sea (Brazen Sea) took the place of the Laver of the Tabernacle of Moses. The Sea was a place of washing for the Priests while the sacrifices were cleansed in the ten smaller Lavers. The believer, in addition to being a living sacrifice, is also a Priest and has a place at the Molten Sea. In Christ we become offerer and offering, giver and gift, Priest and sacrifice (Hebrews 5:1-5). Notice the following in connection with the Molten Sea:

   a) It was for the *Priests* to wash to be sanctified for ministry in the Temple of the Lord (I Corinthians 3:16; II Corinthians 6:16 and Ephesians 2:19-21).

   b) It was *ten* cubits in diameter. Ten is the number of Law and Divine Order as seen in the Ten Commandments. This number is fulfilled in us by the Law of the Spirit of Life in Christ Jesus. This is His imparted righteousness (Romans 8:1-4; 10:1-5).

   c) It was upheld by a foundation of *Twelve* Oxen of Brass (II Kings 16:17). Twelve is the number of Apostolic Government which is the foundation of the Church.

   d) These Oxed faced *North, South, East* and *West* (Matthew 28:18-20).There message was worldwide in outreach(Mark 16:15-20; Acts 1:8).The power and cleansing in the Gospel and Word of Christ is world-wide and extends to the four corners of the earth.

   e) The height measured *five* cubits which direct us to the Atonement and the Grace of God which provide the Water for cleansing.

   f) The circumference was approximately *thirty* cubits. Thirty is the number of consecration to Priestly Ministry (Numbers 4:1-3; Luke 3:23). Remember the Molten Sea was for the Priest to wash.

   g) It had ornamentation of flowers of *lilies.* The lily speaks of the beauty, purity and fruitfulness of Christ by the Spirit (Song of Solomon 2:1-2).

   h) It held *2000 baths* of water (I Kings 7:26) when in use and *3000 baths* of water (II Chronicles 4:5) when full. These numbers are significant of the Church Age which is capped by the fulness of the

Kingdom Age.

i) It was made of *Brass without weight.* The power of the Gospel of Christ to cleanse from sin is beyond human comprehension.

All this finds fulfillment in Christ and His Church in the power of the cleansing Word.

3. **The Sea of Glass in Revelation** Revelation 4:6; 15:1-2 — Notice the people who stand upon it and the fact that it was in the Outer Court (Revelation 11:1-3).

4. **The Lord Jesus Cleanses His Disciples** John 13 — This chapter should be especially studied in connection with the Laver and the cleansing power of the Word. Christ, the **Word** made flesh, washed His Disciples' feet. God gave us His cleansing Son to be an example. We are to in like manner *wash one another's feet* (Matthew 18:15; Luke 17:3, 4; James 5:16; Galatians 6:1).

Christ has ministered to us the initial cleansing. It is our responsibility to maintain that daily cleansing by exposing ourselves to the Word. We are to minister that cleansing water to one another in the Spirit of Christ and true humility. The Church is to be sanctified, cleansed and made holy by the **Washing of Water by the Word!**

The Cloud of Glory

Scriptures to read: Exodus 40:1-38; Numbers 9:15-23.

In this final section we consider the crowning glory of the finished work which God gave Moses to do.

When the Tabernacle and all its furnishings was completed, the builders brought it all to Moses for him to inspect it to see that it all had been made according to the pattern.

In the closing chapters of Exodus (Exodus 39-40), we are told, 17 times, that everything had been made **"according as the Lord commanded Moses."**

Moses then set up the Tabernacle, positioning the furniture in its Divinely appointed place, sprinkling it all with blood and anointing it all with the holy oil. Thus **"Moses finished the work"** (Exodus 40:33).

All of this was done on the Day of the Dedication of the Tabernacle in the Wilderness.

What was the end result? The Scripture tells us that **"A cloud** covered the Tent of the Congregation, and **the Glory** of the Lord filled the Tabernacle"** (Exodus 40:34).

Not even Moses could stand to minister in the Presence of that Glory-Cloud. This was the seal of God upon that which originated in Himself, and that which had been built by the wisdom and Spirit of God through chosen vessels, according to that pattern shown to Moses in the Mount of God.

From that time on, the whole of the pilgrimage of the nation was governed by the Glory-Cloud.

The Glory-Cloud speaks of the Presence of the Holy Spirit. He is the Cloud of God's Presence who fulfills, in His Ministry and Operation, all that the typical Glory-Cloud shadowed forth in Israel.

The following is a brief outline tracing the history, function and ministry of "The Cloud" as it relates to the Children of Israel and the Tabernacle, both of which constitute "The Church in the Wilderness" (Acts 7:38).

1. The Lord led Israel by a Cloudy Pillar of Fire out of Egypt to the Promised Land. This is the first mention of The Cloud (Exodus 13:21-22). Note the blessings of the Presence of this Cloud.

    a) The **Lord** went before them. He goes before the Church.
    b) The **Lord** led them. So the Holy Spirit leads the Church.
    c) The Cloud gave them light by night. Light in the surrounding darkness.
    d) The Cloud was a Pillar of Fire, giving them warmth.
    e) The Cloud was a Shade for them from the heat of the day.

    All that the Cloud was to Israel, the Holy Spirit is to the Church.

2. The Cloud led Israel through the Red Sea. The Cloud was darkness to the Egyptians but it was light to the Israelites, God's people (Exodus 14:19-31), compare II Corinthians 2:15-16. The Lord was in that Cloud. God was in the type. It was a visible manifestation of the Presence of the Lord to the nation. Paul tells us that the nation was "baptized in the Cloud and in the Sea" (I Corinthians 10:1-4).

3. The Glory of the Lord appeared in The Cloud (Exodus 16:10).

4. The Cloud eventually brought Israel to Mt. Sinai and settled on the Mount. The voice of God spoke to the nation out of this Cloud, at the Feast of Pentecost (Exodus 19:9-19; Deuteronomy 5:22).

5. Moses went up onto Mt. Sinai into the Glory of the Cloud and was there for 40 days and 40 nights. There in the Presence of that Cloud Moses received the 10 Commandments and the revelation for the construction of the Tabernacle (Exodus 24:15-18; 34:5-7).

6. At the Dedication of the Tabernacle, The Cloud of Glory (The Hebrews refer to it as 'The Shekinah') left Mt. Sinai and came and dwelt over the Tabernacle, upon a Blood-stained Mercy Seat, in the midst of God's people, Israel (Exodus 40:34-38).

7. The Lord appeared in that Cloud upon the Mercy Seat and there the audible voice of God spoke to Moses the Divine communication (Leviticus 16:1-2; Numbers 7:89).

8. The Glory-Cloud governed all the journeyings of Israel in the Wilderness, finally leading them to the Land of Canaan.

When the cloud moved they moved. When the Cloud stayed, they encamped. The eyes of the Priesthood had to be continually on the Cloud, day and night. The Priests could blow the trumpets in order for the Camp of Israel to move on with God, whether it was by day or night, whether it was in a day, a month, or a year (Numbers 9:15-23; 10:1-36; Deuteronomy 1:33; Nehemiah 9:9; Psalms 78:14). The message for all Israel was **"Follow the Cloud."**

9. When Solomon's Temple was built, the Cloud of Glory came to it, dwelling upon the Ark of the Covenant which had been previously taken out of the Tabernacle of Moses, and the Tabernacle of David (I Kings 8:10-11; II Chronicles 5:13-14).

10. The tragic end of the history of the Cloud in the Old Testament, relative to the Nation of Israel, is seen in the fact that the Glory-Cloud eventually departed from the Temple which had become polluted with filthy abominations. God allowed this Temple to be destroyed because of these defilements. (Read Ezekiel 10:1-22, and compare with I Corinthians 3:16-17; 6:19, 20). The Glory-Cloud could never again return to a material Temple.

However, this is not the final revelation in the Bible of that which pertains to the Cloud. The New Testament gives to us the glorious climax of this truth.

When Jesus Christ, the **True** Tabernacle and the **True** Temple, went up into the Mount of Transfiguration, the record tells us; "A **Bright Cloud** overshadowed them, and behold **a voice** out of The Cloud, which said, This is My Beloved Son, in whom I am well pleased; hear ye Him."

Read carefully Matthew 17:1-9; Luke 9:28-36; Mark 9:1-7.

That Glory-Cloud which had left the defiled material Temple under the Old Covenant (Old Testament) now descended upon the New Testament Temple, or Tabernacle; the Lord Jesus Christ. Once more God's voice was heard out of The Cloud, pointing to His Son.

In relation to Christ we see:

1. The *Bright Cloud* of Glory overshadowed Him in the Mount of Transfiguration (Matthew 17:5).
2. A *Cloud* is seen in His Ascension back to the Father (Acts 1:9).
3. He is clothed with a *Cloud* (Revelation 10:1).
4. He is seated upon a *White Cloud* (Revelation 14:14-16).
5. He will come in a *Cloud of Glory* (Luke 21:17).
6. He will also come in the *Clouds of Glory* with His saints, who are in Clouds of Glory. That is, the Glory-Cloud (Mark 14:62; Matthew 26:64; I Thessalonians 4:17; Hebrews 12:1).
7. The **Glory** that was in that **Cloud** will be the eternal joy of the redeemed in the City of God, the New Jerusalem.

Until that time, let us **Follow the Cloud** of the Holy Spirit whose ministry it is to lead us to the City of Eternal Rest and to **The Glory of God.**

New Testament Local Church Pattern

There are many ways of viewing the Tabernacle of Moses. There are many facets of truth that are revealed in the Tabernacle. In this section we present a brief outline of the Tabernacle and furniture setting forth a picture of truth as seen in the New Testament Local Church.

God's whole plan of redemption may be summed up in the word which God gave to Moses for the Nation of Israel at Mt. Sinai, "I bare you on Eagles' Wings, and brought you unto Myself"(Exodus 19:4-6).All of history is seen as the Grace of God coming to redeem fallen man and bring him to Himself. The order of approach in the Tabernacle of Moses gives us a wonderful picture of the Grace of God in the Plan of Redemption. It sets forth the order of the believer's experience "in Christ."

In the same way, the Tabernacle arrangement is a prophetic type of the Restoration or Recovery of truth since the time of the Reformation; each visitation of God bringing back to the Church some facet or portion of truth that had once been delivered to the saints (Jude 3).We offer the following outline of this portion of truth as an impetus to further study:

1. **The Way of Approach** — The **Gate** of the Court. This is the sinner's introduction to the plan of God. It is the first place he must actualize in his experience.

   Restoration Truth: The Gate directs us toward the Doctrine of Repentance from Dead Works (Hebrews 6:1-2).

2. **The Way of Justification by Faith** — The **Brazen Altar.** This is the place of Bloodshed where sin is judged. The sinner approaching by way of the Gate receives reconciliation through sacrificial blood.

   Restoration Truth: The Brazen Altar points us to the Doctrine of Faith toward God (Hebrews 6:1-2).The first two steps were recovered to the Church in the reformation.

3. **The Way of Separation and Sanctification** — The **Brazen Laver.** It was at the Laver that self was judged, there was cleansing by water and the Priest was purified. As we come to God by faith we must experience the same.

   Restoration Truth: The Brazen Laver typifies the Doctrine of Water Baptism (Acts 2:38-41; Matthew 28:19-20; Mark 16:15-20), Holiness and Sanctification.

4. **The Way of Entrance** — The **Door** of the Holy Place. No one could minister in this area without the **Garment** of the Priest. This Priestly garment which prepares us for ministry before the Lord is the Baptism of the Holy Spirit. Jesus told the disciples to tarry in Jerusalem until they be endued (Literal Greek "Clothed") with power from on high (Luke 20:49; Acts 2:4; 1:8).

   Restoration Truth: The infilling or Baptism in the Holy Spirit, the receiving of the Priestly Garment and the entrance into Priestly Ministry was secured for the Church under an outpouring at the turn of the last century. The Doctrine of Holy Spirit Baptism was recovered to the Church (Hebrews 6:1-2).

5. **The Way of Illumination** — The Golden **Candlestick.** Once inside the Holy Place the believer-priest receives light, illumination, anointing and insight by the 7-fold Spirit of the Lord in the Church and the revelation of the Word of God.

   Restoration Truth: The Candlestick speaks generally of the recovery of all seven (seven lamps) of the Principles of the Doctrine of Christ. It points particularly to the recovery of the Doctrine of the Laying on of Hands (Hebrews 6:2).

6. **The Way of Communion** — The Golden Table of Shewbread. Divine healing, health and life were in the Table of Shewbread. There is healing, health and life as we discern the Lord's Body both physically and spiritually at His Table.

   Restoration Truth: The Doctrine of the Lord's Table and the Communion is seen to be restored in the Tabernacle picture. It is at the Table of the Lord that the truths of life, health and Divine healing are to be recovered. It is here where the Lord's body is to be discerned and the unity of the body of Christ is to be experienced (I Corinthians 11:23-24; Matthew 26:26-28). In the Table we see the New Covenant relationship with Christ and the members of the Body of Christ.

7. **The Way of Prayer, Worship and Intercession** — The Golden **Altar** of Incense. As we minister before the Lord, prayer, praise and worship are to ascend within the veil(Psalms 141:1-2; Revelation 5:9-10; 1:6;l Peter 2:5-10).

Restoration Truth: It is here that the spirit of Prayer, Praise and Intercession are restored to the Church. Jesus said His House was to be called "of all nations a House of Prayer"(Mark 11:17).Once again the Church is moving into worship in Spirit and in Truth as God restores the Altar of Incense (John 4:24).

8. **The Way of Access into the Glory of God** — The **Veil** of the Most Holy Place. By the Blood of Jesus the believer has access within the Veil into the very Holiest of All (Hebrews 9:1-10; 10:19-22; 6:19-20).

Restoration Truth: There is a time coming to the Church which is typified in the ceremonies of the Great Day of Atonement in National Israel in which the Church (Spiritual Israel) will come into access to the very Glory of God. It will be an occasion when much of our 'positional' truth becomes 'experiential' truth. There is a hope which enters wthin the Veil. Jesus, our Forerunner, has entered in for us.

9. **The Way of Glorification** — The **Ark** of the Covenant. This is the final piece of furniture to be touched and points us to the finished work of redemption, the perfected saint (Hebrews 6:1-2; Romans 8:26-30).

Restoration Truth: This points to the ultimate in God's Plan of Redemption, the Glorification of the Church and the believer. It directs us to a time when the Shekinah Glory of God will be present in the midst of His redeemed people (Revelation 21:1-5).The contents of the Ark point to various aspects involved here:

a) The Manna — Christ is our Eternal Life and Immortality (II Timothy 1:9-10).

b) The Rod — Christ is our Eternal Priest after the Order of Melchizedek (Psalms 110:1-4).

c) The Law — Christ is our Eternal Law-Giver. His Law is written in our hearts. We will be everlastingly obedient to His will (Isaiah 33:22).

In the Plan of Redemption the believer proceeds from the Outer Court (the Brass), to the Holy Place (the Silver and Gold) and, finally, into the Holiest of All (the Gold). All this is typical of the believer's walk and experience "in Christ" from justification to glorification, from earth to glory. The Tabernacle as a whole can therefore be seen as **The Way of Worship and Ministry.** The Tabernacle speaks of Christ and the Church. Its significance can be summarized in the following way:

a) The Tabernacle was the only place where God recorded His **Name** (II Samuel 6:1-2).

b) The Tabernacle was the only place of **Worship** (John 4:24).

c) The Tabernacle was the place for all Priestly Ministry unto the Lord (Revelation 1:6).

d) The Tabernacle was God's Habitation Place. He dwelt in the midst of His people in the Pillar of Fire and the Cloud.

All these things find fulfillment in the New Testament Church. The Church is the only place where God records His **Name,** accepts true **Worship,** receives Priestly Ministrations and dwells in the midst by the Cloud and Fire of His Presence in the Person of the Holy Spirit (Matthew 18:20; I Corinthians 3:16; II Corinthians 6:16).

In the Local Church the truths distinctively typified and set forth should be seen, preached and enjoyed. Since the Reformation the Lord has been restoring to the Church that which was lost in the "Dark Ages" of Church History. Every New Testament Local Church should contend for the "Faith once delivered to the saints"(Jude 3).Everyone should seek the Lord that every piece of furniture will be set and established in the Church and that the spiritual truth will be entered into by all who come the **Way** of the Lord.

It is God's desire that every Local Church measure up to the **Pattern** shown in the Mount, for He can only fully bless and place His Glory in that Church which measures up to the Divine Standard as laid down in His Word. His Word is the Pattern by which every New Covenant or New Testament Church will be measured.

The Lord will establish His House (Isaiah 2:1-4).

Christ in the Heavenly Sanctuary

The Tabernacle has been viewed in relation to Christ Jesus Himself and His ministry in redemption. It has also been considered in relation to the believer and the Church. In this chapter we offer a brief survey or outline concerning the typical importance of the Tabernacle in relation to Christ's Ministry in the Heavenly Sanctuary.

While all of the previous facets examined in the Tabernacle are true, the Epistle of the Hebrews is based upon the thoughts contained in this present chapter. The writer to the Hebrews presents Christ, our Great High Priest after the Order of Melchizedek, as ministering to the Heavenly Sanctuary.

This is a vast subject and can in no way be covered adequately in such a short treatment. We simply offer a seed outline that the Teacher and Student may develop as he examines God's Word in this area. We offer the following as a stimulus to further study in this area:

1. **The Heavenly Sanctuary — A Reality** — The Scriptures clearly and distinctly show that there is a True and Heavenly Sanctuary of which the earthly or worldly Sanctuary was but the shadow. That which Moses built by the pattern of God was a mere copy or outline of things in the Heavens. Everything that took place in the earthly Sanctuary points to the ultimate ministry of Christ in the Heavenly Sanctuary. Examine the following Scriptures in this regard: Hebrews 8:1-5; 9:1-15; 23-24; Revelation 11:19 and 15:5-8.

2. **The Three Places or Apartments** — The earthly Sanctuary had three Places or Apartments including the Outer Court, the Holy Place and the Most Holy Place. These three places together formed the **One** Sanctuary or **One** Tabernacle which was the place of Aaron's ministry. It was in these three areas that the High Priest functioned in behalf of the people. These three Places correspond to the *three Places* in the Heavenly and True Sanctuary. They refer to the *three Heavens*. The three Heavens could be outlined as follows:

   a) The Atmospheric Heavens — This is the first Heaven and would correspond to the Outer Court.
   b) The Planetary Heavens — This is the second Heaven and corresponds to the Holy Place.
   c) The Heaven of Heavens — This is the third or highest Heaven which is pictured for us in the Most Holy Place.

   Jesus Christ, our Great High Priest, ministers in the *third* Heaven, in the immediate Presence of God for us. It was to this third Heaven that Paul was caught up when he heard things not lawful for him to utter. This third Heaven is the very Paradise of God (compare II Corinthians 12:1-4; Luke 23:43; Hebrews 9:24.),

   In His Ascension, Christ "passed through (literal) the Heavens" (Hebrews 4:14) into the third Heaven. Heaven's Most Holy Place and sat down on the Right Hand of the Majesty on High. From there He ministers in the Heavenly Sanctuary.

   In this picture given us in the Tabernacle, the earth corresponds to the Wilderness in which Israel, the Church in the Wilderness walked.

3. **The Great High Priest** — Jesus is our Great High Priest after the Order of Melchizedek. Aaron's ministry as High Priest in behalf of the nation of Israel foreshadowed the ministrations of Christ in behalf of the New Testament or New Covenant Church, which is His Body. The Epistle of Hebrews sets forth this Priesthood of Christ. He is King-Priest. He is ruling, reigning, interceding and ministering in the behalf of His own people who are also called to be King-Priests unto God in the same Order (compare Hebrews 4:14-16; 5:1-10; 7:1-28; 8:1-5; I Peter 2:5-9; Revelation 1:6; 5:9-10.)

   Christ ministers "within the Veil" (Hebrews 6:19-21; 10:19-22). Spiritually the believer may enter within the Veil by the Body and Blood of Jesus. Here Christ ministers salvation and redemption to His people.

   When we look at the Tabernacle from this portion of Truth it will make the Epistle of Hebrews more meaningful to the worthy searcher after the Truth of God (Proverbs 25:2).

108

The Metals of the Tabernacle

In several places throughout this study we have referred to the importance of the various metals when seen in relation to the Place in which they were used. In order to summarize our thought, we offer the following:

1. **The Outer Court** is emphatic in is use of *Brass*. Its furniture was of Brass, the Pillars stood in Sockets of Brass, and the pins were of Brass. Brass is symbolic of the Holy Spirit and His Ministry. He is the "Spirit of Judgment" (Isaiah 4:4; John 16:7-9). There are many pictures of Brass in connection with judgment. We consider the following:

   a) The Fiery Brazen Serpent was constructed in relation to judgment on sin (Numbers 21:7-9).
   b) The Feet of the Man were as brass in a furnace (Daniel 10:16; Revelation 10:1; 1:15).
   c) The heavens were as Brass when Israel was disobedient to God's Word (Deuteronomy 28:13-23).
   d) The Censers of the "sinners against their own souls" were made of Brass. They brought judgment upon themselves (Numbers 16:36-40).

   In our spiritual experience we begin with the *Brass*. That is, sin must first be judged. Conviction of sin, righteousness and judgment is brought about by the ministry of the Holy Spirit.

2. **The Holy Place** is noted for its Gold, but the entire structure of the Tabernacle was grounded in Sockets of *Silver*. Silver is symbolic of Atonement Money, Ransom Money and the price of a soul. It speaks of the Redemptive Ministry of the Son of God (Exodus 30:11-16). Silver is seen in the following places:

   a) Joseph was sold for Silver (Genesis 37:28).
   b) Slaves were sold for Silver (Exodus 21:32).
   c) Jesus was sold for Silver (Matthew 27:1-9; Zechariah 11:12-13).

   From the Brass of the Outer Court we move to the Silver of the Holy Place. From the place of judgment against our sin we move to the place of redemption. We were not "redeemed with corruptible things, as silver and gold . . . but with the precious Blood of Christ" (I Peter 1:19-20).

3. **The Most Holy Place** or Holiest of All is emphatic in its use of *Gold*. Gold is symbolic of the Father. The Word 'Gold' in the Hebrew literally means "from it shining." It is symbolic of the Shekinah Glory of God. Gold is always associated with the True God, gods, idols or objects of worship. In relation to the True God, it speaks of Divine Glory, Nature and Being. In relation to the Saints, it speaks of the Divine Nature, character and glory of God which is inwrought and outworked in them (Isaiah 31:7; Song of Solomon 5:11; Acts 17:29; Revelation 21:18, 21; II Peter 1:4; I Peter 1:7; Job 23:10).

   This is the last metal we experience spiritually — the Glory of God.

   Thus our approach to God is typified in the three Places of the Tabernacle. The three Places point us to our spiritual progression and experience in God. We begin with the **Brass** in the Outer Court and experience judgment on sin and self. From there we experience the **Silver** of the Holy Place and the Redemption by the Blood. Finally we come to the very Glory of God, and we experience the **Gold** of the Holiest of All.

The Prophetic Significance of the Tabernacle Measurements

A further facet of truth in the Tabernacle is that which is seen in its measurements. These very measurements were Divinely given and were part of the "Pattern" given to Moses in the Mount. Hence God had some truth or portion of truth in mind. God never does anything promiscuously. Every Word that proceeds out of the mouth of God is a revelation of Divine Truth. Every Word that He spoke to Moses has its particular portion of revelation.

The Tabernacle as such contains many facets of truth. Not only does the Tabernacle reveal prophetic truth concerning Christ and the Church, but it may also be viewed in relation to the Ages of time relative to the Plan of Redemption. We have such revelation in the measurements of the three places; the Outer Court, the Holy Place and the Holiest of All.

The Scripture tells us that the "ages" (Greek, Aionios) were framed by the Word of God (Hebrews 11:3). It tells us that God the Father sent His Son to make an end of sin "in the end of the Age" (Greek, Aion, Hebrews 9:26.) It reveals that it was by the Son of God that "He made the Ages" (Greek, Aionios, Hebrews 1:2.) Paul tells us that we are the people upon whom the ends of the Ages (Greek, Aionios) are come (I Corinthians 10:11), and often refers to the Ages to come (Ephesians 2:7). Even though at times these are translated "world" or "worlds," the Greek word is the same in each case. The word "Aionios" simply means "a period of time, a course, or a Messianic period." Hence the Prophetic Significances in this section will be spoken of as "Ages" or "Arrangements."

1. The **Law Age** or **Arrangement** — **The Outer Court**

The Outer Court and its linen enclosure had the measurements as given in Exodus 26:9-19.

The North side measured 100 cubits in length,
the South side measured 100 cubits in length,
the West side measured   50 cubits in width and
the East side measured   <u>50</u> cubits in width,
giving us a total of   300 cubits around.

The linen curtain that comprised the wall around the Outer Court was to be five cubits in height. The Gate of the Court was also five cubits in height. To determine the linen area of the Outer Court we would multiply 300 x 5. The Area of the Linen Curtains (including the Gate) was 1500 square cubits.

This is typical and prophetic of the 1500 years of the **Law Age,** from Moses to Jesus or from the Exodus of Israel out of Egyptian bondage to the crucifixion of Christ Jesus at Calvary. It is in this section that we see the 60 Pillars in Brass Sockets, capped with silver and connected with silver connecting rods. These speak of the 60 men in the Blood-line from Adam to Messiah which are recorded in the geneologies in Matthew and Luke's Gospel.

The distinctive metal of the Outer Court was brass — typical of the Law Age, the Age of Judgment, the "Brass Age." However, these 60 men were "Faith men," connected by the silver rod of the Atonement by faith in the coming Messiah of God. In this picture of the Outer Court the four Pillars in the Gate become typical of the four Gospels.

The Brazen Altar (Blood) and the Brazen Laver (Water) were the two distinctive articles belonging to the Outer Court. When Jesus Christ died on the Cross, Blood and Water flowed from His wounded and pierced side (John 19:33-34), thus fulfilling and abolishing these articles of brass. He was judged for our sins on the Cross, providing the means of true cleansing by that very Blood and Water (I John 5:6-8).

Thus the Outer Court has the typical characteristics impressed upon it of all that represents and pertains to the **Law Age** or the pre-Cross time.

To summarize these points we offer the following:

a) The 1500 square cubits of linen area are significant of the 1500 years of the Law Covenant from Moses, the mediator of the Old Covenant, to Christ, the Mediator of the New Covenant.

b) The 60 Pillars in the Brass Sockets connected by Silver become significant of the 60 men in the Faith-line or Messianic-line and geneology of Christ from Adam to Christ.

c) The Brazen Altar (Blood) and the Brazen Laver (Water) were absolutely prophetic of that Water and Blood which flowed from His side on the Cross. This closed off the Law Age and introduced the Church Age. It brings us to the Door of the Holy Place.

d) The four Pillars of the Gate of the Court and the four colors correspond to the four Gospels which present to us all the truths that are typified in the above.

Thus the impress of the Law Age is upon the Outer Court, its metals, articles, and measurements in the curtains and Gate.

2. The **Church Age** or **Arrangement — The Holy Place**

The next area in which we consider prophetic significances is the Holy Place of the Tabernacle itself.

The Holy Place measured 20 cubits in length, 10 cubits in width, and 10 cubits in height. Thus 20 x 10 x 10 = 2000 cubical contents.

The distinctive pieces or articles of furniture in this Holy Place were the Golden Candlestick, the Golden Altar of Incense, and the Table of Shewbread.

The structure of boards overlaid with gold stood in the silver sockets of the redemption or the ransom money.

The division was bounded by the two entrances: the Door of the Tabernacle at one end, and the second Veil at the other end. The Door opened into the Holy Place; the Veil closed off the Holy Place, and opened into the most Holy Place.

The Holy Place has the impress and typical characteristics of that which pertains to the **Church Age,** or the Dispensation of the Holy Spirit.

These points may be summarized as follows:

a) The 2000 cubical content of the Holy Place is prophetic of the 2000 years of the **Church Age,** the present Dispensation of the Holy Spirit, ushered in with the death, burial, resurrection, ascension, exaltation and glorification of the Lord Jesus Christ Himself, and the Outpoured Spirit at Pentecost.

b) The Door of the Tabernacle corresponds to the Lord Jesus Christ (John 10:9), the closing off of the Outer Court (Law Age), and the opening and entrance to the Holy Place (Church Age). It is also distinctively linked with the Cross of Jesus, which becomes the **Door** indeed. The **Cross** closes off the Old Covenant Age and the **Law Age,** and it ushers in the New Covenant Age, the **Church Age,** the Age of Grace and Faith and the Age of the Spirit.

c) The five Pillars signify the five New Testament writers of the Church Epistles which tell us of the behavior of the believer-priests who minister unto the Lord in the 2000 cubicle cubits of the Holy Place (the Church Age or Arrangement).

d) The articles of furniture in the Holy Place have significance related to the Church Age.

   1. The Golden *Candlestick* points to the Light of the Church by the anointing, illumination, fruit, and gifts of the Spirit and the Word of God (Revelation 1:20). The only light in the Holy Place was that of the Candlestick. The Church is the only light in this 2000 years.

   2. The Golden *Table of Shewbread* typifies the Lord's Table, the very communion of Christ and the Church which is to be experienced in this 2000 years by the believer-priests (I Corinthians 11:23-24).

   3. The Golden *Altar of Incense* emphasizes the ministry of prayer, praise and intercession that is to be so characteristic of the Church as they move in Priestly function and administration before the Lord (Revelation 8:1-3).

e) There were absolutely no animal sacrifices or animal bloodshed in the Holy Place. All these sacrifices took place in the Outer Court. All was finished there. This is significant of the fact that no animal blood or sacrifices will take place in the Church Age. All such sacrifices and oblations were fulfilled and abolished at Calvary's Cross by Christ's perfect, once-for-all sacrifice for sin. God will never return to what was abolished at the Cross. To do so would be an insult to Calvary. Any such animal sacrifices since Calvary are an abomination to God and an insult to the work of Christ.

f) The Boards of the structure of the Tabernacle were standing in silver Sockets of redemption. This is prophetic and typical of the Church, God's Habitation by the Spirit, standing upon redemption ground. The Church stands in silver, not brass! Sin has been Judged. All in the Holy Place are redeemed believer-priests (Revelation 1:6; 5:9-10; Ephesians 2:19-22).

Thus the impress of the Church Age is stamped upon the Holy Place, its metals, its furnishings and its measurements.

3. The **Kingdom Age** or **Arrangement — The Holiest of All**

The Most Holy Place or Holiest of All measured 10 cubits in height, length and width. It was a cube and foursquare. It had a cubicle content of 1000 (10 x 10 x 10). It had but one lone article of furniture in it, the Ark of the Covenant. The Holiest of All was the very Throne of God in Israel. He dwelt in their midst in this foursquare Most Holy Place.

Upon the Ark of the Covenant was the Blood-stained Mercy Seat upon which the very Presence and Shekinah Glory of the Lord God rested. His Glory filled that foursquareness and covered the *earth* floor of the Tabernacle. The only source of light in the Most Holy Place was this visible Glory of God.

In the Ark of the Covenant there were three articles, the Tables of the Law, the Golden Pot of Manna and the Rod of Aaron that Budded (In Solomon's Temple only the Table of Stone remain. It was here that the staves were finally taken out, (I Kings 8:8-11 and II Chronicles 5:9-10).

All of these facts in connection with the Most Holy Place point us to the Age to come or the Kingdom Age in the full sense of that word. The following summary gives us a glimpse at this age:

a) The 1000 cubicle cubits of the Most Holy Place become prophetic of the 1000 years of the Kingdom in its final aspect relative to the earth and God's Plan of Redemption. (This is spoken of in Revelation 20:1-6).

b) The Ark of the Covenant speaks of the Throne of God and the Lamb which is to be with men in the earth (Matthew 6:9-10; Jeremiah 3:17; Revelation 22:1-2).

c) The foursquareness speaks of the ultimate picture seen in the Foursquare City of God, the Holy City, Heavenly Jerusalem (Revelation 21:1-5).

d) The Shekinah *Glory* and Presence of God on the Ark filling the Most Holy Place and covering the *earth* floor is significant of the *earth* being filled with the knowledge of the Glory of the Lord as the waters cover the sea (Habakkuk 2:14; Isaiah 11:9).

e) The articles in the Ark are significant of the fact that all who enter into that 1000 cubits, the Kingdom Age, will have:

1. partaken of Christ, the Heavenly Manna (Revelation 2:17; John 6:47-58),
2. accepted Christ, the Heavenly Priest after the Order of Melchizedek and come under the fruitfulness of the Rod of God as in Him (Isaiah 11:1-4).
3. The Law of God written in their hearts and minds as under the New Covenant (Jeremiah 31:31-34).

f) Just as none could enter without Blood Atonement into the Most Holy Place (Hebrews 9:7) and to presume to do so meant death, even so none will enter the Kingdom Age without being born again or born from above. "Except a man be born again, he cannot see (or enter) the Kingdom of God"(John 3:1-5).

g) The two entrances of the Tabernacle correspond to the First and Second Coming of the Lord Jesus Christ. The Door was the First entrance and let one into the Holy Place, the 2000 cubits. This corresponds to the First Coming of Christ who opened the Door to the 2000 years of the Church Age and its particular furnishings. The Second Veil corresponds to the Second Coming of Christ. This Veil comes at the close of the Holy Place (2000 years) and lets one into the Most Holy Place (1000 years). It is then that the Scripture is fulfilled in its fulness, "Behold, **the Tabernacle of God is with men, and He will dwell with them, and they shall be His people, and God Himself shall be with them, and be their God**" (Revelation 21:3).

Thus the Holiest of all is seen to have the impress and typical characteristics of the Kingdom Age of 1000 years upon it.

Summarizing the Prophetic Measurements of the Tabernacle, we behold:

1. The 1500 years of the Law Age — Moses to Jesus.
2. The 2000 years of the Church Age — First coming to Second Coming.
3. The 1000 years of the Kingdom Age — Second Coming to the New Heavens and New Earth.

Note: For a summary of these thoughts refer to the accompanying diagram of the Dispensations.

A Word of Explanation

Many people wonder how we arrive at the measurements for the Holy Place and the Most Holy Place since they are not expressly given in Scripture. For this reason we feel that a word of explanation in this regard would be most appropriate. Certain of the measurements are undisputed because of the measurements that are given in the Scripture. These include the following:

1. The height of the Tabernacle Structure including the Holy Place and the Most Holy place is determined by the height of the Boards which were standing upright to compose the sides of the Tabernacle. These Boards were 10 cubits in length (Exodus 26:16). The height of the Tabernacle was therefore *10 cubits.*

2. The overall length of the Tabernacle Structure can be easily determined on the basis of the width of the Boards that made up each side. Each Board, we are told, was to be 1 ½ cubits wide, and there were 20 such Boards on both the North and the South sides. The length of the Tabernacle Structure was therefore *30 (20 x 1 ½ cubits)* (Exodus 26:18-21).

Concerning these two measurements there is no dispute. However, when we consider the width of the Tabernacle and the size of the Holy Place in relation to the Most Holy Place, we have quite another story. Because of the uncertainty of the exact position and size of the Corner Boards, and because of the uncertainty of the Placement of the Second Veil there is much confusion. We feel that the measurements we have used in this study are the most logical. Not only is tradition on our side, but when we consider the measurements of the curtains in relation to the overall structure this conclusion is strengthened. We propose the following:

3. The width of the Tabernacle Structure including the six end Boards (6 x 1 ½ = 9) plus a third width of each of the Corner Boards (½ = ½ = 1) is proposed to be *10 cubits.* This, as we will see is confirmed by the Coverings for the Tabernacle.

4. The Most Holy Place is proposed to be a perfect *cube* placing the Second Veil 10 cubits from the West end of the Tabernacle. The arrangement of the Coverings also confirms this conclusion.

Let us briefly examine the curtains and coverings that were placed on the Tabernacle in relation to the measurements involved. The first curtain to be placed over the Structure or Framework was the Fine Linen Curtain. This was composed of 10 separate curtains that were joined together into two halves of five curtains each. The measurements of each individual curtain was 4 cubits x 28 cubits. When the halves were joined together, as we have indicated, there were two curtains with the measurements of 20 (4x5) cubits x 28 cubits. These two halves were then joined together with fifty loops of Blue and 50 taches of Gold. The whole curtain when joined had the overall measurements of 40 (2x20) cubits x 28 cubits Exodus 26:1-6.

This curtain of Fine Linen was to be draped over the Tabernacle Framework. We are nowhere told exactly how this curtain was to be draped, but by inference from other passages we can get a fairly good idea. We have no reason to believe that the Curtain of Fine Linen extended beyond the door of the Holy Place. The Curtains of Goats' Hair, which we will consider next, did extend beyond the Door, but in this case God told them what to do with the excess. We have no such instruction with regard to the Fine Linen Curtain.

Since the height (10 cubits) and the length (30 cubits) of the Structure are known, we can proceed to place the 40 cubit x 28 cubit Linen Curtains over the Framework. When we place it with the one end beginning at the Door, we find that it would run the full thirty cubits of the length with an additional ten cubits to cover the back wall. If this was done, this would put the connecting taches and loops exactly ten cubits from the West end. If the Most Holy Place was a cube, the taches and loops would be directly over the Veil. What better place for the division to take place?

When we look at the Curtains of Goats' Hair we get a further picture. These Curtains were composed of eleven curtains with the individual measurements of 4 cubits x 30 cubits. These were divided into one group of five and one group of six. The group of five curtains was 20 x 30 cubits while the other curtain was 24 x 30 cubits. These two halves were joined by 50 loops and 50 taches of brass, giving a total curtain measuring **44 x 30**. This curtain went over the curtain of Fine Linen.

As we place this Curtain of Goats' Hair, we want to remember three things. First of all we are told that the extra length of the extra curtain (the sixth curtain) was to be doubled in the forefront of the Tabernacle (Exodus 26:9).Secondly, half of the back five curtains were to hang down the backside of the Tabernacle (Exodus 26:12).Finally, we have no Scriptural grounds for believing that any of the Coverings touched the ground, and yet it is fair to say that all the gold of the Tabernacle was covered and not seen by the outsider.

When these things are considered we are ready to place the Curtain of Goats' Hair. Beginning at the backside, we begin at the ground and cover the 10 cubits of the back wall. The remainder of the half of this first section would extend an additional 10 cubits where it would meet the loops and taches of the Fine Linen Curtain below (Exodus 26:12).The loops and taches of the Curtain of Goats' Hair would be directly over the loops and taches of the Curtain of Fine Linen. The second section of the Goats' Hair Curtain would then finish covering the full 30 cubits of the length of the Framework with an additional 4 cubits left over. This remaining four cubits would be doubled over the front (Exodus 26:9).

When we consider the width of the Goats' Hair Curtains with the thought that they most likely covered or hid all the gold in the Framework, we get a figure for the width of the Tabernacle itself. If these Curtains, which were 30 cubits wide, covered the height of the South wall which was 10 cubits, and it covered the height of the North wall which was 10 cubits, there would have remained but 10 cubits to cover the ceiling of the Tabernacle (10 + 10 + 10 = 30). The Tabernacle therefore would be *10 cubits wide.*

With the Curtains placed in this fashion (which seems the most Scriptural) it is not hard to see why we use the measurements that we do. There is a natural division in these two coverings at the loops and taches. It is difficult to imagine that this would not be the place of the Veil. When this is coupled with the 30 cubit width of the Goats' Hair Curtains our conclusions are manifest:

Holy Place	= 20 x 10 x 10 = 2000 (Church Age)
Most Holy Place	= 10 x 10 x 10 = 1000 (Kingdom Age)
Overall	= 30 x 10 x 10 = 3000.

The dimensions of the Tabernacle itself speak to us of the 3000 years of Time from the Cross, the First Coming of Christ to the Second Coming and on through to the New Heavens and New Earth and the Eternities of God and the Lamb.

God did not give these measurements without spiritual signficiance!

Christ Typified in the Materials of the Sanctuary

"In the volume of the Book it is written of Me." (Hebrews 10:5-7)
"Every whit (every bit of it) utters His Glory." (Psalms 29:9)

Symbol of Type	Christ Seen
1. Gold	His Divine Glory and Nature, His Deity.
2. Silver	His Redemptive ministry and power, the Atonement.
3. Brass	His capacity to endure judgment for sin.
4. Blue	His Heavenly origin, the Lord from Heaven.
5. Purple	His Royalty, His Kingship, the New Creature, the God-Man.
6. Scarlet	His Sacrificial ministry and glory of the Cross.
7. Fine Linen	His Holiness, righteousness, of His sinless humanity.
8. Goats' Hair	His Atonement, our Sin-offering.
9. Rams' skins dyed red	His Consecration to the Father's will, substitution.
10. Badgers' skins	His protection, and unattractiveness to the unregenerate man.
11. Shittim wood	His incorruptible humanity, the Root, the Branch.
12. Anointing Oil	His Anointed Ministry, the Christ of God, the Messiah.
13. Incense Spices	His Fragrant Life of Prayer and Intercession, His Graces.
14. Precious Stones	His Priestly Glories and Perfections on behalf of His People.
15. The Gate	Christ — the Way.
16. The Brazen Altar	Christ the Sacrificed One, our Justification.
17. The Brazen Laver	Christ the Cleanser, our Sanctification, our Separation
18. The Door	Christ — the Truth.
19. The Golden Candlestick	Christ the Light, Illuminator, the Word, in whom dwells the Fulness of the Spirit of God.
20. The Table of Shewbread	Christ our Nourishment, Food, Sustainer, Communion.
21. The Altar of Incense	Christ our Intercessor, Advocate, Mediator.
22. The Veil	Christ our Life, Access to God the Father.
23. The Ark of the Covenant	Christ the Fulness of the Godhead Bodily.
24. The Ten Commandments	Christ our Law Giver and Keeper
25. The Golden Pot of Manna	Christ our Heavenly Manna, Food, Divine Health.
26. The Rod that Budded	Christ our Appointed, Resurrected High Priest after the Order of Melchisedek.
27. The Tabernacle as a whole	Christ, God's Tabernacle and Habitation with men.
28. The Shekinah Glory	Christ, the Glory of God bodily.
29. The Cloud and Pillar of Fire	Chirst our Leader, and Guide to Heaven.
30. The High Priest in Garments of Glory and Beauty	Christ, our Heavenly High Priest who represents His own in Himself before God the Father.

Significance of Numbers

Numbers or Figures, as used in the Word of God, are never used promiscuously, but take on Spiritual meaning and significance; and for the searcher after Truth there is to be found "the treasures of wisdom and knowledge" (Proverbs 25:2).

All creation is stamped with the "Seal of God" in numerics. God has made man himself a Creature of Time and therefore, a Creature of Number!

And it is consistent with the very Nature and Being of God that His Book, the Holy Bible, should be stamped with this same "Seal" — **Bible Numbers!**

God is consistent throughout His Book, and though the Bible was written by various men of God over different periods of time and generations, yet there is manifest throughout all the Book, the same marvelous meaning and harmony in the use of numbers. This begins in Genesis and flows through each book and consummates in Revelation. All this confirms the fact of Divine Inspiration (II Timothy 3:16; II Peter 1:21).

Following are the basic principles of Interpretation of Numbers. If the student follows the same it will preserve from error or extremity.

1. The simple numbers of 1 through 13 have spiritual significance.

2. Multiples of these numbers, or doubling and tripling, carry basically the same meaning only intensifying the truth.

3. The first use of the number in Scripture generally conveys its spiritual meaning.

4. Consistence of interpretation. God is consistent, and what a number means in Genesis, it means through all to Revelation.

5. The spiritual significance is not always stated, but may be veiled, or hidden, or seen by comparison with other Scriptures.

6. Generally there is good and evil, true and counterfeit, God and Satanic, aspects in Numbers.

Not all of the following Numbers are to be found in the Tabernacle, but many of them are, or multiples of them are there. By constant reference to this section on the Spiritual Significance of Numbers, the reader will become familiar with the truth typified therein.

One. Number of God. Beginning, Source, Commencement, First.
Genesis 1:1; Mark 6:33.
Number of Compound Unity.
Deuteronomy 6:4; "Echad," John 17:21-23; I Corinthians 12:1-14.
Numerical One — "Yacheed." Only one.
Genesis 22:2; Zechariah 12:10; John 3:16.

Two. Number of Witness, Testimony. 1 with 1 = 2.
John 8:17, 18; Deuteronomy 17:6; 19:15; Matthew 18:16; Revelation 11:2-4; Luke 9:30-32.

Number of Division, Separation. 1 against 1 = 2.
Exodus 8:23; 31:18; Matthew 7; Genesis 19; Genesis 1:7-8; Matthew 24:40-41.

Three Number of Godhead
I John 5:6-7; Deuteronomy 17:6; Matthew 28:19; 12:40.

Number of Divine Completeness, Perfect Testimony.
Tri-angle. Ezekiel 14:14-18; Daniel 3:23-24; Leviticus 23.
Three Feasts. Exodus 12:7; Exodus 3:6.

Four. Number of Earth, Creation, World. Proceeds from three, dependent thereon.
Genesis 2:10; Leviticus 11:20-27; Mark 16:15; Jeremiah 49:36; Ezekiel 37:9; I Corinthians 15:39.
Four seasons, Four winds, Four corners of earth.

Five. Number of Cross, Grace, Atonement, Life.
Genesis 1:20-23; John 10:10; Leviticus 1:5.
Five Offerings. Ephesians 4:11; Exodus 26:3, 9, 26, 27, 37; 27:1, 18; Exodus 13:18,
Margin: Joshua 1:14, margin.
The 5 "I wills" of Satan.
The 5 wounds of Jesus on the Cross.
Note: five in the Tabernacle.

Six. Number of Man, Beast, Satanic.
Genesis 1:26-31.
6th Creative Day. Genesis 4:6.
Six generations, Cain.
I Samuel 17:4-7; II Samuel 21:20; Numbers 35:15.
Time — 6000 years.

Seven. Number of Perfection, Completeness. 3 + 4 = 7.
Genesis 2:1-3. 7th Day.
Hebrews 6:1-2; Jude 14; Joshua 6; Genesis 4:15; Leviticus 14:7, 16, 27, 51.
Note the "Seven Times Prophecies."

Number of Book of Revelation.
Revelation 1:4, 6, 12, 20; 4:5; 5:1; 6; 8:2; 10:3; 12:3; 15:1-7; 17:9-10.
Seven is used about 600 times in the Bible.

Eight. Number of Resurrection, New Beginning.
Genesis 5. "And he died" 8 times.
Leviticus 14:10-11; Exodus 22:30.
Genesis 17. Circumcision, 8th day. Named.
I Peter 3:20. Noah, eighth person.
II Peter 3:8. New Heavens and New Earth, eighth day.
Resurrection of Jesus. Matthew 28:1; John 20:26.
Music — Octave.
Numerical value of "Jesus," 888.

Nine. Number of completeness, Finality, Fulness.
Final of digits. 3 x 3 = 9
Matthew 27:45. Number of the Holy Spirit.
Galatians 5:22; I Corinthians 12:1-12. 9 Fruits, 9 Gifts.
Genesis 7:1, 2; Genesis 17:1.
9 months for the "Fruit of the womb."

Ten. Number of Law, Order, Government, Restoration.
Genesis 1. "God said."
Exodus 34:28; Daniel 2. 10 Toes.
Daniel 7. 10 Horns.

Number of Trial, Testing, Responsibility. 2 x 5 = 10.
Matthew 25:1, 28; Luke 15:8; Luke 19:13-25; Numbers 14:22; Revelation 2:10;
12:3; Leviticus 27:32; Exodus 12:3.

Eleven. Number of Incompleteness, Disorganization, Disintegration. One beyond 10, yet
one short of 12.
Genesis 32:22. 11 sons. Genesis 35:16, 18; 37:9.
Matthew 20:6; Exodus 26:7. Goat's hair, sin offerings. Deuteronomy 1:2.
Daniel 7. The 11th "Little Horn."

Number of Lawlessness, Disorder. The Antichrist.

Twelve.	Number of Divine Government, Apostolic Fulness.

Twelve. Number of Divine Government, Apostolic Fulness.
Genesis 49:28; Exodus 15:27; Exodus 28.
The 12 Stones. Exodus 24:4; 28:21; Matthew 19:28
Revelation 12:1; Revelation 21:12, 21; 22:2.
12 Apostles.
12 Loaves Shewbread.
Note: number 12 in "Holy City, Jerusalem."
Revelation, Chapters 21-22.

Thirteen. Number of Rebellion, Backsliding, Apostasy.
Genesis 14:4; Genesis 10:10 — Nimrod, 13th from Adam.
Genesis 17:25; I Kings 11:6; Esther 9:1.

Number of Double Portion.
Genesis 48. Ephraim, 13th Tribe.
Compare Judas and Paul.

Fourteen. Number of Passover. 2 x 7 = 14.
Exodus 12:6; Numbers 9:5; Genesis 31:41; Acts 27:27-33.

Seventeen. Number of Spiritual Order. 10 + 7 = 17.
Genesis 1; Genesis 37:2; I Chronicles 25:5; Jeremiah 32:9; Acts 2:9-11.
"Walk with God." Genesis 5:24; 6:9. Enoch the 7th, and Noah the 10th.
Genesis 7:11; 8:4. Ark rested on the 17th Day.

Twenty-four. Number of Priestly Courses, Governmental Perfection.

2 x 12 = 24.
Joshua 4:2-9; Joshua 4:20; I Kings 19:19;
I Chronicles 24:3-5; I Chronicles 25.
Revelation 4:4-10. 4 Living Ones (24 wings)
24 Elders.
Note in the "Holy City, Jerusalem"
Revelation, chapters 21, 22.

Thirty. Number of Consecration, Maturity for Ministry.
Numbers 4:3; Genesis 41:46; II Samuel 5:4;
Luke 3:23; Matthew 26:15.

Forty. Number of Probation, Testing. Closing in Victory or Judgment.
Numbers 13:25; 14:33; Matthew 4:2; Acts 1:3; Exodus 34:27-28; Ezekiel 4:6; Acts 7:30; I Kings 19:4-8.

Fifty. Number of Pentecost, Liberty, Freedom, Jubilee.
Exodus 26:5, 8; Leviticus 23:25; 25:10-11; Acts 2:1-4; II Kings 2:7; I Kings 18:4: 13; Numbers 8:25.

Seventy. Number prior to increase.
Genesis 11:26; Exodus 1:5; Genesis 46:27; Numbers 11:25; Exodus 15:27; Luke 10:1; Exodus 24:1, 9.

Seventy-Five. Number of Separation, Cleansing, Purification.
Genesis 12:4; 8:5-6; Daniel 12:5-13; Exodus 27:1.

One-Hundred-Twenty. Number of End of all Flesh, Beginning
Life in the Spirit. 3 x 4 = 120.

Genesis 6:3; Deuteronomy 34:7; Leviticus 25;
120 x 50 = 6000 years of time.
II Chronicles 3:4; 7:5; 5:12; Acts 1:5.

One Hundred Forty-Four. Number of God's Ultimate in Creation
12 x 12 = 144. Revelation 21:17; I Chronicles 25:7; Revelation 7:1-6; 14:1-3.

One Hundred Fifty-Three. Number of Revival, and the Elect.
John 21:11; 9 x 17 = 153.

Three Hundred. Number of Faithful Remnant.
Genesis 5:22; 6:15; Judges 8:4; 15:4.
Note, Three Entrances to Tabernacle, 3 x 100 cubits.

Six Hundred Sixty-Six. Number of Antichrist, Satan, the Damned.
Triplicate. 666. Daniel 3; I Samuel 17; Daniel 7.
Revelation 13:18. Connected with Number 11.
Revelation 14:9-11.

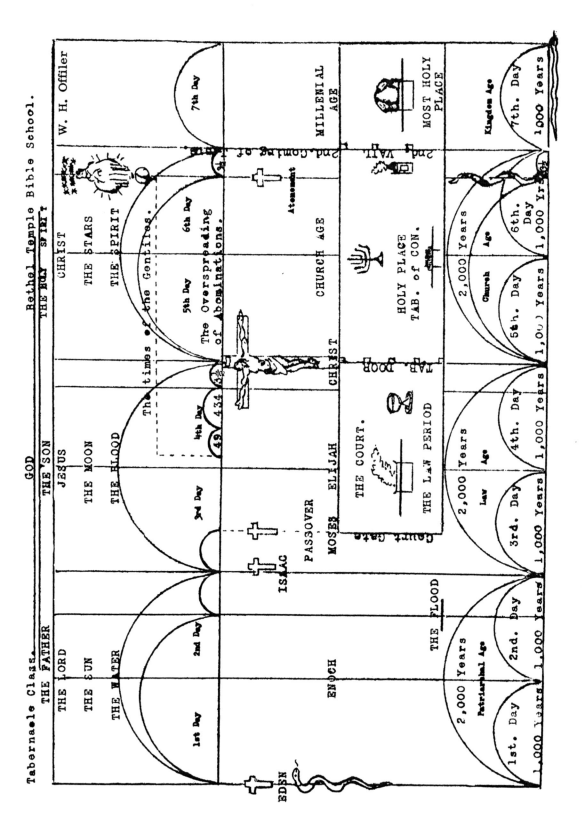

Bibliography:

1. Reference Books:

Made According to the Pattern	C. W. Slemming
The Path of the Just	B. Maureen Gaglardi
Gleanings in Exodus	Arthur W. Pink
The Tabernacle, Priesthood and Offerings	Henry W. Soltau
The Holy Vessels and Furniture of the Tabernacle	Henry W. Soltau
The Law Prophecied	R. H. Mount, Jnr.
The Tabernacle	M. R. DeHaan
Keys to Scripture Numerics	Ed. F. Vallowe
Number in Scripture	E. W. Bullinger
Christ in the Tabernacle	Frank H. White
Tabernacle Alphabet	Charles E. Pont
Lectures on the Tabernacle	Samuel Ridout
The Tabernacle, Priesthood and Offerings	Dr. I. M. Haldeman
Typical Truth in the Tabernacle	W. S. Hottel

2. Lecture Notes:

The Tabernacle of Moses	Ern Baxter
Tabernacle in the Wilderness	Violet Kiteley
Studies in the Tabernacle	Bethel Temple Bible School
The Tabernacle	W. W. Patterson
Notes on the Tabernacle	Ray S. Jackson
Use of the Old Testament	B. Maureen Gaglardi
Significance of Numbers	Ray S. Jackson
Significance of Numbers in Scripture	W. W. Patterson

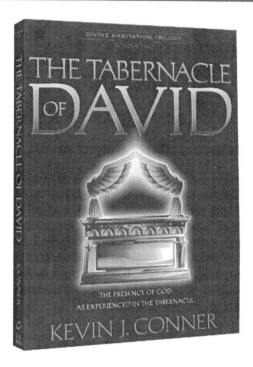

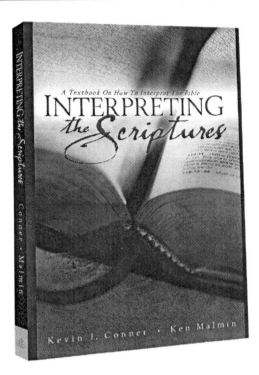
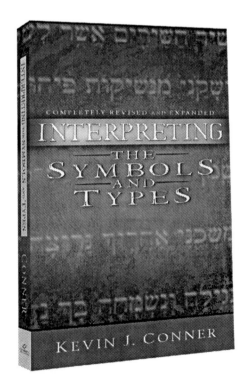

The Name of God

Kevin J. Conner

Revealing God Through His Name

This volume endeavors to set forth the glory of the Triune Name of the Triune God. Its insights are provocative, especially in the area of the application of "The Name" in Water Baptism. This book sincerely seeks to present a balanced approach to the biblical revelation of the Triune God and his Triune Name.

Biblical Studies
Softcover, 192 pages, 7½" x 10", ISBN 1-59383-030-0

The Covenants

Kevin J. Conner & Ken Malmin

God's Covenantal Plan Exposed

This textbook introduces covenant theology through a systematic study of the divine covenants found in Scripture. Perhaps better than any other subject, *The Covenants* give us a biblical framework for our understanding of the administration of God's dealings with mankind throughout all of human history.

Biblical Studies
Softcover, 113 pages, 7" X 10", 0-914936-77-8

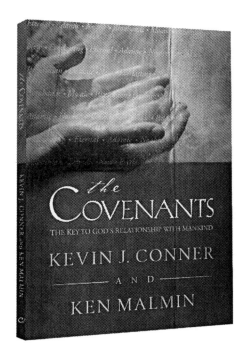

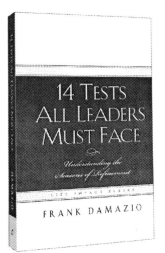

14 Tests All Leaders Must Face
Frank Damazio

Understanding the Seasons of Refinement

Discover 14 tests God administers to release the full potential of those He anoints. These often-difficult trials of Christian leaders include tests of motivation, time, servitude, and character. It is encouraging to know that God uses these tests not to tear you down, but to increase your capacity and strength through a deeper relationship with Him.

Life Impact Series - Leadership / Pastoral Helps
Hardcover, 105 pages, 4¾" x 6½", ISBN 1-59383-029-7

52 Offering Prayers & Scriptures
Frank Damazio

Encouraging the Heart of Giving in the Church

This powerful book on giving is the fruit of Pastor Frank Damazio's three decades of ministry in leading churches in the area of finances and giving. Included are 52 sets of scriptures and prayers to assist pastors and leaders in guiding their congregations in faithful giving.

Life Impact Series - Leadership / Pastoral Helps
Hardcover, 152 pages, 4¾" x 6½", ISBN 1-886849-73-0

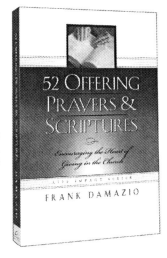

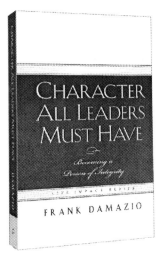

Character All Leaders Must Have
Frank Damazio

Becoming a Person of Integrity

Why is character of such importance in God's kingdom? In this short, but powerful book, Frank Damazio explains how character can cause one to either fulfill or forfeit the call to leadership. Emphasizing moral purity, this book will deeply encourage you to prioritize integrity in your life.

Life Impact Series - Leadership / Pastoral Helps
Hardcover, 104 pages, 4¾" x 6½", ISBN 1-59383-028-9

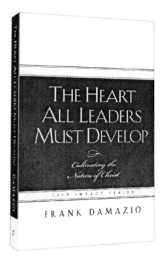
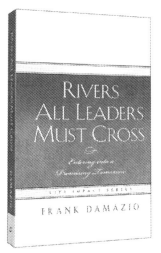

CPSIA information can be obtained at www.ICGtesting.com
Printed in the USA
BVOW021959070513

320103BV00001B/1/A